Praise for *The Identity and Mission of the Korean American Church*

The Identity and Mission of the Korean American Church exemplifies the multifaceted role of an immigrant Christian community: toward its own ethnic group, for the well-being of the host church, and as a catalyst of Christian mission. Korean American Christianity also has a call to renew its mother church at home. This book's 360-degree view produces a unique spiritual narrative that can encourage other immigrant churches to have a close look at theirs. The book is a timely and valuable contribution!

—Wonsuk Ma, executive director of the Center for Spirit-Empowered Research, and distinguished professor of Global Christianity, Oral Roberts University

An exceptional and timely volume on the subjects of identity, mission, and the Korean American church, authored by an impressive interdisciplinary group of scholars in missiology, theology, history, and the social sciences. A must-read for those interested in Korean American identity, missions, and its church in multiple local, national, and global contexts.

—Rebecca Y. Kim, professor of sociology and director of the Ethnic Studies program, Pepperdine University; author of *The Spirit Moves West: Korean Missionaries in America*

Although Christianity faces steep declines in most western contexts, Korean American churches remain centers of vital faith. As with other immigrant churches, however, they face a variety of pressing issues related to race, cultural identity, and the second generation. These interdisciplinary theological essays are a model for any immigrant church seeking to move beyond the first generation aim of cultural survival and preservation, to a mission of radical hospitality and becoming a church for others.

—Robert Chao Romero, associate professor, Departments of Chicana/o and Central American Studies and Asian American Studies, University of California, Los Angeles

This collection of essays brilliantly captures the essence of the intersection of faith, ethnicity, migration, theology, and mission of Korean American Christianity, showcasing its history, community, triumphs, and struggles. The book displays a vibrant strand of the global Christian tapestry and offers many valuable insights for all immigrant communities globally. It is a testament to the missionary passion of Korean Christians and to the enduring spirit of Diaspora Christians in the remaking of Christianity worldwide. I am grateful to Sebastian Kim and Enoch Jinsik Kim for editing the proceedings of a Fuller Symposium to make it more widely accessible.

—Sam George, director, Global Diaspora Institute, Wheaton College

THE
IDENTITY
AND
MISSION
OF THE
KOREAN
AMERICAN
CHURCH

THE IDENTITY AND MISSION OF THE KOREAN AMERICAN CHURCH

ENOCH JINSIK KIM AND **SEBASTIAN KIM**
EDITORS

FORTRESS PRESS
MINNEAPOLIS

THE IDENTITY AND MISSION OF THE KOREAN
AMERICAN CHURCH

Copyright © 2024 by Fortress Press, an imprint of 1517 Media. All rights reserved. Except for brief quotations in critical articles or reviews, no part of this book may be reproduced in any manner without prior written permission from the publisher. Email copyright@1517.media or write to Permissions, Fortress Press, PO Box 1209, Minneapolis, MN 55440-1209.

29 28 27 26 25 24   1 2 3 4 5 6 7 8 9

Library of Congress Cataloging-in-Publication Data

Names: Kim, Enoch Jinsik, editor. | Kim, Sebastian, editor.
Title: The identity and mission of the Korean American church / edited by Enoch Jinsik Kim and Sebastian Kim.
Description: Minneapolis : Fortress Press, [2024] | Includes bibliographical references and index.
Identifiers: LCCN 2023043202 (print) | LCCN 2023043203 (ebook) | ISBN 9781506496795 (paperback) | ISBN 9781506496801 (ebook)
Subjects: LCSH: Korean American churches--Congresses. | Protestant churches--United States--Congresses. | Christianity and culture--United States--Congresses.
Classification: LCC BR563.K67 I34 2022 (print) | LCC BR563.K67 (ebook) | DDC 280/.4089957073--dc23/eng/20231222
LC record available at https://lccn.loc.gov/2023043202
LC ebook record available at https://lccn.loc.gov/2023043203

Cover design: Alisha Lofgren
Cover image: © Jong-Won Heo. Old Catholic Church. Getty Images 2024.

Print ISBN: 978-1-5064-9679-5
eBook ISBN: 978-1-5064-9680-1

CONTENTS

Acknowledgments   vii

Introduction   ix
   Enoch Jinsik Kim

1. In-between Korean Immigrant Identity Formation and the Positionality of Asian Immigrants: Reconstructing Leadership of the Korean Immigrant Church   1
Choi Hee An

2. Cooking *Bahb* and Missional Christian Education in the Korean North American Churches   25
Nam Soon Song

3. Korean Christianity and the Korean War   45
Helen Jin Kim

4. Ascetic Spiritual Formation for the Mission of Korean Immigrant Churches in the Post-Pandemic Era   69
Euiwan Cho

5. The Situational Roles of the Korean American Church in Its History: From Community Centers to Bridges   93
Enoch Jinsik Kim

6. The Paradigm of Diaspora Missiology and
   Missiological Implications for Korean
   Immigrant Churches in the United States   111
   Enoch Wan

7. Race and the Korean American Church   137
   Daniel D. Lee

8. Immigration and US Congregations:
   Contemporary Trends and Issues   169
   Allison L. Norton

9. Exploring Diaspora Mission in the Context
   of the Latin American Mission to North
   America with the Second Generation   199
   Alexia Salvatierra

10. Concluding Remarks: The Identity and Mission
    of Korean American Churches   217
    Sebastian Kim

Index   231

ACKNOWLEDGMENTS

This book has been made possible by the commitment of many people and churches. The 2022 symposium hosted by the Korean Studies Center at Fuller Theological Seminary and this resulting book were made possible by the support of the Fuller Korean Studies Center Advisory Council. We are grateful to the Fuller Korean Advisory Council for their financial support.

We are also grateful to Dr. Amos Yong, Dean of the School of Mission and Theology, for his support for the symposium and for his encouragement to the organizing group. We would like to thank Rev. Joshua Choon-Min Kang of New Life Vision Church for his message to Korean American churches at the symposium. His spiritual challenge and financial support were much appreciated. We are grateful to the professors who presented papers at the symposium and submitted manuscripts for this volume, including Choi Hee An, Nam Soon Song, Helen Jin Kim, Euiwan Cho, Enoch Jinsik Kim, Enoch Wan, Daniel D. Lee, Allison L. Norton, Alexia Salvatierra, and Sebastian Kim. Their presentations are the outcome of their diligent research and passion for the subject areas.

We would like to thank Rev. Huh Changdo, Dr. Cho Euiwan and the director, Helen Lim, of the Korean Studies Center for their hard work as part of the organizing committee. The Events Team, led by Chantelle Gibbs, and the Chapel Team, led by Julie Tai, took ownership of the event and cooperated diligently with the organizing committee. Their service and proactive communication behind the scenes made the event run smoothly.

Finally, we would like to thank Fortress Press Acquisitions Editor, Dr. Jesudas M. Athyal, and the rest of the staff for their support in the publication of this volume. The staff at Fortress has been very kind and helpful, and their guidance has made the entire editing and publishing process a smooth one.

We give God the glory for making it all happen.

INTRODUCTION

There are over six thousand Korean diaspora churches worldwide, and about four thousand are in the United States.[1] The Korean Methodist Church was the first Korean American Church, started by Koreans who came to Oahu, Hawaiʻi as sugar cane farm laborers. Starting from the Oahu church in 1904, Koreans established the LA Korean Methodist Church four months later in mainland United States. Since then, after 120 years, Korean Christians have now solidified their identity as Korean immigrants, Asian Americans, children of God, and a missional entity. Despite this, Korean American churches struggle with their cultural and theological identities. Part of the reason is that the theology and faith of the Korean homeland churches have heavily influenced the Korean American churches. Requiring a tremendous amount of energy for the theologizing process is also a burden for them because such a process requires enormous human intelligence and financial resources.

With this background, this book weaves together contributions from a group of scholars recognized in North America and internationally who were brought together for the 2022 Korean Studies Center Symposium at Fuller Theological Seminary with the theme of "The Identity and Mission of the Korean American Church." In the symposium, nine presenters introduced their

---

1 Sŭng-hun Kim and Wonsuk Ma, *Korean Diaspora and Christian Mission*, Regnum Studies in Mission (Eugene, OR: Wipf & Stock, 2011), 181–206.

research results—which were achieved using sociological, missiological, psychological, and theological methods—to identify Koreans, Korean Americans, and Korean American churches and their mission. The result addressed the following: who the Korean American churches are; God's vision for the Korean American churches; how to interpret the Korean American church's journey in immigrant church history; what heritage sustained them and continues to sustain them; what the immigrant church should consider in post-pandemic times; and the hopes of the next generation.

The symposium concluded by suggesting mission practices responding to their identity and missional responsibility before God. Its result will also contribute to developing Korean immigrants' contextualization in the United States. Furthermore, because of Koreans' similarities with other Asian American churches, it will also provide insights into the identity and mission of other Asian American churches.

Authors expect a new and vital discourse of missiology and theology with *The Identity and Mission of the Korean American Church*. In an age of confusion regarding immigrant churches, the time is ripe for theologizing the Korean immigrant churches and understanding their role in the *missio Dei*.

Each chapter includes the most recent theological and social sciences scholarship. In addition, chapters also have contemporary or historical narratives or stories that express the concept or thesis of the chapter. Although different authors wrote each chapter, they all raise the significant themes of migration, Korean identity, and Korean churches. This book consists of three areas for the process of theologizing the Korean American churches: identity formation, missional and spiritual formation, and intercultural formation.

We begin by identifying Korean American Christians from sociological, ethnological, and historical approaches. Three authors analyze the cases of Korean Americans' lives and transcend them to biblical meanings. Choi Hee An sees the Korean American's identity and position from the perspective of in-betweenness. She sees Korean immigrants as those who live at the intersection of having to relearn their identity as immigrants from Korea to the United States and of being Asian immigrants as the third other. Choi addresses how this intersectionality has challenged Korean immigrants and their leadership in the church. Using the metaphor of "우리" (*woo-ri*) and "깍두기" (*gaag-du-gi*), Choi explains how intersectionality brought up Korean identity struggles and developed their identities. She sees Koreans as a part of Asian immigrants and their challenges. Cho concludes by identifying this intersectionality as an exploration of how the Korean immigrant church reconstructed its leadership for a better future.

Interestingly, Nam Soon Song explores the ritual and practice of cooking *bahb* (rice) as a Christian education in Korean North American churches. Song symbolizes that *bahb*—both figuratively and literally—is the source of life and the very essence of identity for Koreans. According to Song, the Korean's *bahb* is also a metaphor for Jesus giving life to the full, Christian mission (sharing, harmony, affection), and a localized yet globalized Christian education for the North American Korean church context.

Uncovering the historical background of Korean Christianity, Helen Jin Kim rediscovers the root of the Korean Christian diaspora movement. For this, Kim peels back the forgotten history through the history of the Campus Crusade for Christ, a transpacific parachurch organization. Kim brings up several forgotten influences for the revivals in Korea: the Korean war, white fundamentalism, Cold War orientalism, and anti-Black and authoritarian politics in the United States. Finally, Kim points out that today's parachurch movements highlight only successful sites, affecting the identity of Korean Christianity and its diaspora in the United States.

In the second section, Euiwan Cho and Enoch Jinsik Kim discuss spiritual and missional formation in their chapters. First, Cho introduces the ascetic spiritual formation as the foundation to form a postcolonial self and pursue a missional life in the dominant society. Cho also encourages the reader to pay particular attention to the ascetic self-formation of the desert fathers and mothers from the third to sixth centuries. For the desert fathers and mothers, *agape* was the progeny of *apatheia*. Cho also presents a case of the *Apophthegmata Patrum*, in which the desert fathers and mothers ceaselessly practiced withdrawal, stability, and radical honesty to reach the stage of *apatheia*. Cho argues that the practice of these three stages of self-formation is appropriate for Korean immigrant churches striving to achieve a postcolonial self through radical hospitality.

Enoch Jinsik Kim uses historical records and sociological methods to identify today's Korean American Christians and their missional responsibility. Based on William Petersen's theory, Kim categorizes Korean American immigration stages into four types. Kim also differentiates the role of the immigrant church as the society changes in its nature. Using Shirley Achor's theory, Kim brings up the importance of mobilization groups within ethnicities for their dual identities. As we enter the global age, Korean American churches must have the next step of identity that goes beyond the image of the traditional churches in the traditional ethnic enclaves. When immigrant churches become missional and situational churches, they may have an identity of in-betweenness. Kim emphasizes that this in-betweenness brings Korean American Christians to be members of the global church, to become a part of a mosaic in the global era, and to contribute to the multiethnic society with the blessings given to Korean churches.

Based on an ethnographic understanding of traditional and diaspora Korean culture, Enoch Wan introduces an integrated understanding of the Christian mission and the missiological diaspora paradigm. Wan addresses Korean American immigrants who have providentially come out from the "hermit kingdom" of their homeland to be redeemed and reconciled by the Triune God vertically. Wan appeals to Korean American churches to practice Christian mission within the existential reality of the diaspora experience in a contextual Korean way.

Finally, three scholars discuss the intercultural formation of Korean American churches. First, Daniel D. Lee discusses race and the Asian American immigrant church. Lee brings up the cultural heritages, migration experience, dynamics of assimilation and acculturation, and generational differences and tensions as the analytic toolbox toward critical evaluation and constructive proposals for the context, experience, and ministry of Asian American immigrant churches. Lee also addresses the often-excluded category of race as a hermeneutical approach to Asian American immigrant churches. This interpretive exclusion occurs by those in the Asian American immigrant church and others who observe it from outside. Finally, Lee offers some contributions that the racial concepts can make in the ministerial and theological reflections regarding the Asian American immigrant church.

Allison L. Norton provides an overview of significant trends and issues related to immigration and congregational life in the United States and explores how migrants and their descendants, directly and indirectly, are reshaping the religious landscape. Norton outlines how migration studies and theory can contribute to and expand our understanding of the Christian migrant. Norton also advances a conversation at the juncture of three intertwining topics in the study of immigration and religion that brings new light to long-standing questions posed by religious leaders and scholars.

Alexia Salvatierra introduces the Latin American Mission to North America and the second generation as a case study to cast a light on the Korean American church's identity and mission. Vigorous growth in non-Catholic churches in Latin America has provoked a movement of migrant missionaries creating Latinx immigrant churches throughout the United States. Salvatierra examines how they transmit this vibrant faith to the second generation and the best practices for success in this objective. Salvatierra emphasizes that immigrant churches must be intentional about incorporating and supporting the leadership of emerging generations, which may require changes in language, culture, and ministry activities. She also brings up offering whole-life mentoring, opportunities to participate in active community ministry, and that the consciousness of transnational globalism and social justice should be the priority in serving the second generation effectively.

In the concluding chapter, coeditor Sebastian Kim discusses the key concepts and perspectives from the previous chapters and brings them into dialogue with the contemporary discussion of world Christianity. Then, going one step forward, Kim introduces a grand and multidisciplinary perspective to the Korean American churches through the historical, biblical, and phenological lens. By this concluding chapter, the readers will see God's providential plan for the Korean American churches.

Since 2000, there has been a growing body of literature that addresses Korean American Christianity. In acknowledging their contribution, the editors believe this book is unique in its combination of a focus on Korean Americans, a missiological perspective, and its particular focus on immigrant churches with attention to intergenerational relations.

Academic integration is another contribution of this book. For identifying the Korean American church, the current volume integrates multiple disciplines such as psychology, theology, history, sociology, anthropology, world Christianity, and missiology to address their identity and mission. Each author knows well how his or her expertise fits into the mosaic of missiology. It also brings sensitivity to the issues of identity and inter-generation of immigrants, and finally, this book provides helpful insight into the church's mission practices.

Authors and editors undoubtedly recommend the current volume as a required or recommended reading for courses at Christian institutions to understand the immigrant church at an in-depth level. However, the academic and ecclesial breadth of the contributors also makes it a quality resource for a wider readership of faculty, students, and researchers in theology, missiology, migration studies, ethnic studies, and urban studies.

BIBLIOGRAPHY

Kim, Sŭng-hun, and Wonsuk Ma. *Korean Diaspora and Christian Mission*, Regnum Studies in Mission. Eugene, OR: Wipf & Stock, 2011.

1

IN-BETWEEN KOREAN IMMIGRANT IDENTITY FORMATION AND THE POSITIONALITY OF ASIAN IMMIGRANTS
Reconstructing Leadership of the Korean Immigrant Church

Choi Hee An

INTRODUCTION

When I moved to the United States and learned how to speak English, the most difficult word that I had to use was "I." In almost every sentence, I realized I had to use "I." People kept asking, "What do *I* want? How do *I* feel?" It was very uncomfortable for me to use the word, *I*, all the time. In the first week of my first semester in the United States, one of my American friends asked me about my family. I answered, "Our husband is in Korea." My friend laughed at me and said, "We do not share a husband. Your husband." Experiencing great embarrassment, I could not laugh. In Korean, *our* husband was the right sentence because Koreans often use *our* instead of *my* in many colloquial sentences. However, in English, it was considered a critical error in terms of grammar and culture. As I remembered this unlaughable embarrassment, but laughable moment, I started my academic journey to understand how my Korean immigrant mind has traveled from Korea to the United States.

KOREAN IMMIGRANT IDENTITY FORMATION

Understanding who I am, the self, is the most difficult, unavoidable, and indispensable part of our physical, psychological, and spiritual journey. As our body matures and ages, we explore our maximum physical strength and experience the limits of human finitude. When our body changes, our psychological and spiritual development is deeply impacted. Many psychological development theories such as child development theories, cognitive development theories, and psychosocial theories are good examples explaining how human minds develop as they go through bodily changes over time. Then, how about space? When our body experiences different spaces, how do our mind and soul respond? How does our whole self react to different spaces? How does our whole self experience different spaces over time?

When people migrate and meet a new reality, they go through not only physical challenges to adjust to the new place but also tremendous psychological and even spiritual challenges to know where they are and who they have to be now. As soon as people walk on the new journey crossing boarders and entering new territories, a new identity formation process starts. From the beginning of immigrants' lives, every immigrant identity is questioned under suspicion, not only by others but also by themselves. A new identity formation process occurs with or without self-awareness. Each identity formation process is different and complex depending on each individual and communal culture.

The process of Korean immigrant identity formation is a good example to demonstrate this complexity and uniqueness of how immigrants form and develop their identity based on their unique colonial/postcolonial past and the current immigrant present. In my book *A Postcolonial Self: Korean Immigrant Theology and Church*, I have explained Korean immigrant identity formation in three different parts: A Korean Ethnic Self (We), A Marginalized Self (I as the Other versus We as the Other), and A Postcolonial Self (I and We with others).

Even though there are many ways to explain the Korean ethnic self, I have focused on the concept of *woori* (we) as one of the most critical parts of forming a Korean identity. The core meaning of woori starts with I, you and others who listen to I are referred to as I.[1] It is similar to the meaning of we in English. However, unlike English, it includes a certain hierarchy of relationship. It is used when people talk to those who are not higher than them in terms of social positions. It also includes people's expressions of their intimate relationships with someone or some group to the people who are not higher than them.[2]

However, the meaning of woori goes beyond these definitions. As Korean colonial and postcolonial experience has greatly influenced and formed Korean language, such as colloquial usages of military terms, the concept of woori has been emphasized in two different ways. First, woori has been used to refer to people who are "on the same side."[3] In a colonial and postcolonial sense, woori

---

1   Korean National Language Institute, *Standard Korean Big Dictionary*, (Seoul: Korean National Language Institute, n.d.), https://tinyurl.com/4k9m7ezw.
2   Korean National Language Institute, *Standard Korean Big Dictionary*.
3   Shin Ki Cheol and Shin Yong Cheol, *Sae Woorimal Kun Sajeon* (Our New and Big Language Dictionary) (Seoul: Samsung Press, 1985), 2512; Choi Hee An, *A Postcolonial Self: Korean Immigrant Theology and Church* (New York: State University of New York Press, 2015), 10.

became an exclusive representation of who we are as Koreans, as the colonized who sought liberation and the independence of Korea as a nation. The concept of belongingness as Koreans is a serious part of the formation of woori. Forming woori starts "from the practice of knowing who we know before forming a notion of who we are."[4] It is to know "who we are *not*," that is, different from the colonizers and who we are, that is, "*not*" the colonized. *Woori*'s practice of knowing who we know starts from claiming woori as the citizens of an independent nation whose freedom and independence were originally their own. At the same time, it questions who others are. The practice of knowing who we know is the precondition of defining who we are. Out of survival from the colonial reality, Koreans had to discern who they know and who they can invite in or hide from. In this colonial context, woori often referred to Koreans as the only representation of the Korean race. Promoting woori leads individual Koreans into one national Korean body. Woori became a Korean colonial communal self. Distinguishing Koreans from Japanese and Chinese colonizers, calling themselves woori formed their racial identity of *minjok* (the Korean race) and evoked great patriotism for independence. On the one hand, woori gives Koreans agency to form their communal identity to survive and fight for freedom and justice against the colonial others. It emphasizes togetherness. On the other hand, it provokes extreme obsessions with nationalism and patriotism as a colonial defense. It manipulates exclusivism as the rights and power of the colonized.

Second, woori has been used as the representation of individual I at the expense of erasing the voice of the powerless. It simultaneously presents the voice of the powerless as the voice of the powerful. Even though the word woori was not originated from these exclusive colonial ideologies, colonial experience and

---

4 Choi, *A Postcolonial Self*, 13.

history influenced the meaning of woori in a more exclusively colonial form. The voice of woori often was delivered from the voice of the political military dictators and economically higher colonial class even within the colonized Korean groups. It was easily manipulated by these corrupted leaders for their own privileges and wealth. In the name of woori, sacrifices of the powerless groups such as the poor, women, and children were forced and easily decorated as an honor and glory for the nation. However, at the same time, woori is a voice of the powerless in power. When people without economic wealth and political power cannot present their voices as individuals, they use woori as a collective voice to demonstrate their power and will. Implanting we in an open space to invite each other, woori exercises its communal relationship to extend its members beyond individual self. It calls out individuals to hold each other in the space of power to stand up for their common good.[5]

In summary, the concept of woori has been formed by both colonial and anticolonial/postcolonial movement processes in Korean colonial history. It is often used in tension between a patriotic colonial elite leadership and a postcolonial communal leadership. It was often represented as the voice of community over individuals as it required standing on the same side of thoughts and movements as the citizens of the Korean nation during the Korean colonial era. The process of forming woori started from survival against colonial violence as the patriotic colonial elite leadership demanded individual sacrifices to save the communal body. At the same time, it became a force to call individuals to collect their power to fight against the oppressor and deliver their voice with power. It is one of the most unique Korean communal selves that reflects Korean colonial and postcolonial history and

---

5   Choi, *A Postcolonial Self*, 9–64.

culture. This identity formation, history, and culture differs greatly from experiences Koreans encounter in the United States.

When Koreans move to the United States, the first strange experience that they mention is they are called Asians or Asian immigrants, not Koreans. As their bodies are categorized as Asians, not necessarily Koreans, at the gate of the airport, they are confused about who they are and how they have to perform in a new land. From their language to food, clothes, and culture, they are asked to learn every sentence and move in ways that are different from what they knew before. As they learn "I" as the subject to change their habit of speech instead of woori (we), they accept "I" as the identity to adopt. As they learn how to speak "I," they have to learn how to think and behave as "I." Then, the concept of woori is immediately questioned and under suspicion. However, the more they learn how to be "I," the more they realize they cannot be "I" because the "I" that they can be is not the "I" that they learn. They realize that they are not the "I as the center" like white people, but the "I as the other," the marginalized.[6] The assimilation process to learn and adopt "I" is not successful, but instead a failure because it sets up boundaries around social privileges. "The accomplishment of becoming an independent, autonomous, imperial, white "I" comes at the expense of alienating their individual self from their ethnic self ("woori")."[7] They experience loss of both individual and communal selves in this process.

At the same time, as Korean immigrants experience and learn the marginalized self, they seek space to protect themselves from this marginalization. Korean church is one of the most popular and powerful spaces to offer support and help, not only spiritually, but also psychologically, socially, and physically. Through worship, small group gatherings, and fellowship, Koreans

---

6   Choi, *A Postcolonial Self*, 65–87.
7   Choi, *A Postcolonial Self*, 80.

experience woori again, but not as the center in this society. Instead as the communal marginalized self. It is the process of we as the other.[8] As they learn "I" as the other, they relearn "we" as the other through remembering woori and re-membering individuals as a part of Korean immigrant churches. Forming their immigrant self, from a marginalized individual self to a marginalized communal self, is a unique process of Korean immigrant identity formation. However, this process does not end at the formation of the marginalized communal self. It leads to the development of a postcolonial self, which is "I and We with Others."

A postcolonial self is developed by both the institutional ideology of postcolonialism and the power of people who create embodied knowledge to survive and thrive. As immigrants learn and hear others, "developing somatic consciousness of one's environment, and conjuring images and words to describe new insights and perceptions" in their immigrant communities, Korean immigrants develop somatic consciousness of their communal but marginalized situation through Korean immigrant church, and conjure images and words of woori to claim their new hybrid identity.[9] From "I" to "we" and from "we" to "with others," they take a serious turn toward finding who they are individually and communally in relation with others. Forming a postcolonial self is not a natural identity formation process, especially moving the attention from "I and we" to "I and we with others." It is a synthetic process of intentional learning. It requires radical hospitality to grow into this self. Otherness in a postcolonial self is not the other as the opposition of "I and we" because "the presence of others exists within and with the existence of the I and we."[10]

---

[8] Choi, *A Postcolonial Self*, 88–114.

[9] Kwok Pui-lan. *Asian and Asian American Women in Theology and Religion* (Asian Christianity in the Diaspora), Springer International Publishing. Kindle Edition. 215 of 5921.

[10] Choi, *A Postcolonial Self*, 132.

The Korean immigrant identity process that I explained in this research is neither a staged nor linear development process. Some Korean immigrants experience these identities in different times and spaces, or they experience all of them at the same time. This process is formed in a synthetic, dialectical, and cultural manner that happens at different times and throughout lived experiences of being immigrants. It is a simultaneously natural and intentional process for Korean immigrants to experience and learn. As they struggle to find who they are in this identity process within the Korean immigrant community, they realize where they are in this society in relation with others. Thus, the positionality of Koreans as Asian immigrants in the United States is experienced and considered with and without critical analysis.

THE POSITIONALITY OF ASIAN IMMIGRANTS AS THE THIRD OTHER

When first-generation Korean immigrants learn they are categorized as Asians and not by their nationality of origin, they encounter their new immigrant identity in the United States for the first time. When second- and third-generation Koreans are born in this country, they accept their racial ethnic identity as Asian naturally as primary to their Korean identity. Although understanding their identification as Asian takes a different path between first and second generations, both generations learn how this society sees and classifies them. Asian immigrants' positionality in US social systems begins as once they step onto US soil by way of immigration or birth, often without conscious awareness. What is their positionality? Where do they find themselves in this society? In my new book *A Postcolonial Relationship: Challenges of Asian Immigrants as the Third Other* (2022), I explain their position as the third other.

Many feminist, liberation theology, and postcolonial studies use otherness as a way to describe identity and existence of women, the marginalized, the powerless, and the colonized. In sociopolitical cultural settings it creates a clear division between the "I" and "the other." One of the most powerful and clear paradigms to exemplify this otherness is explained through the Black/white racial binary divide. Deeply rooted in the relationship and history between the enslaved and the enslavers, this divide is one of the most powerful leading paradigms for discussing racism in the United States. As the Black/white binary locates white at the top and Black at the bottom, it invents a clear racial hierarchy not only for Black and white groups, but also for all other racial groups. It "cultivates fear from nonwhite racial ethnic groups of associating with blacks" and this "fear creates an irreconcilable distance from black(ness)."[11] In this sense, the Black/white binary divide becomes the Black/nonBlack binary divide. Discussing justice issues that support Black groups within the Black/white binary divide then becomes *the* paradigm of racial discourse.

There are three purposes of inventing the Black/white binary. First, this paradigm dominates the racial justice discourse. By focusing on only one group, Black people, it minimizes and dismisses other racial issues such as anti-Asian sentiment and anti-Latinx issues. Second, as this paradigm produces fear to stay away from blackness, it glorifies liberal white middle and upper class social justice work as the noble superior behavior which legitimates white privileges. Emphasizing Black people's suffering and white people's sacrifices to support Black people in white liberal movements, the binary puts the position of blackness

---

[11] Choi Hee An, *A Postcolonial Relationship: Challenges of Asian Immigrants as the Third Other* (New York: State University of New York Press, 2022), 30.

as permanent victimhood and whiteness as constant savior/supporter repeatedly. Third, giving more privileges to one racial group over other groups, the Black/white divide manipulates and covers white privileges. Instead of dismantling white privileges, it makes people bring more attention to temporary political advantages and advancement for their own groups.[12] Developing and disseminating these purposes, the Black/white binary divide becomes the "one single power paradigm in control."[13]

Korean immigrants experience this paradigm as the norm of this society. They accept this anti-Black prejudice and tend to dissociate from blackness. Without critical understandings of the Black/white binary, Koreans are put in the position to learn to be white and not to be Black. Many Korean immigrants see this divide as the parameter in US racial discourse. However, as they recognize and accept this paradigm, they often find themselves invisible. They realize that they are or cannot be neither white nor Black. In this divide, they do not exist.

The native/alien binary divide is another divide to explain Asian immigrants' positionality in this society. From the beginning of US immigrant history until 1965, Asian immigrants were never allowed to stay permanently. They were legally foreigners. The "foreigner" was not just a symbol. It was their legal sociopolitical status for decades. And it remains Asian immigrants' status in many respects in contemporary US sociopolitical discourse. They are never accepted as full members of US society. "Seen as forever foreigners, their otherness is treated as non-transferable, nonassimilable to be natives by any means."[14] Their Asian bodies and Asian accents have been the target of discrimination. Manipulating the images of Asian immigrants to be seen as the people who steal jobs from natives, especially

---

12 Choi, *A Postcolonial Relationship*, 9–33.
13 Choi, *A Postcolonial Relationship*, 32.
14 Choi, *A Postcolonial Relationship*, 121.

from white and Black groups, and threaten national wealth and security based on nativism, this divide is invented to control Asian immigrants by producing anti-Asian sentiment and the model minority myth.

Anti-Asian sentiment is deeply associated with foreignness, resulting in many anti-Asian violence cases existing without proper visibility to the public.[15] Anti-Asian violence had rarely been recognized as violence against Asians. Rather, it is often dismissed as the problems of crazy individuals against individuals who accidentally happened to be Asians. The existence of anti-Asian violence has long been denied. However, during the COVID-19 pandemic, many cases of anti-Asian violence dramatically occurred and were finally named as anti-Asian violence in the eyes of public.[16] Coercing anti-Asian sentiment, the native/alien binary divide legitimizes anti-Asian violence as the problem of foreigners, not the problem of natives.

At the same time, this binary divide portrays Asian immigrants as the model minority. Inventing the model minority myth, the binary lifts images of Asians as the successful immigrants. Emphasizing the success stories of upper-class Asians, the binary creates harmful competitions among non-white racial groups, dismisses the multi-layered suffering that Asian immigrants experience, and produces misperceptions of Asians as white.[17] Further, the model minority myth draws the boundary around Asian immigrants as the successful *minority*, and not majority. It manipulates the belief that Asians are smart enough to make their advancement this far, but not smart enough to make it all the way to the top. Using the model minority myth, this divide sets up Asians

---

15   Choi, *A Postcolonial Relationship*, 66–78.
16   According to the 2020–2021 national report at Stop AAPI Hate reporting center, 3,795 incidents were reported from March 19, 2020 to February 28, 2021. https://tinyurl.com/y499x6fr.
17   Choi, *A Postcolonial Relationship*, 84.

as the permanent second class. Their successes achieved by the elite upper-class Asian groups is emphasized in media whereas the sufferings of different Asian immigrant groups are never recognized. The more the public emphasizes this success in media, the more it provokes rage among natives to believe that aliens, especially Asian foreigners, threaten their lives.

However, when the native/alien divide engages with immigrant issues, it gives more attention to Latinx groups. Many immigrant issues are considered issues between natives (white groups) and aliens (Latinx groups). As the Black/white binary divide makes Asian immigrants neither Black nor white, the native/alien divide makes them neither native nor alien. Ironically, despite their foreignness emphasizing their treatment as aliens within the native/alien binary, Asian immigrants are also treated as not alien enough in this divide. Within the intersection of the Black/white and native/alien binary divides, Asian immigrants experience "double in-betweenness" because they are considered imperfect and incomplete others in both paradigms.[18]

> Regardless of their socioeconomic and political status, within these intersections and interactions, they were treated as the imperfect, incomplete other. The effects continue to exist. They are neither completely black nor white. They are neither near white nor near black. They are neither completely aliens nor natives. They are neither completely minorities nor nonminorities. They are never recognized as the complete other. Rather, they are treated as the invisible other who exists but never identified as the other at the opposite end. They are *the imperfect other*.[19]

---

18 Choi, *A Postcolonial Relationship*, 4.
19 Choi, *A Postcolonial Relationship*, 98–99.

Existence of their otherness is denied. Binary paradigms dismiss their otherness as nonotherness because their otherness is positioned as the middle in binary relations and in third space in multirelations. I call it *the third other*. Asian immigrants are the third other. Their otherness is different from otherness in a binary sense. They are the other in a third sense. They are the other in between spaces. Their otherness is not the reflection of "I" or "the other." The third other is not the "shadow other" behind "I" and "the other," even though sometimes it does stand behind. Asian immigrant groups' otherness exists in interstitial spaces. Their otherness exists beyond the space of the other. It is otherness in margins and peripheries that do not hold the strong binary sense of otherness but picture the otherness in a saturated sense in limited capacity. Their otherness is saturated in the form of permanent guests and invisible citizens from multiplications and intersections of binary paradigms. This saturated otherness is presented in the sense of temporary, fragmented, localized universalities and repressive sociopolitical structures.[20]

The reality of this third otherness is particularly unique to Korean immigrants because of their conflictive relationship with Black people. Embodying the Black/white binary as the norm, Korean immigrants see Black people as the group with whom they should not associate. At the same time, placing the minority myth on Korean immigrant groups within the native/alien paradigm, Black groups see Korean immigrants as the group that takes away economic opportunities from their neighborhoods. Instead of critically analyzing the multidimensional approaches to understand

---

20 Choi, *A Postcolonial Relationship*, 99.

their complicated relationships, many first-generation Korean immigrants often use their third otherness as a means of not dealing with this cross-racial tension. Because of their embodied Black/white binary and misunderstanding/miscommunication with Black people, potentially due to their limited English capacity, they are hesitant to extend their postcolonial self to be with others, especially Black groups. As a result, they disconnect themselves from Black communities. However, because of their shared experiences of suffering, Korean immigrants, especially the second generation, should show their solidarity with others, especially Black and Latinx communities. Standing together in various social justice movements like Black Lives Matter, Stop AAPI Hate, and the US Immigrant Rights Movement opens opportunities for Koreans and Korean Americans to demonstrate their postcolonial self by including others in woori.

Korean immigrants' third otherness encourages the isolation of their marginalized self (we as the other). It prevents the growth of their communal self through the process of an inclusive, open postcolonial identity. Woori becomes an exclusive "we" again based on fear of relationships with Black and Latinx communities, along with Koreans' experience of being a third other in both Black/white and native/alien paradigms. However, the position of Korean immigrants' third otherness simultaneously encourages them to stand for issues of justice and equity with others because they are aware of their own isolation and marginalization. Their marginalized but imperfect otherness makes them realize that they cannot get out of this otherness without collaboration and solidarity. Because of this third otherness, they are encouraged to seek others and extend their communal self of woori beyond their racial and ethnic boundaries.

The question then becomes, where can Korean immigrants transform their marginality into inclusivity? I found the answer in Korean immigrant church. Korean immigrant church can be the place where many Korean immigrants turn their third otherness toward openness and inclusivity. Although it is a space that reveals many individual and communal conflicts and even evokes additional complicated sociopolitical problems, it is a space that forms communal power toward solidarity with others. Thus, Korean immigrant church is the site of the formation of the communal marginalized self and its transformation into the postcolonial self. It is the foundation of forming exclusivity and inventing inclusivity simultaneously. How, then, can Korean immigrant church transform their exclusivity into inclusivity? What does it have to do to lead this transformation?

FROM MARGINALITY TO INCLUSIVITY: RECONSTRUCTING LEADERSHIP OF THE KOREAN IMMIGRANT CHURCH

As K-pop, K-food, K-film, K-drama, and K-culture lead and form an important part of global culture, Koreans in Korea demonstrate great sensitivities regarding including others and meeting their needs. They try to learn how to welcome the socially marginalized voices in terms of class, gender, and race. Even though they still hold their exclusive mono racial identity under the strong influences of colonial and postcolonial military culture, they are aware of their advancement and achievement in a sense of globalization and try to create inclusive cultural trends. As they want to preserve their Korean authentic culture with pride, they embrace their hybrid modernized culture with creativity and confidence.

Korean immigrants in the United States are also aware of this new globalization process that Koreans in Korea are experiencing. They also feel proud of this great achievement and identify themselves as Koreans. However, their identity as Asian immigrants in the United States still suffers because they remain marginalized (we as the other) rather than forming/moving toward a postcolonial identity that includes others as a part of their immigrant identity. This marginalized identity then becomes escalated as an exclusive identity in Korean immigrant church. Rather than embracing inclusivity, the church actually emphasizes exclusivity in the name of faith and has failed to extend their inclusiveness beyond a Korean ethnic boundary. My research on Korean immigrant Christian leadership found several problems within Korean/Asian immigrant churches: traditional clergy-centered leadership, lack of ordained clergy women's leadership, difficulties developing social services, dis-communication between the first and the second (and third) generations, fighting with the power of American individualism, and discrepancy on LGBTQIA+ issues to name a few.[21] Specifically in terms of LGBTQIA+ issues, not all, but many Korean immigrant churches show extreme conservative attitudes and bluntly claim LGBTQIA+ members as sinners. Because of these reasons, many Korean immigrants, especially, many second-plus generation immigrants have left the Korean immigrant church. In recent years, including the ongoing COVID-19 pandemic, exit or exile from the Korean immigrant church has escalated.

While the previous section highlights the imperfect nature of the Korean immigrant church—specifically the pain caused among multi-marginalized groups, the production of hierarchal patriarchal colonial attitudes, and the fostering of communal marginalization and voluntary exclusion—it is also true that Korean immigrant church has been a primary space and resource to many Korean immigrants socially, spiritually, and psychologically. It is also a space that teaches and believes inclusivity. Therefore, in order for Korean immigrant church to be the center of transformation and not to lose its prophetic voice as the church,

---

21   Choi Hee An, *A Postcolonial Leadership: Asian Immigrant Christian Leadership and Its Challenges* (New York: State University of New York Press, 2020), 156–179.

it is important for Korean immigrant church leaders to *cultivate inclusivity* and to embrace their third otherness as the position to connect with others.

Here, I would like to introduce a movement that is deeply embedded in Korean culture to show how Korean authentic play culture has benefitted from inclusion. That is *kkagdugi* (깍두기) play. Kkagdugi is well known as a kind of kimchi that has the shape of a square made by a radish. It has another meaning. It indicates the person who cannot belong to either side because of lack of ability to join.[22] However, when children play the game, the position/meaning of kkagdugi transforms in an opposite direction. Players designate a person as kkagdugi, allow this person to belong to both sides, and play for both sides. If there are odd numbers of players preventing teams from dividing equally, or players find someone who cannot play very well because of their young age or physical conditions, they create a kkagdugi position to include the person and play together with them. It gives both teams an opportunity to be equally divided and encourages both teams to include the marginalized and the powerless so they are no longer marginalized and powerless. It is not a fixed concept, but a play and movement that empowers and includes the marginalized. It gives a chance to the powerless to no longer be powerless but to *feel powerful* and play on both sides. Their presence is not dismissed but becomes an important game changer. Because of their position, presence, and double opportunity to play, the game can be continued, and children can participate in the play with more excitement and solidarity. Many people in their childhood remember this position and *experience inclusivity*. With graciousness and generosity, equality is created and the marginalized become the center of play. Kkagdugi centers the center and re-centers both teams in balance.

---

22   Korean National Language Institute, *Standard Korean Big Dictionary*.

Embracing inclusivity is not a new concept, but a new movement to start in the Korean immigrant church. Learning from kkagdugi play, it is important for the Korean immigrant church to incorporate inclusivity into practice, specifically the intentional practice of leadership. I would like to propose two spaces that can incorporate kkagdugi play in leadership: (1) dismantling male dominated church leadership by empowering women in leadership within church and (2) collaborative leadership beyond Korean ethnic boundaries.

First, embracing inclusivity within the church begins with dismantling male dominated church leadership. Korean immigrant church should empower those not in power positions, train them to learn leadership roles, and give them opportunities to exercise their leadership skills. The traditional function of the church emphasizes taking care of the marginalized, poor, and powerless, and looks at these groups as people in need. However, embracing inclusivity transforms the marginalized, powerless, and poor into leaders by recognizing their power and training them to learn new limits about themselves. Instead of centering the clergy and elite lay leaders, it is important to creatively generate leadership positions to include all congregation members and develop leadership training, mentoring, and collaboration.

Empowering women's leadership in the center of Korean immigrant church is one of the most important leadership practices that cultivates movement of kkakdugi play. Korean hierarchical church culture originates from two different roots of patriarchal culture: Korean Confucian patriarchal military culture and western colonial Christian culture. As Koreans went through their colonial history, their leadership was performed under strong colonial military culture, with and without the colonizers' physical occupation. Dictatorship was the main model of leadership and individual charisma was one of the most important characteristics in Korean colonial and postcolonial history. Kings, generals, and individual heroes, such as King Sejong and General Lee Sun-shin were the ideal and most beloved leaders for whom many Koreans show deep respect. Demonstrating strong individual charisma and confidence has also become the first condition to be a leader in both Korea and Korean immigrant contexts, specifically among upper-class, elite males.

However, this traditional culture does not mean there were no women in leadership. Women have been the center of Korean immigrant church life. Without recognizing their leadership, the Korean immigrant church cannot survive. Although they have been excluded from formal leadership roles, women have continuously exercised their leadership throughout history, as many feminists and women scholars claim. Instead of demonstrating top-down individual leadership, many Korean women in Korea and the US Korean diaspora engage in collaborative leadership.[23] And, fortunately, the Korean church has been the place for them to cultivate their official leadership roles, especially during the early Korean church history. While it is true that leadership of Korean immigrant churches is predominantly male clergy-centered in terms of worship, it is also true that many Korean immigrant women exercise their leadership behind the curtain in terms of small group gatherings and fellowship after worship, which sustain essential parts of church life. Through regular small group gatherings, daily bible readings, and prayer meetings, from the early colonial Korean church to the modern postcolonial Korean and Korean immigrant church, women have been the main *force* sustaining the existence of church. And their leadership is shown, not necessarily in the form of individuals, but in the form of communal collaborative movements. Therefore, it is important for the Korean immigrant church to *recognize* women's leadership and their hard work and intentionally create more opportunities for women to take part

---

23 Choi, *A Postcolonial Leadership*, 207–215.

in official leadership roles. Recognizing women's leadership in collaborative work, cultivating women's individual leadership, and intentionally providing the opportunity for women to exercise their leadership in official leadership roles can de-center the center of male leadership and re-center both women and men's leadership. Without this recognition, cultivation, and opportunity for women, it is impossible for Korean immigrant church to transform their marginality to inclusivity.

Second, embracing inclusivity cannot happen without collaborative leadership beyond the Korean immigrant communities. Cultivating collaborative leadership outside of their ethnic boundaries is one of the most crucial practices the Korean immigrant church needs to develop, especially embracing the space to cultivate solidarity between Korean immigrants and Black people. "The historical roots of Asian-Black solidarity" can be traced "back to 1955 with the Bandung Conference, where representatives of people from the Asian continent and folks on the African continent came together to talk about what decolonization was going to look like for both of us."[24] They saw the commonality of their suffering and empowered each other to get through tough immigrant lives. However, these developing collaborative relationships weakened on US soil as immigration policies favored one ethnic group over other ethnic groups, usually in favor of Asian groups over African groups, and vice versa. These shifting dynamics led to Asians and Africans fighting against each other to secure resources and benefits for their own groups. US immigration policies also negatively impacted relationships between Asian immigrants and Black Americans as racial politics contributed to further divisions in competition for social resources. However, in recent

---

24 NPR's Ailsa Chang talks with author Kim Tran about the history of solidarity between Asian and Black Americans and how their movements interact. https://tinyurl.com/58mn8zcs.

years, when there was a call for solidarity from Black Lives Matter starting in 2014-2015. Asians responded and formed Asians for Black Lives and the Asian American Advocacy Fund. And, when anti-Asian violence heightened with the onset of the COVID-19 pandemic, Black Lives Matter stood in solidarity with Asians in the United States.[25]

The Asian American Advocacy Fund stands in solidarity with Black lives and understands the movement for Black lives and liberation as one that works against the oppressive systems of white supremacy. As AAPI's, we must not only continue to educate ourselves but show up for Black communities. The AAPI community continues to benefit from the rights and privileges that are the result of the hard-fought battles by Black organizers and activists. We will not be tools of white supremacy or uphold a racist and violent state. We condemn forms of the model minority myth and recognize the racism and anti-Blackness in this narrative. We are and will always be in solidarity with the movement for Black lives. *We are and will always be in solidarity with the movement for Black lives.*[26]

Standing hand in hand, Black Lives Matter and various movements against anti-Asian violence are playing kkagdugi together. Cultivating collaborative leadership between Asian/Korean people and Black people can create the position of kkagdugi for each other. When they collaboratively work together to bring about solidarity in their movements, they cover each other's marginality and bring their marginality to the intersection's center. They

---

25 NPR, "The History of Solidarity between Asian and Black Americans," https://tinyurl.com/58mn8zcs.
26 "Asian Americans for Black Lives," https://tinyurl.com/2s3ad33f.

include the marginalized from among each other. Then, they are no longer marginalized and powerless but feel powerful together and work on both sides for justice and equity. Their presence can no longer be dismissed in public. They become an important voice to challenge the white colonial racial discourse. They de-center the dominant white culture and re-center both Black groups and Asian immigrant groups in harmony. Cultivating solidarity beyond Korean ethnic boundaries can help the Korean immigrant church transform its position of third otherness and the process of the marginalized self into a space of invitation to connect with others in God's kin-dom on earth.

CONCLUSION

Being Korean immigrants in the United States has been more than tough. It requires the individual and communal life and death of Korean immigrants within the intersection of forming a Korean immigrant identity and being a third other. Fortunately, the Korean immigrant church has been the most important space for Koreans to survive, not only individually but also communally. However, it is losing its leadership roles among Korean immigrant communities. Because of its own exclusivity without others and the marginalization of women in leadership, many Korean immigrants leave the church. Without re-forming Korean immigrant church leadership and reconstructing the Korean immigrant church, those leaving will not come back. Without leading the transformation from marginality to inclusivity, Korean immigrant church cannot survive and will lose its existence. Therefore, now is the time for the Korean immigrant church to critically evaluate their past and present, and show their prophetic leadership to create hope and vision for a better future.

BIBLIOGRAPHY

"Asian Americans for Black Lives," https://www.asianamericanadvocacy fund.org/asians-for-black-lives

Choi, Hee An. *A Postcolonial Leadership: Asian Immigrant Christian Leadership and Its Challenges.* New York: State University of New York Press, 2020.

———. *A Postcolonial Relationship: Challenges of Asian Immigrants as the Third Other.* New York: State University of New York Press, 2022.

———. *A Postcolonial Self: Korean Immigrant Theology and Church.* New York: State University of New York Press, 2015.

Korean National Language Institute, *Standard Korean Big Dictionary.* Seoul: Korean National Language Institute, n.d.), https://stdict.korean.go.kr/search/searchView.do

Kwok, Pui-lan. *Asian and Asian American Women in Theology and Religion* (Asian Christianity in the Diaspora). Springer International Publishing. Kindle Edition.

NPR. "The History of Solidarity between Asian and Black Americans," https://www.npr.org/2021/04/02/983925014/the-history-of-solidarity-between-asian-and-black-americans

Shin, Ki Cheol and Shin Yong Cheol, *Sae Woorimal Kun Sajeon* (Our New and Big Language Dictionary). Seoul: Samsung Press, 1985.

"Stop AAPI Hate", https://stopaapihate.org/2020-2021-national-report/

2

COOKING *BAHB* AND MISSIONAL CHRISTIAN EDUCATION IN THE KOREAN NORTH AMERICAN CHURCHES

Nam Soon Song

Jesus said to them, "I am the bread of life. Whoever comes to me will never be hungry, and whoever believes in me will never be thirsty."

—John 6:35 NRSV

INTRODUCTION

Bahb! It is a sentimentally loaded word for Koreans including the Korean diaspora. A bowl of bahb (cooked rice) contains the laughs and tears of Koreans—both joy and sadness. We as Koreans hear and say the word *bahb* from the earliest days to the end of our life. Koreans make bahb. Then, bahb makes Koreans. It is the source of life. It is the very essence of Korean identity, regardless of where we live. Christian education is aimed at helping people to "have life in all fullness." Thus, this article seeks to explore Jesus as the bahb of life, characteristics of bahb and mission of God, and suggests a localized yet globalized missional Christian education for the Korean North American church.

JESUS AS THE BAHB OF LIFE

After Jesus had fed a crowd of five thousand on the mountain in Tiberias with five loaves and two fishes, he walked on water and went to Capernaum. People continued to follow him, seeking food. Bread, to be exact. Then Jesus revealed who he was, saying to the gathered crowd: "I am the bread of life" (John 6:35, 48 NRSV) and "I am the living bread that came down from heaven" (John 6:51 NRSV). Jesus declared his true identity as the divine being, and his mission, which was that people might have eternal life. In Jesus's context, the word *bread* meant daily food; in Greek, *artos* [ἄρτος], bread or a loaf, just as it does in much of the Western world. And bread is traditionally an essential source of life, just as bahb is for Koreans, including Koreans living in North America. Jesus used the analogy of himself as bread to highlight the spiritual hunger of his followers. Interestingly, Jesus shared physical bread with his followers numerous times in his ministry, not just spiritual bread, even after the resurrection, to feed their physical and spiritual hunger.

If we were to localize this analogy in Korean or Korean North American context, Jesus would have said, "I am the bahb of life." or "I am the living bahb." Although the Korean Bible translates the word *bread* as *ttok* (rice cake) instead of *bahb*, bahb seems to be a more appropriate Korean contextual word. This is because bahb is a necessity of life consumed daily by all Koreans, regardless of where they live, whereas ttok is usually reserved for special occasions such as traditional Korean holidays and birthdays. For example, a Korean birthday ttok is equivalent to a birthday cake in the Western world. Hence, it is much more appealing and relatable to Koreans, including Korean North Americans, if Jesus says, "I am the bahb of life," or "I am the living bahb."

Takenaka, a Japanese theologian, offers a localized approach to understanding God with the phrase "God is rice," rather than "God is bread."[1] He considers rice the symbol of God's gift of life for Asians.[2] Here he is referring to cooked rice or ready-to-eat rice. Likewise, I have decided to use bahb (cooked rice) instead of *ssal* (raw rice) to reflect the Korean context because Jesus uses bread—a final, ready-to-eat product made from wheat—not wheat itself, which is just a raw ingredient. As mentioned, bread is a symbol of daily food in many parts of the world, especially in the West. Bahb serves as a symbol of daily food in the East and some countries worldwide. Hence bahb has long been considered a gift of God, the very source of life for many people throughout the world.

For the Korean diaspora in particular, bahb becomes an essential part of who we are, a common denominator that binds people together at the root of our collective identity. Upon reviewing archaic rice seeds, one recent study suggests that rice was in Korea between thirteen thousand and fifteen thousand years ago.[3] And many scholars have concluded that Koreans have had bahb as their main food staple for over five thousand years.[4] In her book *The Living Reed*, Pearl S. Buck describes rice as "the food of life" for Koreans.[5] According to Park, King Sejong the Great

---

[1] Masao Takenaka, *God is Rice: Asian Culture and Christian Faith* (Geneva: World Council of Churches Publications, 1986), 17.
[2] Takenaka, *God is Rice*, 21.
[3] Hye Kyung Chung, [Babe inmunhak] *Humanities of Bahb* (Seoul: Taby, 2015), 29–30.
[4] Chung, *Babe inmunhak*, 30.
[5] Pearl S. Buck, *The Living Reed* (New York: The John Day, 1963), 263.

also once said that bahb is "the heaven of people."[6] In the Korean language, the words that refer to the day's meals all have the word *bahb* at the end: morning bahb, noon bahb, evening bahb, and even *sat bahb* (an in-between light meal for farmers). Likewise, the daily greetings exchanged between Koreans often include the word *bahb*, usually along the lines of: "Have you had (eaten) bahb?" This is also the most common greeting between Korean parents and children: "Are you having (eating) bahb well?" And when Koreans first meet, talk, and attempt to build a new relationship with someone, the gateway to an easy conversation is, "Let's have bahb." As the Korean language illustrates, bahb is at the core of life for the Korean diaspora. That is, bahb is still the source of life for Koreans, including those living in North America. Indeed it is an absolute essence of life for all Koreans, regardless of where we live. Bahb is a means of sustaining life and the foundation of Korean social and cultural constructs. Hence bahb is the fundamental element of Korean identity. Bahb encompasses Korean history, Korean sentiment and characteristics, as well as Korean identity. Then indeed, Jesus is the bahb of life and the living bahb from heaven, the life of God, which cannot be possessed but must be shared.

CHARACTERISTICS OF BAHB AND MISSION OF GOD

While bahb has many characteristics in traditional Korean culture, in this article, I limit these to four significant characteristics connecting bahb with the mission of God. The first significant characteristic of bahb concerning the mission of God is *sharing*, which connects to our communalism, our community-oriented society. Chee Ha Kim's poem, "The Bahb is Heaven," reminds us

---

6 Hyun Mo Park, "Sejongchurum," (11, 02, 2012), https://hmparkblog.tistory.com/세종처럼?page=5

that sharing is the fundamental characteristic of bahb: "Just as we cannot have Heaven alone, so bahb is to share. Just as stars of Heaven are shared, so bahb is shared and eaten with many people together."[7] Indeed Kim is right. Bahb's fundamental characteristic is sharing with all those around us. In the olden days, whoever visited a home around mealtime was invited to the *bahbsang* (dining table) and fed a hearty bowl of bahb. Even a single lunch box would be shared among other people, who would just bring extra chopsticks. Korean people would share bahb with close people, such as friends and neighbors, and even strangers. There was no discrimination in sharing bahb. Anyone who needed bahb was welcomed and fed. In recognition of bahb's characteristic of sharing, people today have created a new word, *honbahb*, which means eating bahb alone. This points to the changing nature of Korean society, a shift from communalism to individualism. When we share bahb with others, it becomes that much tastier and enjoyable. Bahb's fundamental characteristic of sharing gives sharers a sense of richness and fullness after the meal, lessening the void and hunger.

Bahb's characteristic of sharing is linked to the hospitality of Koreans. Korean North American churches offer bahb to anyone who visits the church, inviting each newcomer after church: "Please come and have bahb with us before you leave." Korean North American churches are invested in a particular treat: bahb-sharing as an essential cultural ritual. I was involved in a recent study by the Centre for Asian Theology and Ministry aimed to discover the future of Asian Canadian churches in the Greater Toronto Area. We interviewed thirty laypeople and twenty ministers from ethnic-specific and English-language congregants in mainly Chinese, Taiwanese, and Korean churches. The results were published in the book *People of Faith and People of Jeong*

---

7 Vitanova, "밥은 하늘입니다 김지하," (04, 06, 2018), http://designvita.tistory.com/92

(*Qing*) in 2020. Through this process, I discovered how vital bahb is in Korean Canadian church life, not only for the first generation but for the second also. Even the second generation attends church to have bahb with their second-generation Korean friends. Having bahb together builds close relationships, which gives them their shared identity as Koreans.

Korean North American churches are enthusiastic about sharing food at church either as a whole or as individuals, not just on Sundays but on any occasion. This is a unique aspect of our church ministry, so much so that some ministers call the Korean North American church ministry *mokhwe*, an "eating ministry." In this sense, all church members are called church *sikku* (people who eat bahb together living at the same house): people who eat bahb together at church, as if they were eating together at home. This sharing of bahb is an essential aspect of the church's ministry which then moves into God's mission. It is sharing life, the source of life. Sharing bahb opens generosity in people. Like heaven, bahb is graceful. It is a gift of God to be shared with those who do not have it.

Here we are reminded of Rev. Il Do Choi, Minister of *Bahb Puh* (serving cooked rice) of the Dail community, who has shared bahb with those who need it since 1988. He created a *bahbsang* community, began to serve bahb in Chungyangree, Seoul, in 1988, and then in the Dail community, a practice that has expanded to twenty Dail communities in eleven countries worldwide.[8] Through this activity, many people have participated in an essential mission of God, thereby bringing many others to God. Cooking and sharing bahb has expanded to other missions as well, missions taking care of other needs, such as physical sickness and spiritual hunger. In sum, bahb's characteristic of sharing relates to an

---

8   Choong Hun Noh, "최일도 목사 '밥퍼목사 최일도의 러브스토리' 펴내" *Kidokshinmoon*, (06,09, 2021), https://www.kidok.com/news/articleView.html?idxno=211525

essential aspect of God's mission, and sharing bahb expands our *sikku* beyond our own family, and our ethnicity, bringing people from other ethnic groups and reconciling them to God.

The second significant characteristic of bahb concerning the mission of God is the *jeong* that is born from sharing. When we hear the word *bahb* or smell just-cooked bahb, we feel jeong. I can even say bahb contains jeong. From all the stories we heard during the earlier interviews with members of the Asian Canadian churches, we could sense the flow of these two distinctive elements—faith and jeong (*qing*)—characterizing what Asian Canadian immigrant churches are and who Asian Canadian Christians are.[9] We found out this: Because of jeong and a unique faith, second- and third-generation Asian Canadian congregants stay in their ethnic-specific churches, even when facing challenges and difficulties. Because of jeong, we return to Asian immigrant churches even if we leave for a while due to hurtful experiences. Because of jeong, we feel warmth only at ethnic-specific churches. Because of jeong, we feel part of a larger Asian community. And because of jeong, we feel a sense of belonging to the ethnic-specific churches that stand by us.

As noted earlier, Korean North American churches share bahb at church on Sundays and many weekday occasions. In our research, we also found out that when we share bahb at our church, we share more than food—we share jeong and build relationships. The bahb is consumed and disappears from the table, but the jeong remains between people. And this jeong grows with every communal bahb we have at our church. Jeong fosters family-like closeness, solidarity, togetherness, affection, compassion, and care among members. As a result, the church becomes our family or, at the very least, "family-like." Therefore, the church for Korean

---

9   Nam Soon Song et al., *People of Faith, People of Jeong (Qing): Asian Canadian Churches of Today for Tomorrow* (Eugene, OR: Wipf and Stock, 2020), xviii.

North Americans is not only a spiritual home but also a social, cultural, and psychological home. The church is the so-called "home away from home" and the "home for the homeless at home."[10] Jeong comes from and grows in individual relationships as well as in communal relations. Hence there is jeong between people, jeong with our church, jeong with our nation. We are the people of jeong. The Korean North American immigrant church is the body of Christ comprised of people of jeong. This means that our churches display characteristics of jeong both within and beyond their walls.[11] Here we can foster jeongful relationships with people from other ethnic groups to fulfill God's mission. The beginning of God's mission is sharing bahb with strangers around, which eventually builds jeongful relationships as sikku.

The third significant characteristic of bahb concerning the mission of God is making *harmony*. Bahb has an exclusive and inclusive meaning for Koreans. Sometimes bahb does exclusively mean cooked rice, yet bahb also has an inclusive meaning that incorporates all the extra side dishes. The expression, "Let's have bahb," does not only mean "Let's have cooked rice." It means, "Let's have a full meal including all side and main dishes, soup, and others." "I will cook bahb" does not mean only cooking rice. It mostly means, "I will cook the whole meal, including all the other dishes." We often witness wide-eyed reactions when we take non-Koreans to Korean restaurants and they see a table full of extra side dishes. Bahb harmonizes with almost any side dish, even with some western dishes. For example, bahb mixes with any soup, whether Asian or Western, be it soybean, seaweed, or Minestrone. And bahb goes well, not only with kimchi but with any meat, seafood, or vegetable dishes. With the bread of God and the life of God, there is no discrimination based on people's ethnicity, color, or social status. As missional, the church as the

---

10 Song, *People of Faith*, xx.
11 Song, *People of Faith*, 77.

body of Christ harmonizes with those who are different culturally, socially, economically, and generationally.

The fourth significant characteristic of bahb concerning God's mission is its *vanishing* quality. As we eat bahb, it vanishes into our bodies. As bahb vanishes, it becomes energy to be used and part of the body. It restores the body and refreshes the whole person, even the soul. Bahb thus completes its mission of life-giving. This reminds me of the story of Jesus on the road to Emmaus in the Gospel of Luke (24:13–35). After Jesus walked with the two disciples, he shared bread with them and vanished from sight. Although he vanished from their sight, the two disciples were empowered to go back to where the other disciples were and witnessed the risen Christ. I believe that Jesus vanished into their bodies and restored their whole being. It was his ministry of life-giving continuing through his disciples. Bishop Graham Cray reminds us, "Christians who want to share good news need first to be good news, to show genuine concern for others."[12] He says this is the start of an "incarnational mission." Missional church vanishes into the people we participate in God's mission, empowering them for God's mission of life-giving.

Korean North Americans have a distinctive missional identity around the world. The "hermit kingdom" Enoch Wan refers to is now responsible for "kingdom ministry" worldwide through diaspora missions ministering to and beyond the Korean diasporas in North America.[13] God called Koreans from the hermit kingdom to North America to participate in God's mission

---

12   Wendi Sargeant, *Christian Education and Emerging Church: Postmodern Faith Formation* (Eugene, OR: Pickwick Publications, 2015), 26. She quotes from "Fresh Expressions," http:www.freshexpressions.org.uk/.

13   Enoch Wan, "Korean Diaspora: From Hermit Kingdom to Kingdom Ministry," in *Korean Diaspora and Christian Mission*, ed. Kim S. Hun and Ma Wonsuk (Oxford, UK: Regnum in partnership with Korean Research Institute for Diaspora, 2011), 101, 113.

beyond the Korean diaspora in this continent. This missional zeal originates from Koreans' natural character of sharing bahb and fostering jeong through a unique, strong faith in God. As Charles J. Fensham writes, "the church exists by mission as a fire exists by burning."[14] In its existence, it is a sign of God's larger mission. Van Gelder views the church as a missionary in its very nature. He also contends that every context is a missional one, and every congregation is a missional congregation responsible for participating in God's mission in that context.[15] Through our research, we found that Korean Canadian churches participate in God's mission for underprivileged people other than Koreans in the Greater Toronto Area. It is a source of hope that some churches see their identity as missional.

Letty Russell identifies that mission is not created by the church or from the church but is participation in the mission of God, the *missio Dei*.[16] According to Lesslie Newbigin, the mission is not something burdensome but is a kind of explosion of joy, much like that experienced by the two disciples on the road of Emmaus.[17] Newbigin stresses that "the beginning of the mission is not an action of ours, but the presence of a new reality, the presence of the Spirit of God in power."[18] Thus, the church is not the agent of God's mission but a participant in the mission of the spirit of God. The Trinitarian God is the agent of mission.

---

14 Charles J. Fensham, *Emerging from the Dark Age Ahead: The Future of the North American Church* (Ottawa: Novalis, 2008), 148.

15 Craig Van Gelder, ed., *The Missional Church in Context: Helping Congregations Develop Contextual Ministry*. Missional Church Series (Grand Rapids, MI: William B. Eerdmans, 2007), 27.

16 Letty M. Russell, *Church in the Round: Feminist Interpretation of the Church*. (Louisville, KY: Westminster/J. Knox Press, 1993), 88.

17 Lesslie Newbigin, *The Gospel in a Pluralist Society* (Grand Rapids, MI: William B. Eerdmans, 1989), 116.

18 Newbigin, *The Gospel in a Pluralist Society*, 119.

Furthermore, John Hull says mission as God's mission is expressed "most powerfully in the commitment of God in Christ to the point of death." Mission "is expressed through the church as well as through everything that God as creator, as reconciler, and as life-giver are for the world."[19] Therefore, the mission is to share the love of God with all nations, with all human communities, and the whole created world as a sign of the kingdom.

In 2012, the Commission on World Mission and Evangelism (CWME) of the World Council of Churches (WCC) issued a new Affirmation on Mission and Evangelism: "Mission—as a common witness to Christ—is an invitation to the 'feast in the kingdom of God' (Luke 14:15). The mission of the church is to prepare the banquet and to invite all people to the feast of life. The feast is a celebration of creation and fruitfulness overflowing from the love of God, the source of life in abundance."[20] The document confirms "mission is the overflow of the infinite love of the Triune God." It also urges us to "commit ourselves together to the fullness of life for all, led by the God of Life!" Life in all its fullness is Jesus Christ's ultimate concern and mission (John 10:10).[21] Based on this understanding, I would say the goal of Christian education is to ensure that all people have abundant life. As this affirmation contends, a shift in mission from "mission *to* the margins" to "mission *from* the margins"[22] indicates a missional zeal for sharing the love of God from the margins. It is a zeal that now arises from sharing bahb, the source of life, which is

---

[19] John M. Hull, *Mission-Shaped Church: A Theological Response* (London: SCM Press, 2006), 30.

[20] Commission on World Mission and Evangelism (CWME) of the WCC, "Together towards Life: Mission and Evangelism in Changing Landscapes," New WCC Affirmation on Mission and Evangelism, 2012, 37.

[21] The CWME of WCC, 41.

[22] The CWME of WCC, 6.

already a traditional custom of Koreans, including Korean North Americans.

Based on these understandings of mission and bahb, I now explore cooking bahb and Christian education in the changing context of North America. How might we cook bahb from a localized understanding of Christian education in globalized North America? In response, I pay particular attention to missional Korean North American churches.

COOKING BAHB AND MISSIONAL CHRISTIAN EDUCATION

Letty M. Russell, a Christian educator and feminist theologian since the 1960s, criticized Christian education "as a possession of the church."[23] According to Russell, Christian education in the hands of many church leaders at that time was considered like a "stone," which does not have life. She criticized that Christian education frequently offered a "stone," or even small pebbles, to God's children instead of the bread of life (Matt 7:9-11).[24] Christian education should instead be "a way of participating in the gift of God's love offered to all [God's] children." It is the gift of God's love and grace to all people. God offers all people—children, youth, and adults—the opportunity and power of participating in God's mission of reconciliation in the world.[25] God's mission is restoring all human beings to their true humanity by reconciling them to God, one another, and all creation. People experience God's love and grace in a witnessing community and participate in sharing God's love through witness and service. The context of Christian education is a witnessing community. In this sense,

---

23 Letty M. Russell, *Christian Education in Mission* (Philadelphia: Westminster Press, 1967), 19.
24 Russell, *Christian Education in Mission*, 21.
25 Russell, *Christian Education in Mission*, 23.

Christian education is missionary education in a missionary community. Therefore, for Russell, Christian education is "participation in Christ's invitation and is related to all other parts of the church life."[26] In Christian education, we share God's love with others through words and action, although "the process of Christian education must always be changing as well." Nevertheless, Christian education remains a gift offered by Christ to all people to join in God's mission.

Sharing the bahb of life is a way of sharing and witnessing the life of God, which is given to all people as the gift of God, the love of God, and the grace of God. No one in the world is excluded from this life of God. John Hull says, "All persons are the potential or actual recipients of God's gift of self; wherever that gift is accepted in human freedom, we have the history of salvation."[27] In my context, Christian education is life-giving, the serving of freshly-cooked warm bahb to others, regardless of who they are. Or, as I used to say, Christian education is baking fresh bread and sharing it with others. Sharing bahb is an essential part of God's mission; it is sharing the life of God, which reconciles all people to God and others, bringing the fullness of life. Bahb regularly sustains the body, which in turn helps our whole being flourish. Christian education helps people "to have life to the full," as Jesus, the bahb of life, declared. If Christian education is life-giving for the fullness of life, how should we conduct Christian education? Drawing on the metaphor of cooking bahb, I suggest how to carry out Christian education in a missional way in this changing, globalized, and pluralized world.

---

26 Russell, *Christian Education in Mission*, 24.
27 John M. Hull, "The Holy Trinity and Christian Education in a Pluralist World," The National Society's Religious Centre Annual Lecture 1994, Published by The National Society (Church of England) for Promoting Religious Education, 1995, 16.

First, we need to cook bahb from an understanding of the multi-cultural context of North America. Whenever we cook bahb, we care for the people who will eat bahb, whether they are sikku or guests. Depending on the taste of the people who are going to eat it, we cook bahb differently. We cook bahb to taste good to the people at the table. We understand that North Americans come from all over the world. This means that the cultures of the people for whom we cook are different from ours. Even in the Korean North American churches, we are challenged by the different cultures of the first generation, second generation, and beyond. Our research showed clearly that severe problems between the generations of our churches have arisen from cultural differences. Through deep conversation, and before we cook bahb, we can understand the cultural differences between the generations in our Korean North American churches.

In the North American context, in particular, we need to consider the culture of the people who are going to eat bahb. These days many people in the world eat bahb. Nevertheless, bahb itself and how people cook and eat it are different. In North America, there are several types of rice with which we can prepare bahb, such as brown rice, wild rice, and jasmine rice. The amount of water, heat, and time applied to cook the rice depends on the type of rice we choose. Some people in North America eat bahb made with the long grain jasmine rice, and some prefer to eat the wild rice bahb. Some people dislike the traditional Korean-style sticky bahb with side dishes such as kimchi, and instead serve bahb with butter. Some Asian people prefer fried bahb over plain steamed bahb. Some eat bahb with curry or beans. Others simply do not include bahb in their meals. Therefore, before cooking bahb, we need to understand where people are from and cook according to their types of bahb and their way of eating bahb. We sometimes cook from the assumption that all people eat the same bahb or from the prejudice that they should eat whatever bahb we offer.

However, for some people we need to bake bread, not cook bahb. Aesop's fable "The Fox and the Crane," provides a good lesson and sound wisdom.

So too, in missional Christian education for life-giving, we also need to understand people's diverse cultural backgrounds before we witness them or offer any kind of service. We need to accommodate people who are culturally different from us. Then, through Christian education, people can have a full life of reconciling with God and with other people.

Second, we need to cook bahb creatively, understanding how fast the world changes in a globalized world community. As the world changes, we too need to adapt and change how we cook bahb. Although bahb remains the main food staple in Korea, the overall food culture as it relates to diversified resources, cooking, and putting a meal together has been changing, which is reflective of a globalized food chain and economic growth at the macro level. At the micro level, with more options to choose from, Korean people's taste preferences have changed and evolved over time. In the contemporary global food supply system, a growing variety of produce and local food products are now being sold worldwide. For example, traditional ethnic food staples like kimchi seem to be widely available in many parts of the world. These days, such ethnic food staples have reached new global markets and consumers, spawning new kinds of hybrid cuisines including sushi pizza and tofu burritos. Therefore, we need to be creative, using new cooking resources available to us and applying different ways of cooking many dishes in a globalized context. Since we live in a pluralistic society, we also need to be creative, adaptive, and flexible in our cooking.

So too, with Christian education in a globalized changing world: We need to consider how ways of teaching and learning have changed, reflecting changing cultures, and we need to make ourselves current. Although the word of God remains the same, the process and means of education need to change in terms of technology and ways of engaging in conversation with others. We may think of all this as side dishes. We must continually develop how we engage with people from diverse cultures. We learned a great lesson about adapting teaching and becoming a missionary church during this COVID-19 pandemic. There is a mistake we commonly make when we consider mission, which is that mission is teaching or preaching or giving something to others. The mission is not only teaching or giving to others but is learning from others also.

In a globalized world, we need to learn from various local cultures and how these local cultures integrate into other global cultures. There is no one right way of teaching or learning the gospel. Before we teach and serve, we first need to learn how other traditional cultures are rooted. Teaching the gospel needs to come from various cultural forms: art, music, events, performance, and crafts. Thus, if we want to present God to Indigenous peoples through witnesses, we first need to learn about their culture, arts, crafts, music, etc. We need to understand how these art forms relate to their life and education. Then we can present the love of God by applying it to their cultural artifacts.

Third, we need to cook bahb by caring for the sikku's well-being as whole persons. When we cook bahb, we always consider the well-being of the sikku. So we like to use fresh, natural, and organic ingredients as much as possible, and we like to cook balanced food with full nutrition to meet the needs of the sikku. As if bahb is heaven, various side dishes with bahb are necessary precious elements for humanity's well-being, not only physical well-being but also holistic being. Cooking bahb with side dishes is a very precious, joyful, and valuable activity for both men and women. And it requires wisdom for the balanced well-being of sikku.

When we cook bahb, we think of the sikku who will eat together. We tend to cook for the tastes of others, not for our tastes or preferences. We cook bahb with love for others. When we serve bahb, it is served with a loving heart. There is sincerity, care, and love, which we can't exchange for other things. Also, as we eat bahb, we express deep gratitude to the person who made bahb for us. Love, care, sincerity, gratitude, and respect are exchanged mutually. Ultimately cooking bahb enhances our relationships with the sharers of bahb; it is caring for the well-being of other persons so that they might become whole beings, which in turn leads to jeong. I would dare to say that cooking bahb is God's holy service.

Likewise, missional Christian education cares for the well-being of all participants, having a genuine concern for others. While preparing for witness or service, we think of participants' whole beings and recovering relationships with God, others, and all of creation. Missional Christian education founded on love, grace, care, sincerity, gratitude, and respect for participants heals the world as God created it. It is God's holy service to the world through God's people, reconciling all nations to each other.

CONCLUSION

In conclusion, missional Christian education, cooking, and sharing bahb, Jesus as the bahb of life, and expanding jeongful relationship are God's invitation to us and our ultimate identity. Korean North American churches are called to nurture and equip God's people to participate in life-giving missional Christian education in this world. Hence, life-giving missional Christian education is a sacramental practice from the Trinitarian God, who is the ultimate teacher.

BIBLIOGRAPHY

Buck, Pearl S. *The Living Reed*. New York: The John Day Company, 1963.

Chung, Hye Kyung. *[Babe Inmunhak] Humanities of Bahb*. Seoul: Taby, 2015.

Fensham, Charles J. *Emerging from the Dark Age Ahead: The Future of the North American Church*. Ottawa: Novalis, 2008.

Hull, John M. *Mission-Shaped Church: A Theological Response*. London: SCM Press, 2006.

———. "The Holy Trinity and Christian Education in a Pluralist World," The National Society's Religious Centre Annual Lecture 1994, Published by The National Society (Church of England) for Promoting Religious Education, 1995.

Newbigin, Lesslie. *The Gospel in a Pluralist Society*. Grand Rapids, MI: William B. Eerdmans, 1989.

Noh, Choong Hun, "최일도 목사 '밥퍼목사 최일도의 러브스토리' 펴내" *Kidokshinmoon*, (06,09.2021), https://www.kidok.com/news/articleView.html?idxno=211525

Park, Hyun Mo, "Sejongchurum," (11, 02, 2012), https://hmparkblog.tistory.com/세종처럼?page=5

Russell, Letty M. *Church in the Round: Feminist Interpretation of the Church*. Louisville, KY: Westminster/J. Knox Press, 1993.

———. *Christian Education in Mission*. Philadelphia: Westminster Press, 1967.

Sargeant, Wendi. *Christian Education and Emerging Church: Postmodern Faith Formation*. Eugene: Pickwick Publications, 2015.

Song, Nam Soon, Ben Kuo, Dong-Ha Kim, and In Kee Kim, eds. *People of Faith, People of Jeong (Qing): Asian Canadian Churches of Today for Tomorrow*. Eugene OR: Wipf and Stock, 2020.

Takenaka, Masao. *God is Rice: Asian Culture and Christian Faith*. Geneva: World Council of Churches Publications, 1986.

Van Gelder, Craig, ed. *The Missional Church in Context: Helping Congregations Develop Contextual Ministry*. Missional Church Series. Grand Rapids, MI: William B. Eerdmans, 2007.

Vitanova, "밥은 하늘입니다 김지하," (04, 06, 2018), http://designvita.tistory.com/92

Wan, Enoch. "Korean Diaspora: From Hermit Kingdom to Kingdom Ministry." In *Korean Diaspora and Christian Mission*, edited by S. Hun Kim and Wonsuk Ma, 101–116. Eugene, OR: Wipf & Stock, 2011.

Commission on World Mission and Evangelism (CWME) of WCC, "Together towards Life: Mission and Evangelism in Changing Landscapes" New WCC Affirmation on Mission and Evangelism, 2012

3

KOREAN CHRISTIANITY AND THE KOREAN WAR

Helen Jin Kim

INTRODUCTION

In my new book *Race for Revival: How Cold War South Korea Shaped the American Evangelical Empire* (2022), I argue that Koreans were core to the making of modern evangelical America. I show this through an oral history and archive-based investigation into three evangelical parachurch organizations that have deep transpacific roots, namely World Vision, Campus Crusade for Christ, and the Billy Graham Evangelistic Association. We can trace the late-twentieth century global success of all three back to linkages forged during and through the Korean War (1950–53). Consider, for example, Campus Crusade for Christ, a parachurch with roots hearkening back to Rev. Joon Gon Kim and Rev. Bill Bright's 1950s encounter at Fuller Theological Seminary. When we discuss the past, present, and future of Korean, Korean immigrant, and Korean American churches more broadly, we cannot forget the transpacific networks that figures like Kim and Bright forged to revitalize American evangelicalism and South Korean Protestantism. These networks led not only to the global reshaping of Campus Crusade, and the mass recruitment of missionaries on both sides of the Pacific, but also one of the biggest evangelical "crusades" in the history of transpacific history—Explo '74. In peeling back this forgotten history, we also see the importance of the category of race and the important role that parachurches played in shaping transpacific Cold War religion *and* politics.

So, let's begin with the Korean War. The war triggered a new wave of Korean immigration to the US through which South Korean Protestants and white fundamentalists forged new transpacific networks. Often called the "post-Korean War immigration" period, this moment brought not only Korean military brides and orphans but also students, especially men like Joon Gon Kim, from Korea to the United States for their education. Chang Ahn, or Chuck, is also a notable fictional figure from this time period, as the male protagonist in Susan Choi's acclaimed novel *The Foreign Student*. As an immigrant at the University of the South in Sewanee, Tennessee, he rooms with the son of a Klansmen and falls in love with Katherine, a white southern woman, all while battling the trauma of the Korean War.[1] Chuck's fictional story parallels Joon Gon Kim's narrative of immigration and conversion as a student who inhabited "racial interstitiality" in a Black and white racial hierarchy, respectively in the 1950s Jim Crow South and Southern California.[2] Kim Joon Gon's story remains distinct, however, as he highlights student immigration and conversion at 1950s white-led fundamentalist institutions, namely Fuller and Campus Crusade for Christ.[3] I use the term "fundamentalist" here

---

1 Susan Choi, *The Foreign Student: A Novel* (New York: HarperCollins, 1998). For further discussion on race and the Korean War in Choi's novel, see Daniel Kim, *Intimacies of Conflict: A Cultural Memory and the Korean War* (New York: New York University Press, 2020).
2 Leslie Bow, *Partly Colored: Asian Americans and Racial Anomaly in the Segregated South* (New York: New York University Press, 2010), 8.
3 For a helpful history of Korean Protestant students in the Jim Crow South during the Progressive era, see the example of Yun Ch'i-ho in Chris Suh, "What Yun Ch'i-ho Knew: US-Japan Relations and Imperial Race Making in Korea and the American South, 1904–1919," Journal of American History 104.1 (June 2017): 68–96.

as other US historians such as George Marsden would because, in the 1950s, the terms "neo-evangelical" or "evangelical," did not emerge until the end of the decade.

For Joon Gon Kim (1925-2009), encountering Campus Crusade for Christ while he was a student immigrant at Fuller activated his faith as never before.[4] Kim met Bright, who founded Campus Crusade in 1951 at UCLA. They sought converts, like the quarterback who later became Ronald Reagan's pastor at Bel Air Presbyterian Church. Like Bright, Kim quit Fuller and, after one year, returned to South Korea to launch Campus Crusade in 1958. He was the first nonwhite partner, and he established the first international site for the organization.

It was not as if Korean integration into Cold War American institutions was seamless, though. The outbreak of the Korean War ignited suspicion of a communist overthrow from within the United States. As part of a national sweep of aliens suspected of subversive communist activity, two Korean men, David Hyun and Diamond Kimm, were arrested for their respective engagement with labor activism and the publication of a pro-communist newspaper.[5] Under the auspices of the 1950 McCarran Act, Koreans who questioned US democracy's capacity to ensure freedom and equality for all were arrested and even deported.

---

4   Historian of Korean Christianity Rhie Deok-Joo categorizes Billy Kim and Joon Gon Kim as leaders who represent the "second generation" of Korean Protestantism. The "first generation" of Korean Protestantism constitutes the first wave of converts in the early twentieth century. See Deok Joo Rhie, *A Study on the Formation of the Indigenous Church in Korea, 1903-1907* (한국 토착교회 형성사 연구) (Seoul: The Institute for the Korean Church History, 2001), 34. (translation mine).

5   Cindy I-Fen Cheng, *Citizens of Asian America: Democracy and Race during the Cold War* (New York: New York University Press, 2013), 117-148.

Yet if the US government suppressed viewpoints like those of Hyun and Kim, other narratives, like those of Kim were highlighted. In alignment with the Dwight D. Eisenhower administration's Cold War emphasis on US-Asian integration, Kim's narrative bridged affective gaps between the United States and noncommunist Asia through nonstate institutions within fundamentalist America. Cold War America favored these Korean narratives that intertwined a commitment to the Great Commission—world evangelization—with racialized anticommunism.

By the same token, white fundamentalist America's survival depended on the integration of nonwhite and noncommunist Koreans whose life narratives reflected a commitment to a racialized and religious Cold War.[6] Fuller and Campus Crusade were institutions founded by white Protestants who emerged out of the fundamentalist strand of the fundamentalist-modernist controversy. They targeted white students to fulfill their respective missions, but throughout the 1950s, they also prioritized the inclusion of students of Asian descent, more than any other nonwhite race, reflecting the racial and foreign policy priorities of Cold War America. Kim's narratives of conversion

---

6   Joon Gon Kim and Billy Kim were part of a longer history of Korean students immigrating to the United States for higher education, and specifically, connected to, or for the purposes of, Christian education, including Yun Ch'i-ho and Kim Hwallan (Helen Kim). Joon Gon Kim's and Billy Kim's presence in the United States can be seen as an extension of the education that figures like Yun received in the United States. What remains distinct is that Joon Gon Kim and Billy Kim helped to extend these white fundamentalist networks to South Korea and the United States through Bob Jones, Fuller, and Campus Crusade. For a discussion of Korean immigrant history and the Methodist church, specifically, see Hong Ki Kim, A History of One Hundred Years of the Korean-American Methodism I, Part I (Upland: The Committee on Publication of 100 Year History of the Korean-American Methodist Church, 2003).

into these institutions portrayed an image of racial equality in a liberal democracy, even as those white fundamentalist institutions maintained a system of racial inequality, in which Black students were, by comparison, excluded and Koreans divided into "good" and "bad" racialized categories. Espousing these narratives of faith, however, did not mean Kim achieved equality within white fundamentalist America. His integration relied on Cold War Orientalist dynamics that subordinated him. Kim's story required a polarization of Christian versus communist that exacerbated a divisive line between "good" and "bad" Korean. As a racially interstitial student immigrant who was neither white nor Black, Kim's story ultimately found "uneasy resolution."[7] Through integration into white fundamentalist institutions, his narrative as a survivor of the Korean War was both celebrated and suppressed.

WHITE FUNDAMENTALISM, COLD WAR ORIENTALISM, AND RACIAL SEGREGATION

By way of background, America's Cold War rise to global power was complicated, as nationalists throughout Asia were fighting for decolonization from Western domination. As Christina Klein asserts, the cultural problem became: "How can we define our nation as a non-imperial world power in the age of decolonization?" One of the litmus tests for American democracy, and by extension, the nation's legitimacy as a global leader in the Cold War era, was its claim to racial equality. Projecting to the world

---

[7] Bow, *Partly Colored*, 14. Here I incorporate Bow's theorization of racial interstitiality, as she argues: "Thinking interstitially is a matter of turning one's gaze toward the space of the in-between to envision alternative connections and affiliations that complicate black and white" (5).

that America championed racial equality was crucial for saving face on the Cold War stage, precisely because of the internationally publicized racialized violence against African Americans throughout the 1950s, which communist nations used against the United States. As Klein notes, an imagination of the United States as a racially diverse nation played a critical role in the nation's Cold War expansion: "The United States thus became the only Western nation that sought to legitimate its world-ordering ambitions by championing the idea (if not the practice) of racial equality. In contrast to European imperial powers, the captains of American expansion explicitly denounced the idea of essential differences and hierarchies."[8] America's relationships with noncommunist Asians became a critical way to globally circulate an image of racial democracy. Eisenhower's administration encouraged everyday Americans to engage in people-to-people diplomacy that forged personal attachments with noncommunist Asians through "structures of feeling" that sought "sympathy—the ability to feel what another person feels."[9] Policymakers declared that "differences of language, religion, history and race could be bridged" through an "inescapable interconnectedness."[10] Klein's concept of Cold War Orientalism shows that such narratives, "far from undermining the global assertion of US power, often supported it."[11] Intimate bonds between Americans and noncommunist Asians reinforced "the famed 'Cold War consensus,' the domestic hegemonic bloc

---

8 Christina Klein, *Cold War Orientalism: Asia in the Middlebrow Imagination, 1945–1961* (Berkeley: University of California Press, 2003), 23.
9 Klein, *Cold War Orientalism*, 19. As mentioned, Klein draws on Raymond Williams's understanding of cultural hegemony as generating "structures of feeling" through which "ideological principles that support a given arrangement of power are translated into regularized patterns of emotion and sentiment."
10 Klein, *Cold War Orientalism*, 19.
11 Klein, *Cold War Orientalism*, 58 and 27.

that supported the postwar expansion of US power around the world."¹²

White fundamentalists closely aligned with Eisenhower's vision to establish heart-to-heart connections with noncommunist Asians. The Protestant missionary enterprise, in particular, created a "worldwide institutional infrastructure that enabled millions of Americans, especially in isolated midwestern and rural communities, to understand themselves as participating in world affairs," and to feel "bound to the people of Asia and Africa" in spite of their differences.¹³ For white fundamentalists in particular, heart-to-heart connections had long been prioritized for the sake of the heart's conversion to Christ, a core means for fulfilling the Great Commission. At mid-twentieth century, white fundamentalists insisted on the world's total evangelization, in spite of the critiques of Western missionary imperialism and liberal denunciations of literalist interpretations of the Bible. They were aided by Cold War America's military, economic, and political expansion throughout the world.¹⁴ Fuller and Campus Crusade were key institutional forces in that global effort. While these institutions are often thought of as local institutions with a domestic focus, they were globally minded from their inception, with close connections to non-Western people, including noncommunist Koreans.

Fuller and Campus Crusade insisted on global expansion as the state was refashioning its national identity as a global Cold War power. As much as missionaries went overseas to establish connections with nonwesterners, war abroad also triggered new immigration routes to the United States that created new networks, as in the case of Korean people. Koreans, in part,

---

12   Klein, *Cold War Orientalism*, 16.
13   Klein, *Cold War Orientalism*, 30.
14   George Marsden, *Reforming Fundamentalism: Fuller Seminary and the New Evangelicalism* (Grand Rapids: Eerdmans, 1995), 84.

integrated into fundamentalist networks through the second wave of Korean immigration from 1950 to 1964.

In this second wave, limited immigration routes opened, with about fifteen thousand Koreans immigrating to the United States. Largely through personal connections with US citizens, about six thousand students immigrated from Korea. The National Origins Act of 1924 barred Asian immigration to the United States, and two high-profile Supreme Court cases, United States v. Thind (1922) and United States v. Ozawa (1923), rendered Asians as "aliens ineligible for citizenship."[15] In the 1950s, when the second wave of Korean immigration ensued with the onset of war, Asians in the United States lived under that precarious legal status in an age of Asian exclusion.[16] Yet, throughout the 1950s, Cold War America cultivated Korean leaders—ambassadors of goodwill—through education.[17] The State Department Leadership Grants program, the Defense Department, and private foundations sponsored education for thousands of Koreans and trained hundreds of Korean professionals, exposing them to American-style modernity and capitalism.[18]

Most Korean international students during the 1950s would transfer their immigration status from nonimmigrant to permanent resident, settling in the United States as professionals. Joon

---

15 Ian Haney-Lopez, *White by Law: The Legal Construction of Race* (New York: New York University Press, 2006), 56–77. 9. 10. 11. 12. 13. 14. 15. 16. 17. 18. 19. 20. 21.

16 Shelley Lee, *A New History of Asian America* (New York: Routledge, 2014), 5–26; Erika Lee, *At America's Gates: Chinese Immigration during the Exclusion Era, 1882–1943* (Chapel Hill: University of North Carolina Press, 2003).

17 Jane Jangeun Cho, "Immigration through Education: The Interwoven History of Korean International Students, US Foreign Assistance, and Korean Nation-State Building" (PhD dissertation, University of California, Berkeley, 2010).

18 Klein, *Cold War Orientalism*, 30–31.

Gon Kim, however, returned to Korea, forging transnational networks between white fundamentalists and South Korean Protestants through Fuller and Campus Crusade. In an age when Cold War America feared communist infiltration, his story of student immigration and conversion as a nonwhite and noncommunist Korean gained transpacific significance, as it cohered with Eisenhower's broader call for people-to-people diplomacy.

This was an era when racial segregation and Black exclusion haunted the American educational system. As for Fuller, the school was founded by a nearly all-white faculty and white student body. Fuller's starting class had thirty-two men, nearly all white, with one man of Asian descent. In the 1950s, 105 nonwhite students attended Fuller, of which 93 students (89 percent) were of Asian descent. In 1956, the first Black student attended Fuller, and thereafter, about five more attended throughout the decade. Approximately four Latinx students attended in the 1950s, and of all the nonwhites, about ten were Asian women. Though Fuller did not practice strict racial segregation, as was the case of a school like Bob Jones, the Confederate flag made its way into public school gatherings.[19] As for Campus Crusade, the organization's founder, Bright, discouraged staff and student involvement in the civil rights movement, espousing a more individualistic and heart-centered approach to change, and belatedly created its Black student-centered campus ministry in the 1970s. Yet it forged its first nonwhite partnership with Joon Gon Kim, a Korean national, as early as 1958.

As a racially interstitial student immigrants, Joon Gon Kim was incorporated into transpacific networks with white

---

[19] See image with quotation: "Glenn Anderson proves there are still a few rebels who have not joined the union. Dr. and Mrs. Woodbridge and Ray Kusumoto seem ready to join." Fuller Theological Seminary, 1952 Yearbook. Fuller Theological Seminary Archives and Special Collections, 31, Pasadena, CA.

fundamentalists insofar as he sought to fulfill the Great Commission and celebrate the United States as a racial democracy. The elements of his life that aligned more closely with the racial alienation of Black students and Black civil rights activists was suppressed.

JOON GON KIM, FULLER THEOLOGICAL SEMINARY, AND CAMPUS CRUSADE FOR CHRIST

Joon Gon Kim's narrative came at the cost of perpetuating a racialized anticommunist binary of dividing Koreans into "good" and "bad" racialized categories. The year that Billy Kim left for the United States, Joon Gon Kim witnessed Korean communists from his village kill his wife and father, which led to a conversion more powerful than his initial Christian commitment: "The starting point of my Christian life began when I faced persecution and death under the Communist occupation," he recalled.[20] While enrolled at Chosun Seminary in Korea to become a Presbyterian pastor, he became disgruntled with Korea's growing theological liberalism. In 1957, he immigrated to Pasadena, California, where he attended Fuller and met Bright.[21] Given that they came from markedly different backgrounds, how did they come to establish a transpacific partnership in the Cold War era?

---

20   Bailey Marks, *Awakening in Asia* (San Bernardino, CA: Here's Life Publishers, 1981), 21.
21   Chosun Seminary was started by Kim Jae Jun, who led a liberal Korean theological movement against biblical literalism. Note that, as George Marsden points out, Fuller Theological Seminary was founded by American fundamentalists who subsequently became neo-evangelicals; as he shows, the founding of Fuller Theological Seminary was a part of that theological transformation. Marsden, *Reforming Fundamentalism*.

First, a shared theological anxiety about modernism brought white fundamentalists like Bright and South Korean Protestants like Kim across the Pacific. The fundamentalist-modernist controversy in the US was not only a national theological dilemma, but also one that Christians elsewhere, including in Korea, shared. That Kim shared the critiques of modernism, communism, and liberalism with Bright and those at Fuller allowed him to extend the work of Campus Crusade internationally. Second, Kim's anticommunist conversion narrative in the midst of the Korean War cohered with Cold War concerns for the containment of communism among white fundamentalists, distancing Kim from the "red" cause of North Korean communism. Relatedly, the racial implications of his conversion narrative cohered with Cold War America's vision to integrate noncommunist Koreans, distancing him from the "red" cause of civil rights.

The Critique of Theological Liberalism

Bright had become a Christian at Hollywood's First Presbyterian Church, a wealthy suburban church in the Sun Belt.[22] At Hollywood Presbyterian, he met Henrietta Mears, the influential

---

[22] Clarence Roddy, a professor of homiletics at Fuller Seminary, declared that "Henrietta Mears was the best preacher in Southern California." Note her Presbyterian denominational affiliation would have prevented her from being eligible for ordination, but she was considered the "power behind the throne" of many influential male religious leaders. Though not ordained, Mears was widely recognized as a successful preacher and religious educator who influenced many to go into the ministry. It was, for instance, during a stay at Mears's retreat center, Forest Home, that Billy Graham had a reawakening experience right before launching into his crusade ministry. Mears created Forest Home in 1937. John G. Turner, *Bill Bright and Campus Crusade for Christ: The Renewal of Evangelicalism in Postwar America* (Chapel Hill: University of North Carolina Press, 2008), 20.

Christian educator, under whose tutelage he experienced spiritual renewal. Bright continued to stay active at Hollywood Presbyterian, and in 1946, with Mears's encouragement, he began his seminary education at Princeton Theological Seminary.

Just one year after beginning his studies, however, Bright returned to California to revive his candy business. Fortuitously, in that year Fuller was founded, and Bright transferred from Princeton to join its inaugural class. For Bright, "Effective ministry equaled effective evangelism," and he did not think he learned how to become an effective evangelist through seminary.[23] In 1951, Bright began his campus ministry at UCLA, the first chapter of hundreds, under the name Campus Crusade. Joon Gon Kim, on the other hand, matriculated at Fuller in 1957 in order to gain a stronger sense of "intellectual Christianity." He was interested in studying Christian philosophy because he attributed his lack of evangelistic success among college students and youth to his inability to "make the intellectual mind satisfied." "Liberal influences," he said, brought "great trouble" to the Korean churches for the past ten years, "chiefly through students who studied at liberal seminaries in the United States."[24] Kim was referring especially to the theological tensions at Chosun Theological Seminary, where he initially enrolled in 1946.

US theological institutions were experiencing fundamentalist-modernist rifts, and the Korean theological landscape was shifting along similar lines. Chosun Theological Seminary,

---

23   Turner, *Bill Bright*, 37.
24   Joon Gon Kim, Campus Crusade for Christ, Inc. Campus Crusade for Christ International Archives, Orlando, FL. The date and particular purpose of this writing are unclear. I would estimate, though, that this is a document written shortly after Kim decided to partner with Bright to start the Korean Campus Crusade for Christ; the document was clearly written after they met at Fuller and before the 1972 and 1974 revivals.

founded in 1940 by Korean theologians such as Kim Jae Jun, rejected biblical literalism and sought an alternative to Pyongyang Theological Seminary. In 1947, the same year Fuller was founded in Pasadena, fifty-one Chosun seminary students, including Kim, signed a petition denouncing its theological liberalism. By July 1952, this fundamentalist cadre established the Korean chapter of the National Association of Evangelicals (NAE).[25] Those following Kim Jae Jun's theological orientation created in 1959 a new Korean Presbyterian denomination, historically the most left-leaning in Korea.[26] Though Kim had hopes of finding both a spiritual and an intellectual Christian tradition that would give him the key to evangelistic success and to remedying liberalism in the Korean

---

25   Kim Jae Jun's leadership led to the creation of a new Korean Presbyterian denomination. Hapdong aligned with the NAE and Tong Hap aligned with the World Council of Churches. Joon Gon Kim was the education committee leader for the Korean chapter of the NAE. The NAE's statement of faith was as follows: "We believe the Bible to be the inspired, the only infallible, authoritative Word of God. We believe that there is one God, eternally existent in three persons: Father, Son and Holy Spirit. We believe in the deity of our Lord Jesus Christ, in His virgin birth, in His sinless life, in His miracles, in His vicarious and atoning death through His shed blood, in His bodily resurrection, in His ascension to the right hand of the Father, and in His personal return in power and glory. We believe that for the salvation of lost and sinful people, regeneration by the Holy Spirit is absolutely essential. We believe in the present ministry of the Holy Spirit by whose indwelling the Christian is enabled to live a godly life. We believe in the resurrection of both the saved and the lost; they that are saved unto the resurrection of life and they that are lost unto the resurrection of damnation. We believe in the spiritual unity of believers in our Lord Jesus Christ."

26   Woo Suk Kang, "The Evangelical Movement as Revealed in the Life and Thought of Joon Gon Kim" (master's thesis, Chongshin University, 2015), 8. Korea Campus Crusade for Christ Headquarters, Seoul (translation mine).

church, he was skeptical—was America a secular or a Christian nation? "Frankly speaking," he wrote, "I had never expected to acquire spiritual power from this country."[27] But when Joon Gon Kim arrived at Fuller, he entered a new center for American fundamentalism, one that increasingly reformed itself into the "new evangelicalism."

While at Fuller, Joon Gon Kim met Campus Crusade staff, including Bob Kendall and Bob Johns, who introduced him to Bright, who had already heard about "Kim from Korea."[28] Kim attended their meetings, conferences, and even met Mears. His former prejudices about the US spiritual landscape were transformed when he encountered the organization, for it provided him with the keys to unlocking his failures in evangelism. At the annual staff training conference in the summer of 1957 at Mound, Minnesota, Kim "discovered something which [he] had not realized before."[29] He had failed to proclaim the "basic message" as Campus Crusade had done. The staff members were asked to memorize a twenty-minute evangelistic tool, "God's Plan for Your Life," a precursor to Campus Crusade's signature document, Four Spiritual Laws.[30] It appealed to the intellect, but it was not a form

---

27   Joon Gon Kim, Campus Crusade for Christ, Inc. Campus Crusade for Christ International Archives, Orlando, FL. The date and particular purpose of this writing is unclear. I would estimate, though, that this is a document that was written shortly after Kim decided to partner with Bright to start the Korean Campus Crusade for Christ: the document is clearly from after they met at Fuller and before the 1972 and 1974 revivals.

28   Nils Becker, *Fireseeds from Korea to the World: Tribute to Dr. Joon Gon Kim, Founder of Campus Crusade for Christ* (Orlando, FL: Campus Crusade for Christ International, 2007), 59.

29   Joon Gon Kim, Campus Crusade for Christ, Inc. Campus Crusade for Christ International Archives, Orlando, FL.

30   The Four Spiritual Laws was solidified in 1959 by Bright as the following: (1) God loves you and has a wonderful plan for your life, (2) man is sinful and separated from God, thus he cannot know and

of philosophical or theological jargon. As a "simple, basic message," he believed it to be the "key that God could use to open the hearts of men." He learned that instead of persuading a person philosophically, appealing to the person's mind through a simple, basic evangelistic communication tool could chart a path to the heart's conversion. Kim wrote: "I said to myself, 'Here it is, this is the only key to winning the lost souls to Christ.'"[31] Bright's entrepreneurial knack for packaging the gospel in a simple, reason-based message was relevant for Koreans. As a result of his encounter with Campus Crusade, Kim was convinced to turn from a philosophical to a pragmatic approach in sharing the gospel. In 1958, he internationalized Campus Crusade by establishing its first chapter in South Korea.[32]

Conversion and Racialized Anticommunism

While for Americans anticommunism was rooted in a distant but lingering fear, Joon Gon Kim's anticommunism was rooted in his

---

    explain God's plan for his life, (3) Jesus Christ is God's provision for man's sin through whom man can know God's love and plan for his life, and (4) we must receive Jesus Christ as Savior and Lord by personal invitation. The Four Spiritual Laws is one of the most widely distributed religious pamphlets ever, with approximately 2.5 billion printed to date. "History," Campus Crusade for Christ Online, accessed November 1, 2011. http://campuscrusadeforchrist.com/about-us/history.

31 Joon Gon Kim, Campus Crusade for Christ, Inc. Campus Crusade for Christ International Archives, Orlando, FL.

32 Turner, *Bill Bright*, 151. Bright had also met a Pakistani student named Kundan Massey at Fuller shortly after he met Joon Gon Kim. Massey founded the Pakistan chapter of Campus Crusade. Ray Nethery was the first Campus Crusade director for Asia and then resigned in 1968, handing off the job to Bailey Marks. Marks began to streamline the nine Asian chapters of Campus Crusade, which had been otherwise acting rather independently of each other.

Korean War experience, specifically of witnessing his family die at the hands of communists. Klein notes the fear that occupied the imagination of Americans in cultural productions: "According to The Manchurian Candidate, contact with Asians, either at home or abroad, could only weaken the nation. While American participation in the Korean War halted the spread of communism in northeast Asia, it also opened up a hole in the nation's defenses, allowing the Asian menace to invade and corrupt America."[33] Thus, Bright believed that the "evangelization of Japan and South Korea would inoculate other Asian countries against the contagion of communism."[34] Joon Gon Kim's conversion narrative was relevant to Cold War America, as it assuaged the fears of Americans, showing them that communism could be contained through South Korean Christians like him. Similarly, Kim believed that Korea was the key to saving Asia from communism. He declared, "As Chiang Kai-shek remarked, 'The one who conquers Korea will conquer Asia.' Her position is important not only from the political standpoint, but the spiritual standpoint also."[35] Kim analogized his spiritual strategy to Chiang's political strategy. Mears, Bright's mentor, echoed this sentiment when she warned her parishioners at Forest Home in 1947: "There must be a Christian answer to the growing menace of communism." Mears consequently resolved, "God is looking for women and men of total commitment," and an uncompromising proclamation of the gospel was the solution.[36]

---

33   Klein, *Cold War Orientalism*, 37.
34   Henrietta Mears shared this sentiment when she warned her parishioners at the Forest Home in 1947; Bill Bright and Billy Graham were both frequenters of the retreat site Forest Home. Turner, *Bill Bright*, 98.
35   Chiang Kai-Shek was a Nationalist Party leader in China and a Protestant—who fought against the Communist Party in China, only to be led into retreat in Taiwan with Mao's success in China.
36   Turner, *Bill Bright*, 98.

South Koreans like Joon Gon Kim were crucial noncommunist Asians who could protect Americans from the menacing communist Asians. Kim's anticommunist conversion narrative revealed that he was a trustworthy Cold War ally.

The ideological and theological battle that white fundamentalists and emerging neo-evangelicals fought in seminary classrooms and suburban pulpits had an urgent life-and-death battleground on the stage of the Korean War, which made Kim's conversion narrative especially compelling to white fundamentalists. During Billy Graham's and Harold Ockenga's Boston rallies in the 1950s, communism served as a symbol of satanic and secular influence. They feared communism not only as a threat to the evangelization of the world but also as an apocalyptic sign of the end times. Moreover, intertwined with the Cold War anticommunist theology of this age was an argument against the "red" cause of Black civil rights. In the 1950s, white fundamentalists, or emerging neo-evangelicals, like Graham did not side with King's cause for civil rights because of their individual-centered vision of sin and social change. Graham's conversion-focused individualistic theological paradigm eschewed the institutional change.[37] Graham argued that King moved too fast and should put the brakes on racial reform.

Anticommunism exacerbated white fundamentalists' individualistic theological resistance to civil rights reform. Unproven theories connecting Bolshevik radical activities to Black activists' opposition to white supremacy continued into the 1950s red scare, when King's and other civil rights activists' vision for racial equality was cast as communist and therefore un-American or

---

[37] Curtis Evans, "White Evangelical Protestant Responses to the Civil Rights Movement," *Harvard Theological Review* 102.2 (April 2009): 245–273. See also Carolyn Renee Dupont, *Mississippi Praying: Southern White Evangelicals and the Civil Rights Movement, 1945–1975* (New York: New York University Press, 2013).

anti-American.[38] When Graham preached about the "communist threat" in the 1950s, he linked the fear of communism with the "fiery concern about the Black civil rights activists who were, to their way of thinking, promoting communist ideas and socialism." He connected "communism with civil rights work" and "fear of the end times and the Antichrist," which "instilled fear and determination in evangelists and evangelical listeners alike."[39]

THE LEGACIES OF WAR AND KOREAN CHRISTIANITY

On one hand, the Cold War propelled racial progress in America. As Cold War and civil rights historians have shown, international pressures to "safeguar[d] the nation's image overseas" as a global leader against communism, in part, led to the desegregation of the US military and education.[40] On the other hand, racial progress stagnated through anticommunist fear during the Cold War. White fundamentalists like Graham played a key role in impeding progress. Accusations that Black civil rights activists were communists were not mere rhetoric, but fundamentally truncated their international human rights vision for racial equality, reducing it to a more localized civil rights frame. Anticommunism set limits on Black civil rights activists' 1950s vision for peacebuilding and decolonization in Asia.[41] Moreover, white fundamentalists and

---

38   Anthea D. Butler, *White Evangelical Racism: The Politics of Morality in America* (Chapel Hill: The University of North Carolina Press, 2021), 40.
39   Butler, *White Evangelical Racism*, 41.
40   Mary Dudziak, *Cold War Civil Rights: Race and the Image of American Democracy* (Princeton, NJ: Princeton University Press, 2011), 87.
41   Carol Anderson, *Eyes off the Prize: The United Nations and the African American Struggle for Human Rights, 1944–1955* (Cambridge: Cambridge University Press, 2003).

emerging neo-evangelicals further secured a racial wedge through anticommunist theologies that created a false binary between Black freedom and Asian decolonization.

At this time, Koreans like Hyun and Kimm—arrested under the auspices of the McCarran Act—who protested racial injustice in the United States were also cast as communist. The stigma of communism worked to "discredit and make foreign Hyun and Kimm's struggle against racist practices in the United States."[42] Their case "importantly illustrated that anticommunist hysteria of the early Cold War years was entrenched in fear of the foreign."[43] Yet if Hyun and Kimm were representative of "bad" Koreans, then Joon Gon Kim's narrative represented the "good" Koreans from the gaze of the Cold War America.

Through Kim's narrative, white fundamentalists witnessed that the world's total evangelization was still possible, even in the aftermath of Mao's communist triumph in 1949, and that America still had the potential to be a "city on a hill," a nonimperial beacon of democratic and Christian hope, in spite of the racial realities that suggested otherwise. And yet such a narrative only further distanced Joon Gon Kim from the North Korean communists for whom he professed sincere love. Joon Gon Kim became core to the project of global evangelization as he extended nonstate fundamentalist networks across US borders, modernizing Campus Crusade beyond what modernists imagined through massive crusades, including Explo '72, Explo '74, and WEC '80. Yet it came at a significant cost, especially as Joon Gon Kim's narratives encouraged disavowal of his own racial alienation and the cause for Black freedom, a legacy that would haunt Korean and Korean American Christianity.

For, by 1981, Joon Gon Kim continued to share with Bright his vision of Korea as the "new emerging Christian kingdom."

---

42 Cheng, *Citizens of Asian America*, 147.
43 Cheng, *Citizens of Asian America*, 124.

However, he now added the role of Korean America, for he started to observe a sea change in the United States. Whereas the "US churches" held Sunday service at the coveted 11:00 a.m. and the ethnic churches in the afternoon, they were now changing time slots, taking over prime time: "This is a sign that the Korean church is making the greater impact and needs to have an impact on the American church itself. The Lord gave us the idea that Korean citizens can be a great manpower source in the United States itself." Korean immigrant congregations in the United States had originally rented church space from "US churches," but he observed they were now outgrowing them.[44]

CONCLUSION

Joon Gon Kim visited Los Angeles, San Jose, New York, and Washington, DC, where he held Campus Crusade Leadership Training Institutes and pastoral seminars. In the aftermath of Explo '72, Explo '74, and WEC '80, he saw hundreds attend his trainings, and contended this was a fruitful time for Korean American churches.[45] "We desire to have a second Puritan impact, spiritually speaking, in the United States. The first Puritans landed on the East Coast. The second Puritans will be from the ripe, alive church of Korea," he declared.[46] Channeling his excitement from the transpacific revivals, he announced Korean Americans would mimic South Korea's revivalistic "explosion" by leading Madison Square Garden into a "Jesus '82" revival.

---

44   Darren Dochuk, *From Bible Belt to Sunbelt: Plain-Folk Religion, Grassroots Politics, and the Rise of Evangelical Conservatism* (New York: W. W. Norton & Company, 2010), 178.
45   Deacons went through the Leadership Training Institutes and pastors underwent four-hour training seminars.
46   Kim to Bright Correspondence, July 18, 1981.

Yet his excitement for Koreans to venture into the wilderness as the "second Puritans," was dampened because he understood the suffering caused by the triumphalism of US Protestants who tried to evangelize the American West. The "second and third generation," he noticed, "are not well adjusted as Koreans living in America." He worried: "They are lonely and looking for reality." He continued: "I have noticed that the majority of Koreans have struggled for identity and purpose in the US for several years."[47] South Korean revivalistic success mismatched racialized immigrant realities.

In Bright's response, he praised him as usual. He wrote: "My heart continues to sing praises to our Lord . . . as you went from city to city." He was also eager to have Joon Gon Kim send "10,000 missionaries to Europe, the United States and other countries." But perhaps Bright had read the memo incorrectly, for he cited ten thousand missionaries as opposed to the one hundred thousand that Joon Gon Kim had projected to send.[48] He also made no mention of the struggles of the second and third generation that burdened Joon Gon Kim.

Campus Crusade, an organization at the center of what I argue would become the US evangelical empire, was built by the hands and feet of Koreans, and its very global direction shaped by Cold War South Korea. Koreans, therefore, should have had a rightful place at the center of the organization. Joon Gon Kim had been working with the organization since 1958, when he met

---

47 Kim to Bright Correspondence, July 18, 1981.
48 Bright to Kim Correspondence, September 8, 1981. Campus Crusade for Christ, Inc. Campus Crusade for Christ International Archive, Orlando, FL. Kim ended his letter to Bright echoing a sentiment that the East was the spiritual solution for the secularizing West: "During the next ten years we want to send 100,000 missionaries to Europe, the US and other countries as God opens the doors for our missionaries."

Bright at Fuller, and became Campus Crusade's first nonwhite and international partner. Yet Bright's lack of response mirrored Campus Crusade's historic misunderstanding of immigrant and nonwhite realities. Campus Crusade had invested heavily in overseas work, as in South Korea, when those evangelistic and revivalistic activities prioritized world evangelization through individual salvation—saving people, one by one, for the sake of Jesus Christ. When it turned toward the social and structural needs of "the least of these," including the role and needs of nonwhite staff and students in the United States, that multicultural world vision melted away.

For his part, Joon Gon Kim had been masterful in passing down a Korean tradition centered on individual salvation and personal holiness, but what vision of social salvation and social justice did he offer South Korea and Korean America? While at Fuller, and in his later years at the height of the 1970s revivals, he preached the power of individual salvation for the sake of social transformation. He envisioned world evangelization as the primary route to national salvation for the Korean peninsula. But that vision came at the cost of holding hands with an anticommunist organization that, since the 1950s, positioned Joon Gon Kim against the "red" North Koreans and the "red" cause of civil rights. His vision for world evangelization led to massive gatherings that swayed white evangelicals to devote their lives to lifelong missionary work, but at the cost of linking arms with Park Chung Hee's authoritarian regime. The legacy undermined the possibilities for Korean America—that is, Joon Gon Kim's religious vision had focused on the power of individual conversion, lacking a robust social vision that would account for the limits of race and immigration, which continued to undermine US democracy.

When the people of Kim's nation—those with whom Bright had so closely partnered across the Pacific—immigrated to Bright's home country, the limits of Joon Gon Kim and Bright's synchronous network, were readily revealed. Bright's and Joon Gon Kim's transpacific network flagged in the face of race and immigration. As my book *Race for Revival* shows, South Korean Protestants had their own responses to the US evangelical empire and even sought to supersede its global power. Yet, even as their local agency was powerful—a core argument from the discourse of World Christianity, which I draw upon—the structures of racialized power with which Korean Protestants contended, and continue to contend with, dampened that potential.

BIBLIOGRAPHY

Anderson, Carol. *Eyes off the Prize: The United Nations and the African American Struggle for Human Rights, 1944–1955.* Cambridge: Cambridge University Press, 2003.

Becker, Nils. *Fireseeds from Korea to the World: Tribute to Dr. Joon Gon Kim, Founder of Campus Crusade for Christ.* Orlando, FL: Campus Crusade for Christ International, 2007.

Bow, Leslie. *Partly Colored: Asian Americans and Racial Anomaly in the Segregated South.* New York: New York University Press, 2010.

Butler, Anthea D., *White Evangelical Racism: The Politics of Morality in America.* Chapel Hill: The University of North Carolina Press, 2021.

Cheng, Cindy I-Fen. *Citizens of Asian America: Democracy and Race during the Cold War.* New York: New York University Press, 2013.

Cho, Jane Jangeun. "Immigration through Education: The Interwoven History of Korean International Students, US Foreign Assistance, and Korean Nation-State Building." PhD dissertation, University of California, Berkeley, 2010.

Choi, Susan. *The Foreign Student: A Novel.* New York: HarperCollins Publishers, 1998.

Dochuk, Darren. *From Bible Belt to Sunbelt: Plain-Folk Religion, Grassroots Politics, and the Rise of Evangelical Conservatism.* New York: W. W. Norton & Company, 2010.

Dudziak, Mary. *Cold War Civil Rights: Race and the Image of American Democracy.* Princeton, NJ: Princeton University Press, 2011.

Dupont, Carolyn Renee. *Mississippi Praying: Southern White Evangelicals and the Civil Rights Movement, 1945-1975*. New York: New York University Press, 2013.

Evans, Curtis. "White Evangelical Protestant Responses to the Civil Rights Movement," *Harvard Theological Review*. 102.2 (April 2009): 245–273.

Fuller Theological Seminary, *1952 Yearbook*. Fuller Theological Seminary Archives and Special Collections, Pasadena, CA.

Haney-Lopez, Ian. *White by Law: The Legal Construction of Race*. New York: New York University Press, 2006.

Kang, Woo Suk. "The Evangelical Movement as Revealed in the Life and Thought of Joon Gon Kim." Master's thesis, Chongshin University, 2015, 8. Korea Campus Crusade for Christ Headquarters, Seoul.

Kim, Daniel. *Intimacies of Conflict: A Cultural Memory and the Korean War*. New York: New York University Press, 2020.

Kim, Helen Jin. *Race for Revival: How Cold War South Korea Shaped the American Evangelical Empire*. Oxford: Oxford University Press, 2022.

Kim, Hong Ki, *A History of One Hundred Years of the Korean-American Methodism I, Part I*. Upland: The Committee on Publication of 100 Year History of the Korean-American Methodist Church, 2003.

Klein, Christina. *Cold War Orientalism: Asia in the Middlebrow Imagination, 1945-1961*. Berkeley: University of California Press, 2003.

Lee, Erika. *At America's Gates: Chinese Immigration during the Exclusion Era, 1882-1943*. Chapel Hill: University of North Carolina Press, 2003.

Lee, Shelley. *A New History of Asian America*. New York: Routledge, 2014.

Marks, Bailey. *Awakening in Asia*. San Bernardino, CA: Here's Life Publishers, 1981.

Marsden, George. *Reforming Fundamentalism: Fuller Seminary and the New Evangelicalism*. Grand Rapids, MI: William B. Eerdmans, 1995.

Suh, Chris. "What Yun Ch'i-ho Knew: US-Japan Relations and Imperial Race Making in Korea and the American South, 1904–1919," *Journal of American History* 104/1 (June 2017): 68–96.

Turner, John G. *Bill Bright and Campus Crusade for Christ: The Renewal of Evangelicalism in Postwar America*. Chapel Hill, University of North Carolina Press, 2008.

4

ASCETIC SPIRITUAL FORMATION FOR THE MISSION OF KOREAN IMMIGRANT CHURCHES IN THE POST-PANDEMIC ERA

Euiwan Cho

INTRODUCTION

As the Korean immigrant church in the United States approaches its 120th anniversary, it is critical to examine how it goes beyond a compensatory position of meeting the needs of marginalized immigrants and demand that it continues to do so. The Korean immigrant church must follow God's mission (*missio Dei*) and profoundly participate in the local community to become a church for others. However, in unprecedented times, such as the COVID-19 pandemic, there are concerns about whether the immigrant church can become a church for others. Wouldn't the uncertainty of the pandemic and post-pandemic era quickly turn to fear, causing the Korean immigrant church to return to a focus on ministry for survival rather than service for others?

This chapter argues that ascetic spiritual formation can be the foundation for forming a postcolonial self for the Korean immigrant church in the United States and pursuing a missional life in the dominant society. This study focuses on the importance of spiritual formation, considering how missional activities without a formative foundation tend to be disoriented or even deformed. Asceticism of the desert fathers and mothers is particularly relevant among many traditions of spiritual formation during a pandemic, a time of isolation and physical distance from the church as an institution. Finally, as a practical case study, the ascetic spiritual formation introduced in the *Apophthegmata* (*The Sayings of the Desert Fathers*) as withdrawal, stability, and radical honesty will be briefly explored and reflected in the Korean immigrant churches.

"A POSTCOLONIAL SELF" AND ITS OBSTACLES

In her book, *A Postcolonial Self*, Choi Hee An describes South Korean immigrants in North America as experiencing three drastic changes in their identities: The Korean ethnic self (we), the social ideal self (I), and the marginalized self (I as the other).[1] This unstable change in identity explains why there are so many Christians among Korean immigrants.[2] Korean immigrant churches create a sense of belonging and serve as compensation for the immigrants not acknowledged in the dominant society. The unique position of the Korean immigrant church is leading the

---

[1] Choi Hee An, *A Postcolonial Self: Korean Immigrant Theology and Church* (Albany: Suny Press, 2015), 71. See also chapter 1 of this text.

[2] In Korean society, Christians make up about 20 to 25 percent of the total population, whereas more than 70 percent of Korean immigrants in America are Christians. Kwang Chung Kim and Shin Kim, "Ethnic Roles of Korean Immigrant Church," in Ho-Youn Kown, Kwang Chung Kim, and R. Stephen Warner, eds., *Korean American and Their Religions: Pilgrims and Missionaries from a Different Shore* (University Park: Pennsylvania University Press, 2001), 87.

church to provide services in almost all areas, such as economics, culture, education, health, leisure, and core religious functions. In other words, the Korean immigrant church "functions as a safety net or an ethnic enclave within the larger society."[3]

Choi analyzes the characteristics of these Korean immigrants and emphasizes that the immigrant church should play an advanced role in shaping the postcolonial self. In other words, immigrants must go beyond "I as the other" and form a new identity as "I with the other." To achieve this, she suggests that immigrant churches practice radical hospitality above all else. The church must embody radical hospitality as the body of Christ to become an immigrant church with the other that does not remain in the ghetto but moves toward an incarnate life in the dominant society. An argument like this is essential but not new. The missional church movement, which many Korean immigrant churches are interested in these days, also emphasizes moving beyond the ghetto to the local community. It challenges church communities to step outside their comfort zones, discover God who is already working outside the church building, and participate in God's mission in their neighborhoods.[4] In addition, it urges communities to find a way to realize biblical *philoxenia* (love for strangers)—the right direction for the identity of the immigrant church as a postcolonial self—beyond exclusion and hatred as xenophobia.

However, two years in, the pandemic continues to wear on us. These are deeply disorienting times. No matter how much we know exactly where we are going, global fears such as a pandemic suffocate us and cause us to lose direction. In a situation where

---

3   Choi, *A Postcolonial Self*, 99.

4   Michael Frost argues well in his book about the role of the missional church in an excarnate world lacking a lack of commitment or engagement. Michael Frost, *Incarnate: The Body of Christ in an Age of Disengagement* (Grand Rapids, MI: IVP, 2014).

"not to give up on gathering" (Hebrews 10:25) becomes a social nuisance, the fears of the pandemic have shifted to individual responsibility. This privatization of fear accelerates our panic. Many of us have lost loved ones. In addition, physical, mental, economic, and cultural devastation is amplifying in the aftermath of the prolonged pandemic and social distancing efforts.

These factors also apply to Korean immigrant churches. According to the census of Korean American churches conducted by the Korean American Christian Mission Foundation (KCMUSA), 658 Korean American churches have closed due to the pandemic in the past two years.[5] In addition, according to Barna Research conducted on North American pastors in 2021, 29 percent of North American pastors seriously considered quitting their ministry during the pandemic.[6] These findings cast a more pessimistic outlook that 53 percent of pastors do not have time to invest in their spiritual development in their ministry.[7]

No one would disagree with the need to practice radical hospitality as a believer willing to live a life imitating the incarnate Christ. However, in the lives of terrified immigrants, it is still not easy to put radical hospitality into core practice. So, for example, suppose our radical hospitality is only triggered by a sense of inferiority coming from not being able to join the dominant society.

---

5   As a result of a survey conducted by KCMUSA across the Americas from July to September 2021, 338 churches were newly registered, and 1,022 churches were canceled compared to 2019 (3,456 in total). As a result, the number of churches decreased by 658 compared to 2019, before the pandemic, and 2,798 Korean American churches are currently active. Accessed March 13, 2022. https://tinyurl.com/2s47ddwb

6   Carey Nieuwhof, "29% of Pastors Want to Quit: How to Keep Going When You've Lost Confidence in Yourself," accessed May 9, 2022, https://tinyurl.com/mr3jpbr9

7   Glenn Packiam, *The Resilient Pastor: Leading Your Church in a Rapidly Changing World* (Grand Rapids, MI: Baker Books, 2022), 66

In that case, its successful implementation will be far away in the future amid the fear of the post-pandemic era. The sense of inferiority to the center never achieves the transformation of identity into a new self, and it only continues to exhaust us from the periphery. Also, the sense of inferiority toward the center makes Korean immigrant churches in the United States accustomed to unwanted deformative habits such as self-pity, distraction, immediacy, and palliative living in their relationship with mainstream culture.

First, immigrants are prone to self-pity. Most Korean immigrants were highly educated and socially and economically stable professionals in Korea. However, most immigrants cannot maintain the same level of occupation in the United States due to language and cultural barriers. As a result, most immigrants experience downward mobility. Unrecognized in mainstream American society, they find compensation through the immigrant church.

Pyong Gap Min argues that Korean immigrants who have been deprived of status and power in mainstream society are provided with social status through immigrant churches as well as fellowship, ethnic identity, and social services.[8] In fact, according to his survey of fifty-four Korean immigrant churches in New York City, 78.5 percent of individuals hold lay positions. In addition, it is noticeable that the titles indicating church positions, such as elders, exhorters, and deacons, are also commonly carried outside the church.[9] Because their past careers, education, relationships, and conversational skills are useless in American society, Korean immigrants gather in the immigrant church in anticipation of social, psychological, emotional, and relational compensation. It

---

8   Pyong Gap Min, "The Structure and Social Functions of Korean Immigrant Churches in the United States," *The International Migration Review*, Vol. 26, No. 4 (Winter, 1992), 1371–1372.

9   Min, 1389.

is a condition that can trigger collective narcissism by becoming a "church as the other."[10] This is why there have been relatively more conflicts and schisms within the Korean immigrant churches in this context.

The second deformative habit of the Korean immigrant church is a distraction in the mainstream consumer culture. Immigrants are exposed to the consumerist habits of mainstream American society. In addition, they tend to become persistently dissatisfied with religious consumerists who expect compensation for what they have yet to receive in the dominant society.[11]

The symptoms are already well-revealed among second-generation Korean Americans. In her research on Korean American second-generation spirituality, Sharon Kim points out their religious consumer orientation as follows: Second-generation Korean Americans "chose their churches on the basis of which church would provide them with the best 'benefit package.'"[12] She continues, "The topics of church hopping and church shopping are talked about very matter-of-factly and casually by the second generation. There seems to be no hesitation, guilt, or shame over a lack of commitment to a particular church."[13] The breeder as a consumerist is none other than the first-generation parents. In many first-generation immigrant churches, especially in large cities, the leading cause is increased inflows from other churches rather than increasing the number of converts. The danger of consumerism for Christians is not simply because of materialism

---

10   Choi, *A Postcolonial Self*, 101.
11   Rodney Clapp, "The Theology of Consumption and the Consumption of Theology," in *The Consuming Passion*, ed. Rodney Clapp (Downers Grove: InterVarsity Press, 1998), 188.
12   Sharon Kim, *A Faith of Our Own: Second-Generation Spirituality in Korean American Churches* (New Brunswick, NJ: Rutgers University Press, 2010), 97.
13   Kim, *A Faith of Our Own*, 97.

but because their way of the Christian life is like that of religious consumerism. Many immigrant church shoppers move from church to church. Rather than being loyal to one, they have equated numerous distractions and ceaseless busyness with progress and growth. Accordingly, the church tends to respond with a bustling hyperactive ministry that caters to the tastes of these religious consumers.

The third deformative habit is the idol of immediacy. Immigrants move relatively often because they have no roots. As a result, many immigrant churches stray from long-term discipleship training and appeal to rootless immigrants with glittering programs that showcase immediacy. Immediacy offsets discipleship and commitment and anchors a seemingly attractional church. As Dallas Willard mentions, "You must ruthlessly eliminate hurry from your life . . . Hurry is the great enemy of spiritual life in our day."[14] The idolatrous desire for instant gratification constantly seduces immigrant churches suffering from a scarcity of resources. Pastors are obsessed with the compulsion to bear fruit in a hurry, and discipleship and spiritual formation, which require a relatively long process for genuine transformation, cannot fully take root under such soil.

The fourth deformative habit for the Korean immigrant church is palliative living. Korean-born German philosopher Byung-Chul Han defines modern society as a "palliative society," asserting that "a universal algophobia," that is, a generalized fear of pain, dominates today.[15] We live in a society where tolerance of pain is rapidly weakening. The consequence of this algophobia is

---

14 Quoted in John Mark Comer, *The Ruthless Elimination of Hurry* (Colorado Springs, CO: Waterbrook, 2019), 19.
15 Byung-Chul Han, *Palliative Society*, trans. D. Seuer (Medford: Polity Press, 2021), 1–2, Kindle.

permanent anesthesia. Accordingly, all relationships are oriented in a palliative manner.

Sung-Deuk Oak points out that while major Korean churches in the Los Angeles area are making some progress in social engagement, they are still insensitive to the dominant society's suffering and have become ghettoized.[16] Oak correctly criticizes the fact that the Korean American Church, which has grown rapidly along with the increase in immigration since the new immigration law took effect in 1965, has been proclaiming a similar message of prosperity theology for the past forty years along with immigrant Christians who are trying to achieve the "American Dream." In other words, they have equated believing in Jesus with being in the middle class and have emphasized that believing in Jesus means having a good job and a good family.[17]

Ignoring the dominant society's suffering, Korean immigrant churches are used to an ambiguous middle ground and distance to avoid pain and conflict. As a result, they avoid tough conversations and intense debates with one another. They bypass agape and disengage in life with their neighbors, which often comes at the cost of suffering. They prefer quick-acting painkillers regularly.

The common problem in the aforementioned deformative habits of immigrant churches is that they weaken the attentiveness toward God, neighbor, and authentic self. Self-transformation into a postcolonial self is never achieved in a narcissistic, hyperactive, immediate, and algophobic status.

---

16   Sung-Deuk Oak, "The Korean American Churches and Civic Responsibility," *Korean Christianity and History*, vol 29 (September 2008), 178–179.
17   Oak, "The Korean American Churches and Civic Responsibility," 179.

ASCETIC SPIRITUAL FORMATION: ATTENTIVE TO GOD AND STRANGE TO THE SELF

An essential function of spiritual formation is to find the authentic self through "intentional God-ward re-orientation and re-habituation of human experience." It means "gradual transformation from a biological and socially mediated self into the true self,"[18] and spiritual formation does not happen overnight. No matter how intense our missional aspirations may be, if separated from the formative impulse to develop a relationship with God, our lives will only be activistic, populist, and pragmatic, dominated by the urgency of the moment.[19]

Since humans are constantly being formed by their given contexts, Christians should engage in an intentional process of becoming more fully united with Christ. Spiritual formation breaks the false self from passions such as fantasies, delusions, obsessions, shame, fears, anger, and depression that are constantly formed in the dominant powers and systems. Surprisingly, this kind of spiritual formation was first introduced in the early Christian world as a radical form of asceticism. In the fourth and sixth centuries, desert fathers and mothers pioneered these ascetic practices in Egypt, Judea, Gaza, and Sinai. It is no exaggeration to say that desert asceticism sheds significant new light on one

---

18 This description of the function of spiritual formation is based on Evan B. Howard's definition of Christian spiritual formation. According to Howard, Christian spiritual formation is "the intentional and God-ward re-orientation and re-habituation of human experience." Evan B. Howard, *The Brazos Introduction to Christian Spirituality* (Grand Rapids, MI: Brazos Press, 2008), 269.

19 Jeffrey P. Greenman, *Life in the Spirit: Spiritual Formation in Theological Perspective* (Downers Grove, IL: IVP Academic, 2010), 35.

of the most lasting and influential developments in the history of Christian spirituality.[20]

Antony, an eremite (*anchorite*) who lived an ascetic life, was known to the world through Athanasius of Alexandria, who wrote *Vita Antoni*, the first desert literature. Athanasius once said, "the desert was made a city," in reference to how much the ascetic life significantly impacted his time.[21] Unlike today, in the early Christian era, asceticism was regarded as a universal and ideal Christian way of life. The ascetic life was an alternative life to follow as faithful disciples of Christ due to two significant factors. First, the era of martyrdom came to an abrupt end. After the end of persecution from the Roman Empire, realizing that not all Christians are called to real martyrdom, Christians identified the purpose of dying for Christ with the purpose of living a good life for Him. Second, as Christianity gained legal status and Constantine's favoritism in the Roman empire after the Edict of Milan (CE 313), it was difficult for the church to maintain the old standard of discipleship of the previous era. In that sense, desert asceticism represents "both a protest and an affirmation—a protest against a decadent and overly institutionalized ecclesiastical body and a

---

20 The International Conference on the Ascetic Dimension of Religious Life and Culture held at Union Theological Seminary in New York in 1993 made a monumental contribution to contemporary scholarship on asceticism. In one plenary session, Kallistos Ware ends his "The Way of the Ascetics: Negative or Affirmative?" with the decided affirmation: "Without asceticism none of us is authentically human." His affirmation is an explicit Christian understanding of ascetic discipline to form a Christian individual. In *Asceticism*, eds. Vincent L. Wimbush and Richard Valantasis (Oxford: Oxford University Press, 1998), 13.
21 Athanasius, *The Life of St. Anthony*, trans. Robert C. Gregg (New York: Harper Collins Publishers, 1980), 18.

restatement of the gospel teaching to fit the changed conditions of the times."[22]

The Greek term *askesis* is defined as "disciplined exercise and deliberate repetitive practice undertaken for a specific purpose."[23] The term initially applied to athletes. In the Greco-Roman philosophical tradition, the term was used as a practice necessary to pursue moral excellence, *arete*, or virtue. Christian asceticism is distinguished in that it ultimately aims for union and intimacy with God rather than simply striving for moral perfection like Greek and Roman philosophy. In other words, the goal of Christian asceticism is to transform a holistic life through attentiveness and ceaseless prayer by controlling desires, obsessions, habits, and will that hinder the achievement of intimacy with God.

In general, asceticism is understood as severe self-restraint. Today it is frequently perceived as being something fanatical and involving self-torture, forever withdrawn from ordinary human life. Such a distorted and prejudiced attitude toward asceticism in modern society relentlessly removes the ascetic elements from our spiritual life and makes us grow worldly without guilt. In real life, however, asceticism guides us to self-mastery and to achieve the goals we set for ourselves. "Without this ascetic concentration of effort," Kallistos Ware asserts, "we are at the mercy of exterior forces or of our own emotions and moods; we are reacting rather than acting."[24] The Christian life would never be inwardly free without the elements of the ascetic life. Paul's description of "those who are Christ's have crucified the flesh with its passions

---

[22] Thomas M. Gannon and George W. Traub, *The Desert and the City* (Chicago: Loyola University Press, 1969), 23.

[23] Luke Dysinger, "The Ascetic Life" in *The Oxford Handbook of Mystical Theology*, ed. Edward Howells and Mark A. McIntosh (Oxford: Oxford University Press, 2020), 164.

[24] Ware, "The Way of the Ascetics," 3.

and desires" (Gal 5:24) is none other than an ascetic struggle, continually forcing oneself to perform good works by uprooting evil dispositions, evil habits, and evil will be rooted in our soul and body.

A recent study of the asceticism of the desert fathers and mothers' notes that Christian asceticism was not simply an emphasis on renunciation of the body but rather a discipline related to self-formation to control the mind.[25] In the late antique society, the mind was not simply a locus of thought. Instead, it was the center of human experience, which we often call the self. In the second to fourth centuries, new anthropology became increasingly concerned with an individual's inner life and made possible the emergence of a "new reflective self." This late antique anthropology also influenced the desert fathers and mothers active in Egypt and Palestine. Their self-formative ascetic practices protected the monks from the tyranny of afflictive thoughts (*logismoi*) and helped them become attentive.

Asceticism, which helps increase attentiveness toward God through control over evil thoughts, is not content with cultivating privatized self-formation. Poemen, one of the desert fathers, said, "Instructing one's neighbor is for the man [sic] who is whole and without passions; for what is the use of building the house of another while destroying one's own?"[26] Poemen emphasized the importance of paying attention to God. His words do not mean that caring for others is not essential; rather, they remind us that a

---

25 Paul C. Dilley, *Monasteries and the Care of Souls in Late Antique Christianity* (New York: Cambridge University Press, 2017); Inbar Gravier, *Asceticism of the Mind: Forms of Attention and Self-transformation in Late Antique Monasticism* (Toronto: Pontifical Institute of Mediaeval Studies, 2018).

26 Benedicta Ward, trans., *The Sayings of the Desert Fathers: The Alphabetical Collection* (Kalamazoo: Cistercian Publications, 1975), Poemen 127.

more complete self-formation should be forged for serving others. Asceticism, which has an innate counter-cultural function, achieves its integrity in pursuing relational and social transformation beyond personal growth. In that sense, as broadly described by Richard Valantasis, asceticism can be described as "practices intended to inaugurate a new personality, to develop new social relationships, and to support these by the articulation of a new culture, a new worldview."[27]

First, it is required to become a stranger to my old self to form this new self. There can be no asceticism, no new personality, no new social relations, and no newly articulated worldview without first becoming a stranger to the old. Becoming a stranger, therefore, stands at the heart of ascetic activity. Korean immigrants who have learned that their existing ethnic self is no longer effective in the immigrant society are more likely to be exposed to the obsession with the self-image expected by the dominant society and the immediacy, delusion, and hypocrisy to achieve it. They experience frustration and deprivation of themselves that do not meet these social expectations, and they cannot get out of a marginalized life. In that respect, self-formation through ascetic spiritual formation is more critical in an immigrant setting. It is an essential path not for survival but for fulfilling the Christian's responsibility to transform the dominant society with the Gospel.

A CASE STUDY OF DESERT FATHERS AND MOTHERS

Apophthegmata Patrum (*The Sayings of the Desert Fathers*) is arguably one of the oldest documents that gives a glance into the

---

[27] Richard Valantasis, *The Making of the Self: Ancient and Modern Asceticism* (Cambridge: James Clarke, 2008), 174.

critical ascetic practices for attentiveness.[28] Although various types of ascetic practices are reported in the *Apophthegmata Patrum*, this article focuses on three core practices: withdrawal, stability, and radical honesty. It is necessary to conduct *apatheia* (imperturbable calm) that is not easily swayed by external stimuli by continuously reciting these three practices to accomplish *agape* toward God and neighbor. First, withdrawal (*anachoresis*) and detachment from the bondage of the present life are required. Next, through the stability that never leaves their own cell, one must quiet their inner noise and focus on the God who whispers in the silence. Finally, one must radically confess sins to Christ while struggling with the evil thoughts (*logismoi*) that constantly tempt them. Through these repeated practices, the desert fathers and mothers were able to form a new self for humanity.

Withdrawal (anachoresis): The term derived from *anachoresis*, the first step in the ascetic desert movement, is *anchorite*, which refers to an eremite monk. The desert movement eventually developed into the first *cenobitic* communities that formed the basis of the medieval monastic movement. However, the prominent influence of the anchorites initiated the early desert movement. The anchorites chose the desert to break free from their obsession with the world. Doulas said, "Detach yourself from the love of the multitude lest your enemy questions your spirit and trouble your inner

---

28 The *Apophthegmata Patrum* has come down to us in three forms: the Alphabetical Collection in Greek and Systematic Collection, and another Greek collection of anonymous sayings, known as the Anonymous Collection. In this article, I mainly used the Alphabetical Collection. The Alphabetical gathers some 1,000 sayings and brief narratives under the names of one hundred and thirty notable desert fathers and mothers and arranges these according to the Greek alphabet.

peace."²⁹ Excessive attachment to the world deceives the human soul and destroys inner peace. Humans often lose their ways as their thoughts, words, and actions are controlled and manipulated by obsessions, concerns, and fears. Accordingly, the desert fathers and mothers emphasize that they will achieve solitude through withdrawal and be completely forgotten from the world. "Happy is the monk who thinks he is the outcast of all."³⁰ Nilus said, "Go, sell all that belongs to you and give it to the poor and take up the cross, deny yourself; in this way you will be able to pray without distraction."³¹ The ultimate purpose of letting go of everything was to devote ourselves to prayer for the union with God. Contrary to prejudice against them, the fathers and mothers did not withdraw to the desert due to their hatred of the world or their nostalgia for their pastoral life. The withdrawal was the most reasonable choice for them to establish a deeper relationship with God, and in the end, it was to make more room for their neighbors. The desert fathers and mothers were aware of the paradox that genuine openness toward others is achieved through detachment rather than attachment.

Andrew described the three essentials for a monk as "exile (*xeniteia*), poverty, [and] endurance in silence."³² In particular, Andrew's self-consciousness understood withdrawing from people as an "exile" rather than an escaping is noteworthy. If escape is often voluntary, exile implies passivity by an external force. However, the desert fathers and mothers, including Andrew, perceived their withdrawal as "voluntary exile."

Voluntary exile (*xeniteia*) means to be together with others and, at the same time, not to be with them. It does not mean contempt for others. On the contrary, it is free from

---

29 Ward, *The Sayings of the Desert Fathers*, Doulas 3.
30 Ward, *The Sayings of the Desert Fathers*, Nilus 8.
31 Ward, *The Sayings of the Desert Fathers*, Nilus 4.
32 Ward, *The Sayings of the Desert Fathers*, Andrew 1.

excessive consciousness and obsession with others. "Refrain yourself from affection towards many people, for fear lest your spirit be distracted, so that your interior peace may not be disturbed."[33]

Voluntary exile is a necessary spiritual practice for the Pelagian Christians prone to vainglory. Being overly conscious of others is detrimental to our souls. In a culture that distracts attention, we easily fall on the shoulder of the need of others as a pretext. In contrast, the desert fathers and mothers came free from people's recognition and approval in their ascetic lives of deep communion with God. Voluntary exile does not describe their irresponsibility or indifference toward their neighbors but shows their deep *apatheia*.

In that respect, the real emphasis on the withdrawal of the desert fathers and mothers is not on physical relocation but on inner withdrawal. Syncletica warned of the importance of inner withdrawal: "There are many who live in the mountains and behave as if they were in the town, and they are wasting their time. It is possible to be a solitary in one's mind while living in a crowd, and it is possible for one who is a solitary to live in the crowd of his own thoughts."[34] Withdrawal is not complete with a physical distance from the world or by entering a remote cave alone, away from neighbors. Even in a complex city, you can lead an ascetic life with detachment. Conversely, even in the desert, where there is nothing, you can still live without letting go of your obsessions and delusions. Unless internal withdrawal is made, the acts of physical withdrawal have no effect. What harms us is not possessing things or living with people but only excessive attachment to things or people.

Thomas Merton compared how the calling of an ascetic monk differs from that of a Marxist. Marxists are social reformers, whereas monks seek to change human consciousness. A monk is

---

33 Ward, *The Sayings of the Desert Fathers*, Evagrius 2.
34 Ward, *The Sayings of the Desert Fathers*, Syncletica 19.

a marginal person "as (at least ideally) a man who has responded to an authentic call of God to a life of freedom and detachment, a 'desert life' outside normal social structures."[35] This call to the withdrawal deliberately to the margin of society will not be limited to the monks. In modern society, all Christians are called to thrive, not survive, in a prophetic life that does not conform to the dominant society. However, the hectic activity of immigrant Christians who have lost their prophetic power can quickly become obsessed with being anxious to control everything to survive in a dominant society. But, as Merton noted earlier, radical human change only takes place on the margins without a sense of inferiority to the dominant society.

Stability: In the *Apophthegmata Patrum*, several desert fathers and mothers repeatedly emphasize the importance of staying in the cell. Some desert monks who abandoned everything and withdrew into the desert still did not make much spiritual progress. Syncletica pointed out that their problem is not in any other inadequate knowledge or practices but in a lack of stability: "Just as the bird who abandons the eggs, she was sitting on prevents them from hatching, so the monk or the nun grows cold and their faith dies, when they go from one place to another."[36]

A brother, unable to stay in his cell, was caught up in the delusion that his faith would make great progress if he moved elsewhere. So, he went to the two desert fathers in turn for advice. First, Papnutius advised, "Go and stay in your cell; make only one prayer in the morning and one in the evening and one at night. When you are hungry, eat, when you are thirsty, drink; when you are tired, sleep. But stay in the cell and take no notice of this thought." John went further and said, "Don't pray at all,

---

35   Bernard McGinn, "Withdrawal and Return: Reflections on Monastic Retreat from the World," *Spiritus* 6 (2006), 149.
36   Ward, *The Sayings of the Desert Fathers*, Syncletica 6.

just stay in the cell."³⁷ If Paphnutius was admonishing the brother to endure the temptation to leave his cell with minimal spiritual practices, John went one step further and encouraged the brother not to give up on stability even if he stopped all ascetic practices. The importance of stability is reaffirmed again in the instruction given to his disciple by Helacrides, who directly built the room for the disciple: "Each time you are afflicted, eat, drink, sleep; only do not come out of your cell until Saturday."³⁸

While stability was critical to the desert ascetic spiritual formation, the desert monks were frequently tempted to run out of their cells. Often referred to as "the noonday devil," sloth (*acedia*) was a notorious temptation for the desert fathers and mothers to practice ascetic practices in their cells every day.³⁹ For that reason, Anthony recommended that monks always return to their cells in a hurry. "Just as fish die if they stay too long out of water, so the monks who loiter outside their cells or pass their time with men [*sic*] of the world lose the intensity of inner peace. So, like a fish going towards the sea, we must hurry to reach our cell, for fear that if we delay outside, we will lose our interior watchfulness."⁴⁰

A spiritual formation is a place where a great struggle accompanies a great encounter with God. Spirituality does not depend on how many new or powerful spiritual tools I have but on how firmly I stay in the cell. It is only there that we experience inner stillness, listen to God, and become aware of the existence and need of our neighbor.

Self-formation requires stability, not hyperactivity. It is especially true of the Christian faith community, which believes

---

37 Ward, *The Sayings of the Desert Fathers*, Paphnutius 7.
38 Ward, *The Sayings of the Desert Fathers*, Heraclides 1.
39 For a detailed description of the seduction of noonday evil, see Evagrius' *Praktikos* (Kalamazoo, MI: Cistercian Publications, 1981), 18–19.
40 Ward, *The Sayings of the Desert Fathers*, Antony 10.

that our salvation is not in our strength but in God. Stability is a discipline rooted in God's faithfulness. In a consumerist society that encourages numerous opportunities and choices, immigrants become more obsessive and distracted by a sense of relative deprivation. They are thirsty for an ideal place to live, a job, a school, and a faith community. But stability teaches us to abandon our backup plan. Stability comes from trusting in God's plan, which is far better than ours, in acceptance of given circumstances. The key to the spirituality of stability lies in God's faithfulness to us, not our will and choice: we must be rooted in God's steadfast faithfulness here and now rather than searching for an ideal community.

Above all, the great benefit of stability is paying attention to the here and now. It makes us look at the reality in front of us, which is nothing more than a farmer plowing a given field. Stability is a journey of silent trust, believing that daily plowing is the right path for harvest. It is not a grand theology but repeated daily habits that lead us to authentic self-transformation.

A cell does not allow for a quick-fix spirituality. Impatience and anxiety are always uninvited guests of the cell. It is essential not to fall into any temptation of immediacy. Today we see many Christians with theologies that are grandiose but lack real-life holiness. We know our weaknesses, responsibilities, and goals more clearly than ever as immigrant Christians, but knowledge and practice are always separated because of the absence of day-to-day exercises. The key is daily routines and the stability that makes them happen.

Radical Honesty: Poemen once said, "All the virtues come to this house except one, and without that virtue, it is hard for a man [sic] to stand ... For a man to blame himself."[41] Poemen's saying "to blame himself" emphasizes the attentiveness to one's sin. The

---

41   Ward, *The Sayings of the Desert Fathers*, Poemen 134.

desert fathers and mothers warned that smoldering temptations, malice, pride, and other sins must not be sublimated or overlooked, parasitizing our souls.

For early Christians like Clement, self-control (*erkrateia*) is a moral quality that should predominate all areas of a believer's life. Self-control begets all other virtues and thus constitutes the foundation of virtue. The premise for self-control is possible only by acknowledging that one's self is facing external temptations. Therefore, while asceticism cannot be the means of salvation, it is still essential for self-control and attentiveness in a world where sin and temptation are rampant.

As the psalmist confesses, "Our sins are stronger than we are, but you will blot them out" (Ps 65:3). If one does not carefully examine their thoughts, hearts, habits, words, and actions every moment, sooner or later, they will come under the control of evil. Only when we come to God with honesty and sensitivity to our sins will He cleanse us from our iniquities.

The origin of evil is human thought (Mark 7:21–23). Accordingly, the desert fathers and mothers struggled with evil thoughts (*logismoi*) that constantly tempted them in their cells. As Poemen said, "No more can you prevent thoughts from arising, but you can resist them."[42]

Today, the seven critical sins are envy, anger, sloth (*acedia*), vainglory, greed, gluttony, and lust. The daily struggle, meticulous examen, and systematic study against these critical sins originate from the desert fathers and mothers. The harsh environment of the desert became a laboratory where the fathers and mothers faced themselves. Through the radical honesty of their inner thoughts, the monks became the subjects of experimentation and fought against the evils that entered the human mind.

Evagrius describes the importance of careful self-examination and radical honesty as follows:

---

42 Ward, *The Sayings of the Desert Fathers*, Poemen 28.

> If there is any monk who wishes to take the measure of some of the fiercer demons so as to gain experience in his monastic art, then let him keep careful watch over his thoughts. Let him observe their intensity, their periods of decline and follow them as they rise and fall. Let him note well the complexity of his thoughts, their periodicity, the demons which cause them, with the order of their succession and the nature of their associations. Then let him ask from Christ the explanations of these data he has observed.[43]

The desert confession of sin is no mere pretense. The desert fathers and mothers honestly confessed to Christ by examining the flow, cycle, intensity, and change of the evil thoughts that entered them, expressing them concretely. As Augustine famously said, "To be mindful of God is to be mindful of self." Radical honesty with oneself was a core prayer for the desert fathers and mothers. They sought to find their true self through radical honesty and harsh self-accusation. Antony said, "The greatest thing a man can do is to throw his faults before the Lord and expect temptation to his last breath."[44] The integrity of the genuine Christian is continuously formed by accusing themself.

The false self is extremely unstable, mutable, and easily distracted. The false self depends on people's expectations, recognition, and approval to shape their identity. As a result, chronic fear, anxiety, and loneliness lie within. Externally, one is always busy with obsessive and reactive activities. In a heterogeneous culture where even the language is different, Korean immigrants experience more serious identity confusion and instability. Thus, they become more obsessive and sensitive to external stimuli.

---

43 Evagrius, *Praktikos*, 29–30.
44 Ward, *The Sayings of the Desert Fathers*, Antony 4.

In this regard, it is necessary to confess our sins with careful self-examination as a practice to cast off our false selves. Radical honesty is a discipline that urgently needs to be rediscovered, especially when confession of sins is disappearing from public worship, small groups, and private prayer as it is today. God wants us to face our inner reality and bring it to Him in prayer.

CONCLUSION

In this unpredictable post-pandemic era, Korean immigrant churches are in a dilemma: Do they seek radical hospitality, willing to form a new self that lives with others? Or do they live with their old self, deformed by self-pity, distraction, immediacy, and a palliative life? The formation of a new self does not happen overnight. Even if our missionary orientation is clear, it is easy to get lost if it is not accompanied by spiritual formation. Ascetic spiritual formation will lead disoriented immigrants to reorient and re-habituate toward the kingdom of God.

Limiting the ascetic practices of the desert fathers and mothers to withdrawal, stability, and radical honesty may be an oversimplification of the desert movement. However, these three are the vital ascetic practices that lead to the radical hospitality of agape while achieving *apatheia* through attentiveness toward God, self, and others, which are repeatedly mentioned in desert literature, such as *Apophthegmata Petrum*. While experiencing the fear of a pandemic that has never been experienced before, retrieving underutilized and often forgotten practices for attentiveness is more crucial than ever. Otherwise, evil, like vermin, will gnaw at our spirits invisibly. To this end, we must constantly light the divine fire of prayer in our hearts. It is a shortcut for immigrants to transform into a postcolonial self as a missional body of Christ in a dominant society:

> In the beginning, there is struggle and a lot of work for those who come near to God. But after that, there is

indescribable joy. It is just like building a fire: at first, it's smoky and your eyes water, but later you get the desired result. Thus, we ought to light the divine fire in ourselves with tears and effort.[45]

BIBLIOGRAPHY

Athanasius, *The Life of St. Anthony*. Translated by Robert C. Gregg. New York: HarperCollins, 1980.

Choi, Hee An. *A Postcolonial Self: Korean Immigrant Theology and Church*. Albany: Suny Press, 2015.

Clapp, Rodney. "The Theology of Consumption and the Consumption of Theology," in *The Consuming Passion*. Edited by Rodney Clapp. Downers Grove: InterVarsity Press, 1998.

Comer, John Mark. *The Ruthless Elimination of Hurry*. Colorado Springs, CO: Waterbrook, 2019.

Dilley, Paul C. *Monasteries and the Care of Souls in Late Antique Christianity*. New York: Cambridge University Press, 2017.

Dysinger, Luke. "The Ascetic Life" in *The Oxford Handbook of Mystical Theology*, edited by Edward Howells and Mark A. McIntosh. Oxford: Oxford University Press, 2020.

Evagrius Ponticus, *Praktikos*. Kalamazoo, MI: Cistercian Publications, 1981.

Frost, Michael. *Incarnate: The Body of Christ in an Age of Disengagement*. Grand Rapids: IVP, 2014.

Gannon, Thomas M. and George W. Traub, *The Desert and the City*. Chicago: Loyola University Press, 1969.

Gravier, Inbar. *Asceticism of the Mind: Forms of Attention and Self-transformation in Late Antique Monasticism*. Toronto: Pontifical Institute of Mediaeval Studies, 2018.

Greenman, Jeffrey P., ed. *Life in the Spirit: Spiritual Formation in Theological Perspective*. Downers Grove, IL: IVP Academic, 2010.

Han, Byung-Chul. *Palliative Society*. Translated by D. Seuer. Medford: Polity Press, 2021.

Howard, Evan B. *The Brazos Introduction to Christian Spirituality*. Grand Rapids, MI: Brazos Press, 2008.

---

45 Ward, *The Sayings of the Desert Fathers*, Syncletica 1.

Kim, Kwang Chung and Shin Kim. "Ethnic Roles of Korean Immigrant Church." In *Korean American and Their Religions: Pilgrims and Missionaries from a Different Shore*, edited by Ho-Youn Kown, Kwang Chung Kim, and R. Stephen Warner. University Park: Pennsylvania University Press, 2001: 71–94.

Kim, Sharon. *A Faith of Our Own: Second-Generation Spirituality in Korean American Churches*. New Brunswick, NJ: Rutgers University Press, 2010.

McGinn, Bernard. "Withdrawal and Return: Reflections on Monastic Retreat from the World," *Spiritus* 6, no. 2 (Fall 2006): 149–172.

Min, Pyong Gap. "The Structure and Social Functions of Korean Immigrant Churches in the United States." *The International Migration Review* Vol. 26, No. 4 (Winter, 1992): 1370–1394.

Oak, Sung-Deuk. "The Korean American Churches and Civic Responsibility." *Korean Christianity and History*, vol 29 (September 2008): 165–190.

Packiam, Glenn. *The Resilient Pastor: Leading Your Church in a Rapidly Changing World*. Grand Rapids, MI: Baker Books, 2022.

Valantasis, Richard. *The Making of the Self: Ancient and Modern Asceticism*. Cambridge: James Clarke, 2008.

Ward, Benedicta, trans. *The Saying of the Desert Fathers: The Alphabetical Collection*. Kalamazoo: Cistercian Publications, 1975.

Ware, Kallistos. "The Way of the Ascetics: Negative or Affirmative?" In *Asceticism*, edited by Vincent L. Wimbush and Richard Valantasis. Oxford: Oxford University Press, 1998.

Wimbush, Vincent L., and Richard Valantasis, eds. *Asceticism*. Oxford: Oxford University Press, 1998.

5

THE SITUATIONAL ROLES OF THE KOREAN AMERICAN CHURCH IN ITS HISTORY
From Community Centers to Bridges

Enoch Jinsik Kim

INTRODUCTION

International immigration worldwide rapidly grew from 153 million in 1990 to 281 million in 2020.[1] In 2019, about 7.49 million Koreans were living overseas, of which two million were in the United States.[2] The Bible introduces many immigrants. Among them, we have Abraham and his descendants, the Israelites who went to Egypt, Moses and his people who exiled themselves and immigrated back to the land of Canaan, and the diaspora, who scattered to various places in the ancient Near East. As the

---

[1] International Migration 2020 Highlights, United Nations, Department of Economics and Social Affairs, last modified. 2021 January, https://www.un.org/development/desa/pd/.

[2] Abby Budiman, "Koreans in the U.S. Fact Sheet," Pew Research Center, December 9, 2022, https://tinyurl.com/zwud2e6v.

Roman Empire rose and fell, countless Jewish merchants and immigrants moved into the cities of Asia during the Pax-Romana (27 BCE–180 CE). The history of the church also has countless stories of immigrants. God has planned for the people to move for God's providence and missionary vision, and this extends far beyond historical records or natural trends. For letting the unheard in the unfamiliar land hear the good news, God's moving of God's people is natural.

From the Joseon Dynasty's weakening in the nineteenth century, Koreans migrated from the Korean peninsula to the United States, China, Japan, Central Asia, and Mexico. Such immigration allowed the Korean diaspora to contact the gospel; many belonged to the immigrant church. However, as churches in the Korean mainland grew, most of these immigrant churches simply imitated or depended on the churches in the Korean mainland. As a result of this dependency, the immigrant churches could not well develop their immigration theology and continued to struggle to identify themselves. Bearing in mind these needs, this chapter will review the situational roles of the Korean American church in its history and reinterpret it using ethnic-sociological theories. Finally, we will imagine the Korean American church's contextual identity as part of the global Christian mosaic.

This chapter lays the theoretical frame for Charles van Engen. As core areas for theologizing the mission, van Engen conceptualized the biblical basis, the ecclesiological framework, and the social situation.[3] Among the three areas, this chapter will mainly explore the ecclesiology and social science areas.

---

3   Charles van Engen argues these theological disciplines as the key missiological area and named them as World, Word, and the Church. Charles van Engen, *Mission on the Way: Issues in Mission Theology* (Grand Rapids: MI: Baker Books, 1996), 18.

TYPES AND MOTIVES OF IMMIGRATION

Knowing the motivation for immigration is the first step of knowing who the immigrants are. This is because the motive of immigration affects the lives of immigrants tremendously. After people leave their place of origin, they go through several stages of life in a new land.[4] Because of the several stages, the church's role to the immigrants is also situational. This means that to be a situationally appropriate institution, the immigrant church must also pass through stages accordingly with the immigrant society. Now, let's figure out the stages that the immigrant society and their church went through step by step.

First, there is an ecological push when an environment is challenging for people to live in, such as one caused by a natural disaster. This ecologically pushed immigration is quite dangerous and vulnerable to failure because it occurs rapidly, and people must leave without a proper plan. For example, in the history of Korea, the repeated famines in the 1860s and 1870s forced many Koreans seeking fertile land to immigrate to the Kando area near the Tuman and Amnok rivers, to places such as Tonghua (通化), Jian (輯安), Changbai (長白), Sinbin (新賓), and Longjing (龍井).[5] By the 1860s, their numbers had already reached seventy-seven thousand and they gradually dispersed to various areas of northeastern China.

The second type of immigration is due to a country's migration policy. This includes reclaiming new areas or relocating

---

[4] In his book *Mission Strategy in the City: Cultivation of Inter-ethnic Common Grounds*, Enoch Jinsik Kim introduces the process of immigration as five steps, but this chapter simplifies it into four steps.

[5] National Archives of Korea, "Koreans in China (중국의 조선족)," The History of Korean Diaspora (재외 한인의 역사), accessed December 8, 2022, https://tinyurl.com/4mws98v3.

residences due to natural disasters, the relocation of large companies that require workers to work abroad, or intergovernmental immigration agreements. For example, in 1435, for territorial expansion and cultivation, the Joseon Dynasty resettled people from southern regions to northern regions, such as Pyeongando and Hamgildo.[6] In addition, at the end of the Joseon Dynasty, the Japanese military government issued the National Mobilization Law (1938), and the Regulation of the Requisition (1944) brought Koreans to Japan to provide workforces. As a result, 720,000 Korean workers, 360,000 soldiers and civilians, and 200,000 women had moved to mainland Japan and several war zones between 1939 and 1945.[7]

The third type of immigration is a higher aspiration, with new dreams and aspirations to explore a new world. This is the case for a handful of pioneers who ambitiously moved to an unknown territory. The first Korean immigrants in America who arrived in Hawai'i (1903) and California (1904) fall into this category. They were recruited by David Deshler, the owner of the East-West Development Company, to work on sugar plantations with the promise of high wages.[8] Such a suggestion was a dream of overnight riches for Koreans who suffered from drought and famine. Koreans who left for agricultural immigration in Brazil, Argentina, Paraguay, and Bolivia between 1963 and 1971 and the

---

6 National Institute of Korean History, "북방사민정책," The History of Ours (우리 역사넷), March 29, 2017, https://tinyurl.com/mr392bt4.

7 National Archives of Korea, "Koreans in Japan (일본의 재일한인)," The History of Korean Diaspora (재외 한인의 역사), accessed December 8, 2022, https://tinyurl.com/4wxpkvx9.

8 Hawaii's plantation field labor averaged monthly salary was $15 for twenty-six days of work in the early nineteenth century. "History of Labor in Hawai'i" (West O'ahu, HI: University of Hawai'i, Center for Labor Education & Research), accessed November 20, 2022, https://tinyurl.com/2p9y9fz2.

18,600 miners and nurses who worked in Germany between 1963 and 1977 all belong to this type of immigration as higher aspiration.[9]

The last type of immigration is social momentum. It is a mass migration due to attractive social and natural conditions. People often have a less cultural shock in this case because earlier immigrants from the same origin country have already built the foundation for survival. Immigrants to the United States since the early 1990s fall into this category because vast numbers of Koreans already had built social structures and institutions.

FROM SPREADING TO FORMATION

Because of having little social capital and poor cultural knowledge, the influence and presence of immigrants in their early stages are almost invisible. Thus, they tend to be scattered throughout mainstream society like flying flower seeds. Especially if they immigrated to a more developed country than their own, immigrants became vulnerable minority groups and socially marginalized entities.

In the early period of migration history, many guest laborers went abroad alone to work as lower-level technicians or manual laborers.[10] Because their families and relatives are in their home countries, most of the guest laborers returned to their home countries. A small number of them may have married and settled

---

9 National Archives of Korea, "Koreans in Europe (유럽의 한인)," *The History of Korean Diaspora* (재외 한인의 역사), accessed December 8, 2022, https://tinyurl.com/ykzsdy8c.

10 Mark Gottdiener and Leslie Budd, *Key Concepts in Urban Studies*, SAGE Key Concepts (London: SAGE Publications, 2005), 61–65; James A. Tyner, "Global Cities and Circuits of Global Labor: The Case of Manila, Philippines," *The Professional Geographer* 52, no. 1 (2000): 61–74.

locally, but they still experienced enormous cultural difficulties. Due to unstable occupations and low incomes, they usually could not stay in one place for a long time. Their unstable social status, medical care, social security, and children's educational environment also led immigrants to return to their home countries rather than creating their own local societies. As a result, even the few remaining guest immigrants could not sustain their cultural identity but often scattered into the local communities. For example, of the seven thousand Koreans who came to Hawai'i, two thousand returned to Joseon at the end of their contracts, and about one thousand were scattered throughout the continental United States in California, Oregon, and Washington. Most of them mixed with Chinese and Japanese and were absorbed into US society. Later, Koreans who came to the United States as adopted orphans during the war in 1950–53 or from marriages with US forces in Korea also spread out into mainstream society more rapidly.[11]

The existence of an ethnic community becomes a nest of ethnic unity and reduces this ethnic scattering. Even in the early stage of immigration, many Koreans belonged to the Korean community and married within the community. For example, sugar cane workers in Hawai'i married and settled within the ethnic community. Because of the uneven gender ratio, they even invited so-called 'picture brides' from the Korean mainland. Such an effort to maintain the endogamy tradition enabled them to preserve the ethnic community. The miners and nurses who went to Germany to work married each other and settled new roots in Germany is another good example of guest immigrants remaining in the new land.

---

11 Encyclopedia of Overseas Korean Culture (세계 한민족 문화대전), "Koreans' Moving from Honolulu to San Francisco (호놀룰루에서 샌프란시스코로- 초기 한인의 이주 경로)," The History of Korean Diaspora (재외 한인의 역사), accessed December 8, 2022, https://tinyurl.com/ysc7s98u.

Once the immigrant society reaches a certain size and secures social resources, the number of new immigrants increases rapidly and enters the stage of traditional immigrants.[12] The number of chain migrations increases at this stage.[13] This chain migration energizes the immigrants to create a similar niche, providing nutrition to the ethnic enclave. The emergence of this ethnic enclave is meaningful because the enclave can be a platform that effectively collects social capital, networks, information, and technology. The enclave also protects the ethnic culture and language and forms various communities. Though the early Korean immigrants in Hawai'i were typical guest labor immigrants, many of them decided to remain in the United States. This is because they lived together on the Koloa Sugarcane plantation and developed an ethnic enclave. In the enclave, Koreans kept their customs and wore traditional clothes yearly to celebrate Emperor Gojong's birthday, New Year, and Chuseok.[14]

The so-called third era of Korean American immigration began in 1965 when the US government changed the immigration law. Since then, the number of Korean immigrants born in Korea has increased significantly, reaching about 700 thousand in 1990 and about 1.2 million in 2017.[15] As a result of this mass migration, ethnic enclaves could root all over the United States.

For immigrants, the church is a place that means much more than a space for religion. Especially in the early period of

---

12 Tyner, "Global Cities and Circuits of Global Labor."
13 Kim Korinek, Barbara Entwisle, and Aree Jampaklay, "Through Thick and Thin: Layers of Social Ties and Urban Settlement among Thai Migrants," *American Sociological Review* 70, no. 5 (2005): 779.
14 Sungjoon Moon, "The History of Korean Immigration (한인 이민의 역사)," *Joongang Ilbo*, November 5, 2003, https://tinyurl.com/rskw448z.
15 "Origins and Destinations of the World's Migrants, 1990–2017," *Pew Research Center*, accessed December 9, 2022, https://tinyurl.com/yzpb3v7m.

immigration, the lack of social resources and structures makes the church a center of information, culture, institution, relationship, and opportunity. For example, Koreans arriving in Hawai'i had a place of worship within ten months of their arrival. Surprisingly enough, more than half of the first Korean immigrants were Christians. This was because many immigrants were recruited from the church in Korea. George H. Jones, a Methodist Episcopal Church missionary for Korea, had a considerable influence on Korean churches and encouraged Korean believers to join the emigration.[16] As a result, among the first six hundred Korean immigrants in 1904, "three hundred are members of the Methodist Episcopal Church."[17]

However, rather than developing an immigrant theology, the immigrant church copied and repeated the theology of mainland Korea. In addition to this lack of development in immigration theology, Korean churches have always been active in Korean communities, so it has been difficult to overcome the ethnic-centered perspective. This ethnic ghettoization has not changed over time, especially since most churches have been led by the first generation of immigrants.

FROM GROUPING TO BRIDGING

As the size of the immigrant society continues to grow, it crosses a quantitative critical mass. From then on, immigrants become increasingly interested in their identity and culture as a communal dimension. Early urban sociologists assumed that immigrants

---

16 Kale K. Yu, "Hawaiian Connectionalism: Methodist Missionaries, Hawaii Mission, and Korean Ethnic Churches," Methodist History 50, no. 1 (2011): 4–5.

17 Kale K. Yu, "Methodists in Hawaii," *Methodist Magazine and Review* 60, no. July-December (1904): 283, https://tinyurl.com/3cezvyrd.

would naturally assimilate culturally into mainstream society.[18] European immigrants who came to the United States before World War II may have assimilated in such a way. However, Asian immigrants did not experience the one-sided assimilation process Europeans had because of their extensive cultural and biological gap with the West.[19] Instead, Asians have created various choices between assimilation and continuation of their original culture. The direction of the cultural shift is also not necessarily toward mainstream society. Still, it can sometimes be in the opposite direction, mixing moderately or even the creation of a third cultural realm.[20]

As the ethnic enclaves grow, the immigrant societies diversify and create a variety of ramification groups. Among many groups, those who can serve as a bridge between the ethnic group and mainstream society play a crucial role in making the entire ethnic group be a part of mainstream society. This bridge group transports information, benefits, development, and education opportunities between their ethnic group and mainstream society. Urban scholars often use communication channels and cultural preferences to identify this bridge group. Shirley Achor's research

---

18 Nicholas Abercrombie, Stephen Hill, and S. Bryan Turner, "Dictionary of Sociology," in *Dictionary of Sociology* (London: Penguin Reference, 2006), 1; James P. Spradley and David W. McCurdy, *Anthropology, the Cultural Perspective* (New York: Wiley, 1980), 17–22, 179–84; Harvie M. Conn and Manuel Ortiz, *Urban Ministry: The Kingdom, the City & the People of God* (Downers Grove Ill: InterVarsity Press, 2001), 321.

19 Richard D. Alba and Victor Nee, *Remaking the American Mainstream Assimilation and Contemporary Immigration* (Cambridge, MA: Harvard University Press, 2003).

20 Andrew M. Greeley, *Ethnicity in the United States: A Preliminary Reconnaissance* (New York: Wiley, 1974), 309.

on the Mexican ethnic enclave in Dallas, Texas is a good example.[21] By using socio-cultural distances between the mainstream and Mexican societies, Achor categorized four different groups within the Mexican ethnicity (see Table 1). She names these groups insulation, accommodation, mobilizations, and alienators.

		Influence of Mainstream Society	
		High	Low
Influence of Ethnic Group	High	Mobilization	Insulation
	Low	Accommodation	Alienation

Table 1. Analysis of a Mexican Ethnic Enclave in Dallas, Texas.[22]

Some ethnic groups remain isolated and alienated. The isolation and preservation of traditions occur when the voice of insulation is strong. The people in the accommodation group prefer the mainstream environment and dilute their identity to the mainstream. People in the accommodation excessively copy the mainstream culture without acknowledging their origins. Such a dynamic forms easily if the ethnic minority group is ashamed of their original tradition and treats themselves as inferior.

The insulation and alienated stages often unite ethnic groups. For example, the harsh political atmosphere on the Korean mainland, such as the Japanese occupation, led the early

---

21 Shirley Achor, *Mexican Americans in a Dallas Barrio* (Tucson: University of Arizona Press, 1978), 11, 6–21.
22 Achor, *Mexican Americans in a Dallas Barrio*, 15.

stage of Korean Americans to live with a strong sense of patriotism and nationalism in their home country. In 1932, about ten thousand Korean Americans raised $250,000 for the independence movement against the Japanese occupation. The Korean Church had a central role in religious and social life at this time; naturally, people expected the church to take on the same sentiment and burden. The entire Reedley Korean Presbyterian Church of the Central California Assembly actively joined this fundraising campaign. Later, the *Lasung* Assembly supported *Dosan Ahn Chang-ho's* activities and provided independence funds for the Shanghai Provisional Government.[23]

The insulation groups, however, often isolate ethnic groups from mainstream society. The theology of the Korean Mainland Church greatly influenced the Korean American Church. As the churches in the Korean mainland grew rapidly from 1980, most Korean pastors in America had already received theological education in Korea. Naturally, they imitated everything from the mainland Korean churches, including rhetoric, theology, pattern, dynamics, relationship, and ministry priorities. As a result, most members of the Korean American church are quite monocultural and limit the social networks within the ethnicity. Most of those who had received theological education in American seminaries also served in Korean American churches. Consequently, the ministry and interests of the Korean Church remained within the Korean community.[24] While this tendency may have appealed

---

23 "Provisional Government Support from Two Committees (두곳 공동회 림정후원)," *The New Korea* (新韓日報), May 26, 1932, https://tinyurl.com/49e7n2zh.

24 A few representative leaders in the time are Im Doohua, Kim Sungrag, Kwon Heesang, Baek Lihun, Woo Sangbum, Kim Sangtae, Oh Changhee, Kwon Heesang, Lee Dongjin, Choi Youngyong, Kim Dongmyung, and Park Daehee.

to first-generation Koreans and was suitable for cooperating with churches in the Korean mainland, it isolated the immigrant church from mainstream society and their churches.

The separation trend of Korean American churches was not limited to American society. They also remained silent on Korean societal issues, justice and peace, or the North-South reunification, and only paid attention to the church's growth. For example, as the demands for democracy became more vital in the 1970s and 1980s, Korean American society supported the campaigns in Korea. Not only this, but to create a positive atmosphere for North and South Korea's reunification, many Korean American groups took on the role of bridges between the two Koreas. However, most Korean American churches remained silent regarding social issues, much like their counterparts in mainland Korea, and instead only worked hard to grow their numbers.

As such, the isolation and traditional theology slowly cooled the Korean American church's fever to be a community partner. The church continually became "for the first generation only," because it rarely mentioned justice, community, and the social responsibility of the church, which the young generation was interested in. Due to these dynamics plus added influences from mainstream society, the mobilization and accommodation groups—as classified by Achor—left their churches or performed a silent exodus to the English-speaking churches.

The immigrant groups that belong to the mobilization group have frequent interactions and profound attachments to both the immigrant and mainstream society's cultures. They also have leadership and attachment to their ethnic group, enabling them to build bridges with mainstream society. These people who belong to the mobilization group have a great sense of duty and abilities to integrate their ethnicity with others. In other words, its role is not only to provide good things to the ethnic minority group but also to let the mainstream society acknowledge them as a part of society.²⁵ Immigrant populations with many mobilization groups within them quickly become part of mainstream society and maintain their ethnic self-respect and traditions while building trust and synergy with other ethnic groups and developing new cultures.

As the immigrant society grows and produces a variety of groups, each inside group actively chooses its cultural identity. They continually create a new culture, isolate themselves, preserve traditions, or assimilate into mainstream society. Among them, "creating a new culture" is far beyond copying and following mainstream society.²⁶ It is instead creating a new culture with their originality and the mainstream. Creating a new culture is possible when they can overcome a sense of inferiority as a minority, find pride and dignity of in-betweenness as immigrants, and have an open posture and the competence to live in the mainstream society. But most of all, understanding and appreciating their roots is vital for the new culture because this pride is not only a base for protecting one's ethnic identity but also a strong foundation for creating a unique immigrant culture. As such, the matured society and the bridge roles of the mobilization group enable the immigrants to create a third culture. For this third culture to be possible requires many immigrant groups to be in the mobilization stage. In other words, with time, legacy, leadership, and social resources, Koreans are responsible for being a bridge to create the Korean American culture, which is new to both Korea and America. The new culture may give Korean Americans a more appropriate identity and competencies in both

---

25   Grzymała-Kazłowska Aleksandra, "The Role of Different Forms of Bridging Capital for Immigrant Adaptation and Upward Mobility. The Case of Ukrainian and Vietnamese Immigrants Settled in Poland," *Ethnicities* 15, no. 3 (2015): 460–90.
26   The third culture here is a kind of sub and hybrid culture, but not a totally new one.

cultural zones. It can be a springboard for serving others with a God-given uniqueness.

CONCLUSION: CONTEXTUAL IMMIGRANT CHURCH AS PART OF THE GLOBAL CHRISTIAN MOSAIC

What should be the final and ultimate feature of the immigrant church? To identify this, it is crucial to set up the immigrant church's biblical, essential, and cultural identity and address its role in today's age of globalization. What is the church's role in encouraging the Korean America community to create the third culture? What vision should the Korean American church need to have?

First, the immigrant church should become a church of Korean immigrants. And the ethnic church should keep the blessing and anointing that God has given to the Korean church as roots and make it bloom for the immigrants' society. For this reason, the immigrant church must keep trying to find out who they are in the first place. The root here does not refer to the form of worship or the external tradition. Instead, it is a theological formation of the blessings the Korean church has received from its ancestors and the heritage that has been passed on to the descendants.

Second, the Korean American church must be contextual. Heritage is a keystone for the contextualization and the foundation for the church to be a missional institution. The preservation of its heritage should not simply be the preservation of our heritage, but the embedding of the heritage in the process of contextualization. Naturally, this contextual immigrant church differs from the churches in the home country and mainstream society. It is a new and unique church; it is biblical, and has the dynamics from the heritage. The contextualized church understands God's vision for immigrants, preserves its heritage, and creates an appropriate identity to the time and circumstances.

Third, Korean American churches need to provide bridge roles between the immigrant and mainline societies. For this, it is necessary to reemphasize the importance of the mobilizers because they have good potential for bridging. So naturally, these mobilizers are indispensable for letting the immigrant church work as a bridge to create a good circulation relationship.

Apostle Paul and his colleagues Timothy, Epaphroditus, and Silas were all immigrants and played the role of bridges between two or more cultural zones. These multicultural and immigrant leaders were familiar with both immigrant and mainstream society so that they could introduce the gospel contextually. Because of the bridge role of these immigrants, the words of Jesus, which began from the Jewish corner of the world, could be the light of the world. In the same way, the Korean American churches must know that they are responsible for sharing the blessings God has placed on the Korean church with others. For this, the blessings must transform to be sharable and compatible with others. Then the Korean American church will have influence, have something to share, and finally can pay its spiritual debts to other churches worldwide.

The contextualization of the immigrant church becomes increasingly critical in the global age because the world has become highly connected.[27] Such a connected world always greatly demands people who can connect with others. The immigrant church is literally a church in-between. If the immigrant churches of the world can serve as bridges and share the blessings God placed on their home churches, then the immigrant churches

---

27   Smart Alan and Smart Josephine, "Urbanization and the Global Perspective," *Annual Review of Anthropology*, 2003, 265.

become the channel of the blessing, as Abraham had heard from God (Gen 12:2).

Now we must pay attention to the new value of immigrant churches. The immigrant church's role is crucial to let the church in every cultural zone become the source of blessing. God gave unique cultures and histories to every people group, and they become a different lens to view the world and the word of God.[28] Because of the different lenses, every ethnic church can interpret the word of God in their unique way. In this way, the churches of all nations can see God's truth again with their own eyes and discover things that other have not. Therefore, sharing our reflection with other groups becomes a sharing of the blessings that have remained inside our culture. Then, our blessings become present in churches around the world. This way, every church in the world becomes a part of God's mosaic of blessings. May the Korean American church work as the bridge that shares blessings to the churches of the world.

BIBLIOGRAPHY

Abercrombie, Nicholas, Stephen Hill, and S. Bryan Turner. "Dictionary of Sociology." In *Dictionary of Sociology*. London: Penguin Reference, 2006.

Achor, Shirley. *Mexican Americans in a Dallas Barrio*. Tucson: University of Arizona Press, 1978.

Alan, Smart, and Smart Josephine. "Urbanization and the Global Perspective." *Annual Review of Anthropology*, 2003, 263–285.

---

28 Dean S. Gilliland, *The World Among Us: Contextualizing Theology for Mission Today* (Dallas, TX: Word Publishing, 1989), 12, 13; Harvie M. Conn, *Eternal Word and Changing Worlds: Theology, Anthropology, and Mission in Trialogue*. (Phillipsburg, NJ.: P&R Publishing, 1984), 232; Charles H Kraft, "Contextualizing Communication" in *The World Among Us: Contextualizing Theology for Mission Today*, ed. Dean S. Gilliland (Dallas, TX: Word Publishing, 1989), 135.

Alba, Richard D., and Victor Nee. *Remaking the American Mainstream Assimilation and Contemporary Immigration*. Cambridge, MA: Harvard University Press, 2003.

Aleksandra, Grzymała-Kazłowska. "The Role of Different Forms of Bridging Capital for Immigrant Adaptation and Upward Mobility. The Case of Ukrainian and Vietnamese Immigrants Settled in Poland." *Ethnicities* 15, no. 3 (2015): 460–490.

Budiman, Abby. "Koreans in the U.S. Fact Sheet." Pew Research Center, December 9, 2022. https://tinyurl.com/zwud2e6v.

Conn, Harvie M. *Eternal Word and Changing Worlds: Theology, Anthropology, and Mission in Trialogue*. Phillipsburg, NJ: P&R Publishing, 1984.

Conn, Harvie M., and Manuel Ortiz. *Urban Ministry: The Kingdom, the City & the People of God*. Downers Grove, IL: InterVarsity Press, 2001.

Encyclopedia of Overseas Korean Culture (세계 한민족 문화대전). "Koreans' Moving from Honolulu to San Francisco (호놀룰루에서 샌프란시스코로- 초기 '한인의 이주 경로)." *The History of Korean Diaspora* (재외 한인의 역사). Accessed December 8, 2022. https://tinyurl.com/ysc7s98u.

Gilliland, Dean S. *The World Among Us: Contextualizing Theology for Mission Today*. Dallas, TX: Word Publishing, 1989.

Gottdiener, Mark, and Leslie Budd. *Key Concepts in Urban Studies*. SAGE Key Concepts. London: SAGE Publications, 2005.

Greeley, Andrew M. *Ethnicity in the United States: A Preliminary Reconnaissance*. New York: Wiley, 1974.

"History of Labor in Hawai'i." West O'ahu, HI: University of Hawai'i, Center for Labor Education & Research. Accessed November 20, 2022. https://tinyurl.com/2p9y9fz2.

Kim, Enoch Jinsik, *Mission Strategy in the City: Cultivation of Inter-ethnic Common Grounds*, Eugene, OR: Pickwick Publication, 2017.

Korinek, Kim, Barbara Entwisle, and Aree Jampaklay. "Through Thick and Thin: Layers of Social Ties and Urban Settlement among Thai Migrants." *American Sociological Review* 70, no. 5 (2005): 779–800.

Kraft, Charles H, "Contextualizing Communication" in *The World Among Us: Contextualizing Theology for Mission Today*, edited by Dean S. Gilliland. Dallas, TX: Word Publishing, 1989.

National Archives of Korea. "Koreans in China (중국의 조선족)." The History of Korean Diaspora (재외 한인의 역사). Accessed December 8, 2022. https://tinyurl.com/4mws98v3.

———. "Koreans in Europe (유럽의 한인)." The History of Korean Diaspora (재외 한인의 역사). Accessed December 8, 2022. https://tinyurl.com/ykzsdy8c.

———. "Koreans in Japan (일본의 재일한인)." The History of Korean Diaspora (재외 한인의 역사). Accessed December 8, 2022. https://tinyurl.com/4wxpkvx9.

National Institute of Korean History. "북방사민정책." The History of Ours (우리 역사넷), March 29, 2017. https://tinyurl.com/mr392bt4.

Pew Research Center. "Origins and Destinations of the World's Migrants, 1990-2017." Accessed December 9, 2022. https://tinyurl.com/yzpb3v7m.

The New Korea (新韓日報). "Provisional Government Support from Two Committees (두곳 공동회 림정후원)." May 26, 1932. https://tinyurl.com/49e7n2zh.

Spradley, James P., and David W. McCurdy. *Anthropology, the Cultural Perspective*. New York: Wiley, 1980.

Tyner, James A. "Global Cities and Circuits of Global Labor: The Case of Manila, Philippines." *The Professional Geographer* 52, no. 1 (2000): 61–74.

van Engen, Charles. *Mission on the Way: Issues in Mission Theology*. Grand Rapids: MI: Baker Books, 1996.

Yu, Kale K. "Hawaiian Connectionalism: Methodist Missionaries, Hawaii Mission, and Korean Ethnic Churches." *Methodist History* 50, no. 1 (2011).

———. "Methodists in Hawaii." *Methodist Magazine and Review* 60, no. July-December (1904). https://tinyurl.com/3cezvyrd.

6

THE PARADIGM OF DIASPORA MISSIOLOGY AND MISSIOLOGICAL IMPLICATIONS FOR KOREAN IMMIGRANT CHURCHES IN THE UNITED STATES

Enoch Wan

INTRODUCTION: AN ETHNOGRAPHIC DESCRIPTION OF DIASPORA KOREAN CULTURE

This chapter will introduce the paradigm of diaspora missiology after the ethnographic description of Korean immigrant churches in the United States. The missiological implications, along with the action points, will be suggested for possible implementation in the practice of contextualization.

KOREAN DIASPORA IN THE UNITED STATES[1]

There are different waves associated with Korean immigration to the United States. The earliest Korean arrivals happened during

---

1   Part of the following ethnographic description of the Korean diaspora is taken from a previous study by Enoch Wan, "Korean

1903–1924. The final wave of Korean immigration arrived post 1965 when, after a forty-year exclusion policy based on race and nationality, the Hart-Celler Act (1965) brought immigration of entire Korean families.[2] According to a 2012 Pew Research Center report, only 36 percent of all Korean Americans were native born and 64 percent of them were foreign-born.[3]

Ethnographic Description of the Korean Diaspora

Ethnographic profiling of the Korean diaspora begins with Koreans' historical past in their native land. The Korean sense of "community/cooperation" (*jeong* 정) can be attributed to a centuries-long agricultural history and communal living. There is also the time-honored high value placed on developing relational skills and cultivating or nurturing relational networks. Solidarity of the group and collective identity (e.g., family, clan, and nation) are the natural outcomes of the linguistic, racial, and cultural homogeneity of Korean society for many centuries. The positive side of this group's solidarity is patriotism and a sense of ethnic unity and pride. It can also account for the economic accomplishments of South Korea over the last sixty years[4]. The negative side, locally in Korea, is parochialism and racism. Among the Korean diaspora it is the tendency to be socially isolated from other ethnic groups. They also experience hardship in cultural adaptation.

Diaspora: From Hermit Kingdom to Kingdom Ministry," in *Korean Diaspora and Christian Mission*, eds. S. Hun Kim and Wonsuk Ma (Eugene, OR: Wipf and Stock Publishers, 2011), 101–116.

2   Christine J. Hong, *Identity, Youth, and Gender in the Korean American Church*, 1st ed. 2015 edition. (New York, NY: Palgrave Pivot, 2015), 7.

3   Eileen Patten. "2010, Foreign-Born Population in the United States Statistical Portrait." Pew Research Center. February 21, 2012. https://tinyurl.com/5t44kxcr.

4   The rapid economic development of South Korea in today's modern world economy is indeed impressive, becoming the largest economy in Asia after Japan and China.

Korea's sense of *kibun* (기분) culturally can be described in terms of pride, face, mood, or state of mind, and it permeates every facet of Korean life. The imperative to show the proper respect and avoid causing loss of face ensures social harmony. *Inhwa* (인화) is the Korean version of the Confucian concept of harmony that requires consensus in decision-making and collective efforts. "Smooth personal relationships" (SPR) based on mutual trust and benefits are to be nurtured and reinforced at all costs. SPR and social networks are essential to success in both business and ministry.

Korean companies and congregations share the same hierarchical social structure based on age, gender, and social status (i.e., "high power distance" and "collectivism" in the cultural scale of Geert Hofstede's analysis)[5]. The organizational arrangement is highly centralized with authority and decision-making concentrated in senior levels. Personal ties (e.g., kinship, schools, birthplaces, etc.) often take precedence over job seniority, rank, or other factors (e.g., performance and productivity), thus having significant influence over the structure and management of Korean companies and congregations. The rule of reciprocity (e.g., gift-giving, favor, etc.) is to be followed closely to maintain harmonious relationships and social networks. In summary, SPR and social networks are the primary importance, both in traditional Korean culture and contemporary society at home and abroad (i.e., among native Koreans and Korean diaspora).

Korean society is comprised of myriad extended or overlapping relational networks. This is also true of the Christian subculture. Whenever there is a relational problem within the networks, the discord and disharmony will have severe negative impact on the wider system of the organization or congregation. This can help explain frequent occurrences of conflict and fragmentation of Korean organizations. A case in point is the schism within the

---

[5] Geert Hofstede, Gert Jan Hofstede, and Michael Minkov, *Cultures and Organizations: Software of the Mind*, 3rd ed. (New York: McGraw-Hill Education, 2010), 116–118.

Korean Presbyterian Church (i.e., Hap-dong 합동 and Tong-hap 통합), with the irony that all four characters in the two names have implicit meaning of unity or harmony.

One of the key sociohistorical factors in the formation of "Korean-ness" in modern Korean society is called *hangukinron* (한국인론). The term explains the national social ideology between 1987 and 1997, when South Koreans experienced a high level of economic growth and development. Michael Hurt discusses *hangukinron* in relation to Korea's ethnocentrism and explains how this concept implies Korean is a superior race. Many examples can be found in Korean literature including Lee Eo-Ryeong's children book, *Mommy, I'm Korean, Right?* (1997) and the discourse of racially pure, superior Koreanness in *The Economy and the Mythology of Koreans* (1994) by Song Byung Nak.[6] The racial hierarchy is used to elevate the Korean people's intrinsic nature in comparison with the Japanese often due to the historical Japanese oppression experienced in Korea.[7] Another key concept of *hangukinron* that contributes to identifying Koreanness is the term, *jeong*. Using Sang-Hee Lee's literature work on Korean people, Hurt illustrates what this concept means and concludes that the idea of *jeong*, which is a key trait of *hangukinron* is used to self-identify what it means to be a Korean.[8]

Another important concept of *hangukinron* is *han* (한), which refers to a strong internalized emotion of generalized bitterness

---

6   Michael Hurt, "Transmitting the Monumental Style: *Hangukinron*, "Diasporicity," and the Osmotic Flow of Transnational Korean American Identity," in *A Companion to Korean American Studies*, eds. Rachael Miyung Joo and Shelley Sang-Hee Lee (Leiden ; Boston: BRILL, 2018), 361–362, accessed February 5, 2022, 361–362, http://ebookcentral.proquest.com/lib/westernseminary-ebooks/detail.action?docID=5449679.
7   Hurt, "Transmitting the Monumental Style," 363.
8   Hurt, "Transmitting the Monumental Style," 364, 365.

or resentment that defines the Korean way of being. This concept is well used in Korean art, literature, film, and pop culture. Many scholars agree that it originated during the Japanese colonial period as a colonial stereotype, which can be understood as the memory of past collective trauma.[9] Usually, *han* is portrayed in the context of broken families, relationships, and class conflict within the society.

KOREAN DIASPORA CHRISTIANS IN THE UNITED STATES

In comparison to other ethnic groups, first generation Korean immigrants in the United Sates are relatively less likely to be assimilated due to socio-objective factors (e.g., language barrier, racial discrimination, visible minority, social isolation, etc.) and psycho-subjective factors (e.g., linguistic and cultural homogeneity, intern ethnic-solidarity, psychological aversion to loosing-face or risk-taking, etc.). Subsequently, "ethnic Korean congregations in the United States" (hereafter referred to as "KDC"—Korean diaspora congregations) have multiple sociocultural functions, such as social center, language preservation mechanism, "home away from homeland," etc.).

Korean Diaspora[10] and Church Affiliation

One of the unique factors about Korean immigrants in the United States is their strong affiliation with ethnic churches, unlike

---

9   Kim, Sandra So Hee Chi. "Korean 'Han' and the Postcolonial Afterlives of 'The Beauty of Sorrow.'" *Korean Studies* 41 (2017): 253–279. http://www.jstor.org/stable/44508447, 253.

10 "Diaspora" means "a scattering," used to describe the large-scale movement of people from their homeland to settle permanently or temporarily in other countries. Lausanne Committee for World

other religions such as Buddhism. Pyong Gap Min points out that "historical studies (Choy, 1979; Patterson, 1988) suggest that approximately 40 percent of the pioneer immigrants to Hawaii at the turn of the century were Christians prior to immigration, and that the majority of them attended ethnic churches in the United States."[11] He argues that there are three major social functions that made ethnic church a vital community within the Korean American society: (1) providing social services to the Korean community and fellowship for Korean immigrants; (2) maintaining Korean cultural tradition; (3) providing social status for Korean adult immigrants.

Many Korean American church leaders in the United States report that the decline in Korean immigrant population in recent years has caused a decrease in their church membership. However, John J. Oh argues that this interpretation is not valid according to the hard statistics and further points out that the number of Korean diasporas has been steadily growing in the United States but not in the same form. "Unlike the immigrants of the 1970s and 1980s who sought comfort and identity through the Korean churches, the new immigrants of the 2010s no longer feel any need to attend a Korean church."[12] Therefore, the Korean church is not the central place or community that functions as a bridge connecting Korean diaspora in the United States. In the same article, Oh focuses on the following

---

Evangelization Issue Group No. 26 A and B, "Lausanne Occasional Paper 55."

[11] Min, Pyong Gap. "The Structure and Social Functions of Korean Immigrant Churches in the United States." *International Migration Review* 26.4 (1992): 1370-1394.1.

[12] John J. Oh, "From Silent Exodus to Silent Divergence: Changing Immigrant Society, Unchanging Immigrant Church." *Journal of Language, Culture and Religion* 2, no. 2 (2021): 1.

significant changes happening in the Korean diaspora in the United States:[13] (1) The Korean immigrant society's transition to immigrants who are legal permanent residents (LPRs); (2) green card holders include nonimmigrants who are short-term residents such as international students and company personnel; (3) The Korean immigrant society is changing from an offline to an online community, expedited by the pandemic. Also, the population of the Korean diaspora in the United States has changed over time. If most Koreans were green card holders in the 1970s and '80s, the number of non-residents such as international students, professors, visitors, or on work and business visas has been increasing in the recent years. This also shows that people no longer find the church as the resource to help settle down in a new environment because they already have other resources available on the internet or through online communities that share information.

According to the KCMUSA directory, the total number of Korean churches in the United States in 2021 was 2,798 and about 568 churches have closed permanently since 2019. The decline of Korean churches can be found in major cities of the United States. However, this doesn't necessarily support the assumption that the decreasing number of Korean churches is due to the decline in the Korean population in the United States. As John Oh argues, there are other contributing factors that cause Korean churches to lose momentum and decline such as changing trends in Korean immigration and cultural shifts among the Korean diaspora. These findings call for reflection on contextualizing Christian missions in Korean immigrant churches in the United States.

---

13 Oh, "From Silent Exodus to Silent Divergence," 3.

THE PARADIGM OF DIASPORA MISSIOLOGY

Traditional Missiological Paradigm and "Diaspora Missiology Paradigm"

Etymologically, the term "diaspora" is a derivation from the Greek word "*diaspeirein*" which means "to scatter about" (disperse- from, *dia*- about, across + *speirein* – to scatter).[14] Diaspora missiology is a new missiological paradigm, supplementing the "popular missiological paradigm."[15] It informs the Church on how to participate in God's mission locally and globally in view of the new demographic reality of diaspora phenomenon in the twenty-first century.

Demographically people often moved spatially due to educational advancement, economic improvement, famine, war, political and religious oppressions; yet the number of people moving on large scales and at high rates has increased significantly since the last century. Consequently, this brought about an unprecedented number of diasporas, thus the emergence of "diaspora missiology" to cope with this new demographic reality.

The "popular missiological paradigm"[16] is diagrammatically compared with "diaspora missiology paradigm"[17] in the figures 1 and 2.

---

14 From http://www.etymonline.com/index.php?search=dKiaspora+&searchmode=none, accessed August 20, 2011

15 Popular missiology is represented by organizations such as the Missio Nexus, American Society of Missiology, and Evangelical Missiological Society (Wan, "Korean Diaspora: From Hermit Kingdom to Kingdom Ministry," 97–98).

16 "Popular missiology paradigm" is managerial in nature and can be defined as "ways and means of practicing Christian mission in the same manner of secular management in business that might be "biblical" and secularly contextual; but definitely not "scriptural" (Wan, *Diaspora Missiology: Theory, Methodology, and Practice*, 6).

17 "Diaspora Missiology Paradigm" is "a missiological framework for understanding and participating in God's redemptive mission (*missio Dei*) among diaspora groups (Wan, *Diaspora Missiology*, 6).

#	ASPECT	POPULAR MISSIOLOGY ↔ DISPORA MISSIOLOGY	
1	FOCUS	Polarized/dichotomized – "great commission" ↔ "great commandment" – saving souls ↔ social Gospel – church planting ↔ Christian charity – paternalism ↔ indigenization	– Holistic Christianity with strong integration of evangelism with Christian charity – contextualization
2	CONCEPTUALIZATION	– territorial: here ↔ there – "local" ↔ "global" – lineal: "sending" ↔ "receiving" – "assimilation" ↔ "amalgamation" – "specialization"	– "deterritorialization"[18] – "glocal" – "mutuality" & "reciprocity" – "hybridity" – "inter-disciplinary"
3	PERSPECTIVE	– geographically divided: foreign mission ↔ local, urban ↔ rural – geo-political boundary: state/nation ↔ state/nation – disciplinary compartmentalization: e.g., theology of missions / strategy of missions	– non-spatial, – "borderless," no boundary to worry, transnational & global – new approach: integrated & interdisciplinary
4	PARADIGM	– OT: missions=gentile-proselyte—coming – NT: missions=the Great Commission going – Modern missions: E-1, E-2, E-3, or M-1, M-2, M-3, etc.	– New reality in the 21st Century – viewing & following God's way of providentially moving people spatially & spiritually – moving targets & move with the targets

Figure 1. "Popular missiology" vis-à-vis "diaspora missiology" — 4 aspects.[19]

---

18 "Deterritorialization" is the "loss of social and cultural boundaries" due to the large-scale diaspora.

19 Enoch Wan, "Diaspora Missiology," Originally published in Occasional Bulletin, of EMS, Spring 2007:8, posted in "Featured Article" (July 2007), www.globalmissiology.org

#	ASPECT	POPULAR MISSIOLOGY ↔ DIASPORA MISSIOLOGY	
1	MINISTRY PATTERN	OT: calling of gentile to Yahweh (coming) NT: sending out disciples by Jesus in the four Gospels & by the H.S. in Acts (going) Modern missions: - sending missionary & money - self-sufficient of mission entity	- new way of doing Christian missions: "mission at our doorstep" - "ministry without border" - "networking & partnership" for the Kingdom - "borderless church,"[20] "liquid church"[21] - "church on the oceans"[22]
2	MINISTRY STYLE	- cultural-linguistic barrier: E-1, E-2, etc. Thus various types M-1, M-2, etc. - "people group" identity - evangelistic scale: reached→←unreached - "competitive spirit" "self-sufficient"	- no barrier causing worry - mobile and fluid - hyphenated identity & ethnicity - no unreached people - "partnership,"[23] "networking" & synergy

Figure 2. Comparing popular missiology & diaspora missiology in ministry.[24]

---

20 David Lundy, *Borderless Church*, (Los Angeles: Authentic Media, 2005).
21 Peter Ward, *Liquid Church*, (Carlisle: Paternoster, 2002).
22 A church was founded by the chief cook's brother Bong on board the container vessel Al Mutannabi, November 2002, (see Martin Otto, *Church on the Oceans*, UK: Piquant, 2007, 65). From personal communication of March 29, 2007, a staff worker reported that "Last week I met the second cook on another ship, and I was very happy to see that the second cook already started planting a church..."
23 "Partnership" is defined as "entities that are separate and autonomous but complementary, sharing with equality and mutuality." More discussion on "partnership" in another section.
24 Enoch Yee-nock Wan, *Diaspora Missiology: Theory, Methodology, and Practice*, 2nd ed. (Portland, OR: Institute of Diaspora Studies: Western Seminary, 2014), 9.

Popular missions are polarized or dichotomized in focus and territorial with a sharp distinction between here and there spatially; and movement is lineal, meaning it goes one way. It is fixated with geography and unilineal in direction. In contrast, "diaspora missions"[25] focus on holistic missions and contextualization, integrating evangelism and social concern, Great Commandment with Great Commission, evangelism, and social action. It is de-territorialized and simultaneously local and global conceptually (thus "glocal mission"). In perspective, it is borderless; not geographically divided. It is transnational and global.[26]

As seen in figure 3, there are two kinds of diaspora ministry: ministering *to* the diaspora and ministering *along* the diaspora.[27] "Ministry *to* the diaspora" is non-diaspora Christians who participate in the Great Commission through proclaiming the good news and practicing good deeds—focusing on the diaspora by using the strategy of missions "to" and "through" the diaspora.

Kingdom orientation is essential in motivating and mobilizing Christians individually and collectively for Kingdom ministry. Key is the understanding that "a person with Kingdom-orientation is someone who embraces the perspective, sentiment, and motivation of the Kingdom at heart and in action."[28] "Ministry along the diaspora" is mobilizing diaspora Christians as individual "Kingdom workers" (KW) to partner with others to

---

25 "Diaspora Missions" is "Christians' participation in God's redemptive mission to evangelize their kinsmen on the move, and through them to reach out to natives in their homelands and beyond." (see Enoch Wan, "Global People and Diaspora Missiology," presentation at Plenary session, Tokyo 2010—Global Mission Consultation, Tokyo, Japan, May 13, 2010).
26 Enoch Wan and Sadiri Joy Tira, eds., *Missions Practice in the 21st Century* (Pasadena, CA: William Carey International University Press, 2009), 4.
27 Wan, *Diaspora Missiology*, 129
28 Wan, *Diaspora Missiology*, 198.

fulfill the Great Commission (i.e., collaborate Kingdom-partners (KP) beyond their own diaspora people—focusing on other diaspora and non-diaspora peoples by using the strategy of missions "by & beyond" and "with" the diaspora. On the basis of Kingdom-orientation and local congregations can network in operation (of KW) and partner in sharing resources (as KP).

There are four types of diaspora missions in practice, as listed below: (1) Missions *to* the Diaspora—reaching the diaspora groups with forms of evangelism or pre-evangelistic social services, then discipling them to become worshipping communities and congregations; (2) Missions *through* the Diaspora—diaspora Christians reaching out to their kinsmen through networks of friendship and kinship in host countries, their homelands, and abroad; (3) Missions *by and beyond* the Diaspora—motivating and mobilizing diaspora Christians for cross-cultural missions to other ethnic groups in their host countries, homelands, and abroad; and (4) Missions *with* the Diaspora—mobilizing non-diasporic Christians individually and institutionally to partner with diasporic groups and congregations.

If Korean Christians allowed their cultural and linguistic homogeneity of the past to deter them from learning a foreign language or to adjust to the host culture, then they will forever stay within "the cocoon of the Hermit Kingdom." Instead, they should embrace a Kingdom-orientation, embark on the path of cross-cultural competency, and be engage in Kingdom ministry. They should play the role of a "bridge" for the gospel, reaching out to the non-Christian members in the host society or other diasporic groups in close proximity or folks back in their homeland of Korea. This is what is meant by "ministering through and beyond the diaspora."

"Ministering through and beyond diaspora" are two other aspects of practicing "diaspora missions." These two approaches are to be employed in order to seize new opportunities created by the phenomenon of diaspora. KDCs are to be mobilized for

THE PARADIGM OF DIASPORA MISSIOLOGY 123

DIASPORA MISSIOLOGY		DIASPORA MINISTRY			
	Type	ministering *to* the diaspora		ministering *along* the diaspora	
	Means	the Great Commandment as pre-evangelistic and holistic		the Great Commission—imperative and inclusive	
	Recipient	Focusing on diaspora: serving the diaspora by ministering—social and spiritual dimensions		Focusing beyond diaspora: mobilizing diaspora Christians to serve other diaspora people or non-diaspora	
	DIASPORA MISSIONS				
	Type	missions *to* the diaspora	missions *through* the diaspora	missions *by & beyond* the diaspora	missions *with* the diaspora
	Means	motivate & mobilize diaspora individuals & congregations to partner with others: the Great Commission, i.e. evangelistic outreach, discipleship, church planting and global missions			
		Focusing on diaspora		Focusing beyond diaspora	
	Recipient	members of diaspora community	kinsmen in homeland & elsewhere; not cross-culturally	cross-culturally to other ethnic groups in host society & beyond	partnership between diaspora and others in Kingdom ministry

Figure 3. Diaspora Ministry and Missions.

Source: Wan, *Diaspora Missiology*, 8.

Christian mission when individual Christians are motivated and empowered to carry out their missionary duties. This is what is meant by "minister through the diaspora." When members of the diaspora groups have acquired the language and are adjusted to the culture of the host society, they are the natural bridges to "minister beyond them" to reach others of host societies and countries.

The practice of diaspora missiology in Christian mission can be integrated with relational realism as shown in the figure 4.

DIASPORA MISSIOLOGY & DIASPORA MISSIONS	RELATIONAL PARADIGM	
	5 ELEMENTS	5 RELATIONAL ASPECTS
– not programmatic, not entrepreneur, not outcome-based – strong emphasis on relational dimensions between person Being (the triune God) and beings (of humanity and angelic reality) – recognizing the dimension of spiritual warfare	**PARTICIPANTS** • Triune God & Christians carry out the Great Commission • resistant: Satan, fallen angels	**RELATIONAL NETWORK** • Triune God is the originator of relationship; the center and foundation of all networks • two camps: God, obedient angels & Christians ↔ Satan
– vertical dimensions, e.g. "relational accountability" – "glocal" missions in the globalized context – non-spatial, "borderless," no boundary to worry, transnational – different approach: integrated ministry & interdisciplinary study of Missiology – learning of new demographic reality of the 21st Century & strategize accordingly with good stewardship	**PATTERN** (→sending) • Father → the Son & together → H.S. • Father → the Son → Christians (Jn 17: 18), Christians obeying • H.S. sending: Acts 10:19; 13:2 Christians empowered	**RELATIONAL DIMENSIONS / CONTEXT** • vertical dimension to God • horizontal dimensions within the Church & beyond • multi-context: divine, angelic, human; changing human contexts due to globalization, diaspora movement, etc.

Figure 4. Practicing Diaspora Missions Relationally.[29]

---

29 Adapted from Wan, *Diaspora Missiology*, 196.

– new reality in the 21st Century – viewing & following God's way of providentially moving people spatially & spiritually. – moving targets & move with the targets (diaspora)	**PRACTICE** Christians participating in God's mission, carrying out the "Great Commission"	**RELATIONAL REALITY** • God: reconciling the world to Himself in Christ through Christians Satan & fallen angels at enmity with God and His followers.
– micro: love, compassion, Christian hospitality – macro: partnership & networking – holistic Christianity with strong integration of evangelism with Christian compassion & charity	**POWER** God's love transforms Christians and compels them carrying out His mission	**RELATIONAL DYNAMICS** • doing missions out of love for God and compassion for the lost • empowered by the H.S.
"Great commission" + "great commandment" diaspora mission: ministering *to* and *through* and *by/beyond* & *with* the diaspora relational accountability strategic stewardship and partnership	**PROCESS** God: plan of salvation provided & the Church carrying out God's mission	**RELATIONAL INTERACTION** • God's calling, Christ's commissioning, H.S. empowering • Christians obedient to God, • Satan resisting God's mission

Figure 4. (*Continued*).

The discussion and the proposed diaspora missiology paradigm truly carry out the spirit of a previous study by the author entitled, "Korean Diaspora: From Hermit Kingdom to Kingdom Ministry."[30] Diaspora Koreans are culturally akin and

---

30 Enoch Wan, "Korean Diaspora: From Hermit Kingdom to Kingdom Ministry," May 18-21, 2010, Seoul, Korea. In *Korean Diaspora and Christian Mission*. Edited by S. Hun Kim and Wonsuk Ma, Regnum Studies in Mission. 2011:86-101.

psychologically attached to their country of origin—"the Hermit Kingdom," yet they are to be challenged to engage in Kingdom ministry and practice Kingdom partnership.[31]

Leaders of KDC are hereby challenged to review the following action points for possible implementation:[32] (1) Discern the theological soundness of diaspora missiology paradigm; (2) Disseminate the demographic information of Korean diaspora at a global scale for the practice of "missions *by and beyond* Korean diaspora" and "mission *with* the Korean diaspora"; (3) Deliver the education and training of diaspora missiology/missions through theological institutions and lay-training program in the United States and abroad to motivate and mobilize diaspora Koreans for global outreach; (4) Develop a contextualize version of relational mission practice and diaspora missions—culturally sensitive Korean heritage and adaptable to diaspora Koreans elsewhere; (5) Decide to practice "glocal mission"[33] by evangelizing and making disciples simultaneously locally and globally; instead of the traditional dichotomist way of either local (i.e., so called "evangelism") or globally (i.e., so called "foreign missions"). KDC at each

---

31 For detailed discussion, see "Chapter 14—Diaspora Missions, Strategic Stewardship and Strategic Partnership," in Wan, *Diaspora Missiology*, 199–204.

32 Adapted from Wan, "Korean Diaspora: From Hermit Kingdom to Kingdom Ministry," 17.

33 "Glocal missions" is defined as "due to the integration and interplay between the local dynamics and the global scope leading to: (1) local evangelistic outreaches with global ripple effects (2) local action with global vision; (3) global in scope but local in action and in sequence. It embraced the Great Commission as well as acting out the Lukan mandate they call "glocal missions." Enoch Wan, and Sadiri Joy Tira, eds. *Missions Practice in the 21st Century* (Pasadena, CA: William Carey International University Press, 2009), 236.

location can engage in outreach to fellow Koreans in the local community (by practicing "mission *to/through* the diaspora" with global ripple effects. KDCs can engage in the other approaches (i.e., "mission *beyond* the diaspora" to reach non-Koreans locally, "mission *beyond and with* diaspora" cross-culturally with global vision and global in scope but local in action and in sequence; (6) Dare to raise up a new generation of Korean missiologist and mission leaders who are: (i) Attune to the socio-cultural shift (e.g., globalization, post-modernist orientation, demographic trends of the scattering of Korean globally, etc.); (ii) Ready to contextualize relational paradigm, relational interaction paradigm for transformational change.

MISSIOLOGICAL IMPLICATIONS FOR KOREAN IMMIGRANT CHURCHES IN THE UNITED STATES

Based on the above ethnographic description, the cultural characteristics of Korean diaspora communities in the United States are: highly relational in orientation, existentially diaspora, and collectivistic in social interaction. Several missiological implications will be identified below for KDC's practice of Christian mission.

Popular understanding and relational understanding and practice of Christian "mission." According to popular understanding and missiological literature, Christian "mission" is defined as "the Great Commission" based on several favorite texts: Matthew 28:19-20, 24:14 and Acts 1:8 as summarized below:

THE GREAT COMMISSION: (DOING for God): (1) What to do? (Making disciples). (2) How to do it? (Going, baptizing, teaching). (3) Where to do it? (Jerusalem, Judaea, Samaria, end of the earth). (4) When to do it? (Now to the end of the age).

In this paper, "mission" is relationally defined in terms of the *missio Dei*[34] of the Triune God, to be continued and carried out by individual Christians and the organized congregation (and the Church). Its practice is multi-dimensional: spiritually (saving soul) and socially (ushering in shalom), for redemption, reconciliation, and transformation ("missions").

Programmatic Approach and Relational Approach[35]

The key verse for the Great Commission is Matthew 28:19-20 and it is to be carefully examined in light of the narrative structure of the entire book.[36] "The disciples were systematically and relationally trained in Kingdom-orientation (vertical) by Jesus in two stages: each concluded with an imperative, that is, "the Great Commandment" (horizontal) of Matthew 22:37-38 and "the Great Commission" (vertical + horizontal) of 28:16-20."[37] Likewise, Acts 1:8 should be understood relationally that the Father had given

---

34 "*Missio Dei*" is defined as "the Triune God pressing Himself out thus showing forth His nature of love, communion, commission (sending), and glory."

35 "Relational missiology/ministry" can be defined as "Systematic study of mission (missiology) and the practical outworking of relational theology in carrying out the *missio Dei* and fulfilling the Great Commission." (Enoch Wan, "Relational Theology and Relational Missiology." *Occasional Bulletin* 21, no. 1 (Fall 2007). https://www.westernseminary.edu/files/documents/faculty/wan/Relat_theol_missio_OB_21_1.pdf (accessed October 27, 2021).

36 Enoch Wan and Rob Penner, *Missionary Preparation in The Gospel of Matthew in Light of 28:16-20: A Narrative and Relational Study* (Western Academic Publishers, 2022), 16-20.

37 Enoch Wan et al., *Diaspora Mission to International Students* (Western Seminary Press, 2019), 8.

the Son all authority by which He relationally sent the disciples then (and us now) to bear witness for Him.

> "Mission" as *missio Dei* is intrinsic within the Trinity then extended to Christians as stated by Jesus Christ . . . as the Father sent Me, so send I you" (John 20:21). There is a consistent interactive pattern from the Triune God to redeemed/reconciled humanity with the characteristic of reciprocity for sending and submission, witnessing and glorifying.[38]

Relationally, "mission" is firstly God *working in us* (being), then *working through us* (doing) as summarized below.[39]

There are several key concepts embedded in "BEING" as follows: (1) *Imago Dei*—image bearer of the Creator (Gen 1:26-28, 9:1-7); (2) Blessings to nations—Abrahamic covenant (Gen. 12:1-7); (3) Light to the nations—Children of Abraham (Gen 17:1-14) & Israel = God's elect of the OT is to be "light to the nations" (Isa 42:6, 49:6 cf. Matt 4:16); (4) God's children in the NT (four identities: chosen people, a royal priesthood, a holy nation, God's special possession, 1 Pet 2:9)—". . . declare the praises of Him Who called you out of darkness into His wonderful light" OR "new humanity" (Col 1:15, 3:9-11, Eph 2:14-16, Gal 3:28). (e) The "sent ones" such as Romans 10:14-15 (x4 rhetorical questions; Eph 4:11-13 ". . . evangelist . . .").

Christian "mission" is not "either/or" doing/being, but it is "both/and" being + doing, also integrated as shown in the figure below: The integrated approach ("A + B" in figure 5) in Christian ministry/mission is neither dichotomist nor dualistic; rather, "both-and," including *being* and *doing*, personhood

---

38 Wan et al., *Diaspora Mission to International Students*, 17.
39 Wan et al., *Diaspora Mission to International Students*, 23-24.

and performance, witnessing and making disciples, the fulfilment of the Great Commission and the practice of the Great Commandment of loving your neighbor. We summarize it in the figure 5.

	(A) Relational Paradigm Great Commandment + Great Commission	(B) Popular Missiological Paradigm (Great Commission)
1.	BEING: vertically God works **in us** →	DOING: horizontally God works **through us**
2.	PERSONHOOD: Christians being **in Christ** →	PERFORMANCE: Christians doing **for Christ**
3.	MESSENGER: saved/shepherd/sent **by Him** →	METHOD: making disciples **for Him**
4.	WITNESSING: by life & living **(to serve)** →	WINNING: strategize to win the lost **(to save)**
5.	VERTICAL: Triune God & His won →	HORIZONTAL: enterprising & managerial
6.	RELATIONAL: vertical + horizontal →	FUNCTIONAL/PROGRAMATIC: (vertical) horizontal
7.	PROCESS: open-ended and unpredictable, convergence of tri-systems[17] (i.e. theo-/angelic/human) without "excluded middle" →	PROGRAM: structured plan & procedure, lip service to vertical, secularized with "excluded middle"[18]

Figure 5. Relational Paradigm & Popular Missiological Paradigm.
Source: Wan et al., *Diaspora Mission to International Students*, 20.

From figure 5 we can list out the characteristics of the relational paradigm in summary format: (1) Relational paradigm is sequential from A → B; (2) It is processual from the left column → to the right column; not programmatically obsessed with outcomes of the right column. It is not formulaic nor the mere pragmatism of the right column; and (3) It is integrative of both A and B.

HOLISTIC CHRISTIAN MISSION
Christian "Mission"

= *missio Dei* (relational Triune God) + relational ministry
of Christians individually and collectively;
"grace & love" from God to man ↓, then man reconciling to GOD ↑
= vertical + horizontal relationships, i.e., the essence
of Christian faith & practice (Wan 1029:26)

From the above figure, it is clear that the practice of Christian "mission" is to be an integration of both columns and to be holistic as shown in the figure 6 below. It is not a choice of either saving souls spiritually or serving people in multiple ways: socially, financially, and spiritually. Since Korean culture (both traditional and diaspora) is characterized as highly relational, therefore, the relational definition and relational practice will serve as contextual and integrated approach. The same is true with figure 6 below. Also, the Korean mindset of integration (unlike the dichotomist Western mindset, the holistic concept of 음/양 as in the Korean flag and Korean ontology),

Integrated Holistic Christian Missions: Practice

Practice:
Vertically: God's grace & love received, then
Horizontally: charity & sharing with others

GOAL:
- Reconciliation
- Redemption
- Transformation

VERTICAL
Horizontal

evangelism/discipleship
friendship/partnership

Figure 6. Integrated approach of holistic Christian missions in practice.[40]

---

40 Enoch Wan et al., *Diaspora Missions to International Students* (Western Seminary Press, 2019), 22.

The dual-track (of the Great Commandment and the Great Commission) is required for the engine (holistic ministry/missions) to operate. Sharing God's grace and mercies in charity and sharing the Gospel of salvation for spiritual conversion are not to be compartmentalized.

Integrated Holistic Christian Missions: Process

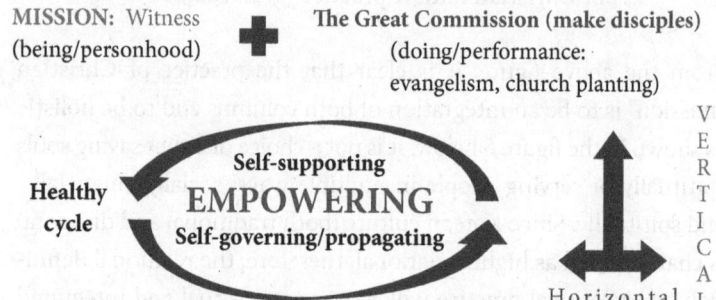

Figure 7. Holistic Christian missions/ministry in process.[41]

Figure 7 shows the process of holistic approach = witness (being/personhood) + the Great Commission (doing/performance/making disciples): (1) is saved by the gospel (Rom 1:16), being transformed by the Spirit (Rom 12:1-2), and can enjoy: (2) *kononia* (Phil 1:5); (3) "body life" (Rom 12:3-21; 1Cor 12); (4) harmony (Eph 1:6), *shalom* (Jn 14:27; 20:19,21,26); and (5) discipleship (Matt. 28:18-19; 2 Tim 2:2).

CONCLUSION

Providentially, Koreans in the United States are immigrants from the "hermit kingdom" of their homeland to be redeemed and

---

41 Enoch Wan (ed.), *Diaspora Missions to International Students*, 22.

reconciled by the Triune God vertically. KDC in the United States are to practice Christian mission *relationally* and *holistically* within the existential reality of diaspora experience in the United States in a contextual Korean way.

BIBLIOGRAPHY

Chong, Chinbo, and Jane Yunhee Junn. "A Wedge between Black and White: Korean Americans and Minority Race Relations in Twenty-First-Century America." In *A Companion to Korean American Studies*. Boston, 2018. https://tinyurl.com/4h97j37u.

Davis, John Jefferson. "What Is 'Perichoresis'—and Why Does It Matter? Perichoresis as Properly Basic to the Christian Faith." *Evangelical Review of Theology* 39, no. 2 (April 2015).

Hofstede, G., Hofstede, G. J., Minkov, M. *Cultures and Organizations: Software of the Mind*. 3rd ed. USA: McGraw-Hill.

Hong, Christine J. *Identity, Youth, and Gender in the Korean American Church*. New York: Palgrave Pivot, 2015.

Hurt, Michael. "Transmitting the Monumental Style: Hangukinron, "Diasporicity." In *A Companion to Korean American Studies*, 2018.

"KCMUSA, '2022 미주한인교회 센서스', 2022 미주한인교회주소록 2022 (Directory of Korean Churches in USA)," 2022. https://tinyurl.com/mr3vruyz.

Joo, Miyung Rachael, and Shelley Sang-Hee Lee, eds. *A Companion to Korean American Studies*. Boston: BRILL, 2018.

Kraft, H. Charles, and Bernard Ramm. *Christianity in Culture*. Maryknoll, New York: Orbis Books, 1979.

Min, Pyong Gap. "The Structure and Social Functions of Korean Immigrant Churches in the United States." *International Migration Review* 26, no. 4 (1992).

Lundy, David. *Borderless Church: Shaping the Church for the 21st Century*. Milton Keynes; Waynesboro, GA: Authentic, 2005.

Oh, John J. "From Silent Exodus to Silent Divergence: Changing Immigrant Society, Unchanging Immigrant Church." *Journal of Language, Culture and Religion* 2, no. 2 (October 2021).

Patten, Eileen. "2010, Foreign-Born Population in the United States Statistical Portrait." *Pew Research Center's Hispanic Trends Project*, February 21, 2012. Accessed February 23, 2022. https://tinyurl.com/42caey3r.

Roberts, Jr., Bob. *Glocalization: How Followers of Jesus Engage a Flat World.* Reprint edition. Grand Rapids: Zondervan, 2016.

Tira, Sadiri Joy. "Glocal Evangelism: Jesus Christ, Magdalena, and Damascus in Greater Toronto Area | Lausanne World Pulse Archives." *Lausanne World Pulse Archives.* Last modified 2010. Accessed February 23, 2022. https://tinyurl.com/2p97vekw.

Wan, Enoch. *Missions Practice in the 21st Century.* Edited by Sadiri Joy Tira. Null edition. Pasadena, CA: William Carey International University Press, 2009.

Wan, Enoch Yee-nock. *Diaspora Missiology: Theory, Methodology, and Practice.* 2nd ed. Portland, OR: Institute of Diaspora Studies: Western Seminary, 2014.

———. "AfriLink: A Case Study of Glo-cal Diaspora Mission in Hong Kong, Reaching Africans Locally." *Global Missiology* 5, no. 1 (January 2020).

———. "A Critique of Charles Kraft's Use/Misuse of Communication and Social Sciences in Biblical Interpretation and Missiological Formulation." *Global Missiology* (October 2004). Accessed October 8, 2019. https://tinyurl.com/2p8enkx6.

———, ed., *Diaspora Missions to International Students.* Western Seminary Press, 2019.

———.. "Global People and Diaspora Missiology." Plenary paper, Tokyo 2010 Global Mission Conference, Tokyo, Japan, May 11-14, 2010. http://tokyo2010.org/resources/Tokyo2010_Plenary_Enoch_Wan.pdf (accessed November 11, 2017).

———. "Korean Diaspora: From Hermit Kingdom to Kingdom Ministry." In *Korean Diaspora and Christian Mission.* Regnum Studies in Mission, 2011.

———. "'Mission' and '*Missio Dei*': Response to Charles van Engen's 'Mission Defined and Described.'" In *MissionShift: Global Mission Issues in the Third Millennium,* edited by David J. Hesselgrave and Ed Stetzer, 41–50. Nashville, TN: B&H Publishing Group, 2010.

———. "The Paradigm of 'Relational Realism." *Occasional Bulletin of the Evangelical Missiological Society* 19, no. 2 (2006): 1–4.

———. "Relational Theology and Relational Missiology." *Occasional Bulletin* 21, no. 1 (Fall 2007). https://www.westernseminary.edu/

files/documents/faculty/wan/Relat_theol_missio_OB_21_1.pdf (accessed October 27, 2021).

———. "Relational Transformational Leadership—An Asian Christian Perspective." *Asian Missions Advance* (2021). http://www.asiamissions.net/asian-missions-advances/.

———. "Rethinking Missiology in the Context of the 21st Century: Global Demographic Trends and Diaspora Missiology." *Great Commission Research Journal* 2, no. 1 (Summer 2010). http://journals.biola.edu/gcr/volumes/2/issues/1/articles/7 (accessed November 11, 2017).

———. "Rethinking Missiological Research Methodology: Exploring a New Direction," *Global Missiology*, (October 2003). http://www.enochwan.com/english/articles/pdf/Rethinking%20Missiological%20Research%20Methodology.pdf (accessed October 27, 2021).

———. "Rethinking Urban Mission in Terms of Spiritual and Social Transformational Change." Paper presented at MSG/WAMS Biennial International Conference, Ghana, October 26, 2021: Pre-publication material: do not duplicate or circulate, 2021.

———, ed., *Diaspora Mission to International Students*. Western Seminary Press. 2019.

———. "Relational Transformational Leadership—An Asian Christian Perspective," *Asian Missions Advance* (2021), http://www.asiamissions.net/asian-missions-advances/.6.

———., "Narrative Framework for Relational Transformational Change," Evangelical Missiological Society, National Conference, Sept. 17–18, 2021:10.

———. "Relational Transformational Leadership—An Asian Christian Perspective." *Asian Missions Advance* (2021). https://tinyurl.com/4rpx5xft.

Wan, Enoch and Mark Hedinger. *Relational Missionary Training: Theology, Theory and Practice*. Edited by Kendi Howells Douglas and Stephen Burris. Skyforest, CA: Urban Loft Publishers, 2017.

Wan, Enoch, and Mark Hedinger. "Transformative Ministry for the Majority World Context: Applying Relational Approaches." *EMS Occasional Bulletin* (Spring 2018). https://tinyurl.com/mryxwz2a https://tinyurl.com/mryxwz2a.

Wan, Enoch, and Rob Penner. *Missionary Preparation in The Gospel of Matthew in Light of 28:16-20: A Narrative and Relational Study.* Western Academic Publishers, 2022.

Wan, Enoch, and Sadiri Joy Tira, eds, *Missions Practice in the 21st Century.* Pasadena, CA: William Carey International University Press, 2009.

Wan, Enoch and Sadiri Joy Tira. "Diaspora Missiology and Mission in the Context of the 21st Century." *Global Missiology English* 1, no. 8 (October 2010). http://ojs.globalmissiology.org/index.php/english/article/viewFile/383/994

Ward, Pete. *Liquid Church.* Reprint edition. Baker Books, 2001.

7

RACE AND THE KOREAN AMERICAN CHURCH

Daniel D. Lee

INTRODUCTION: CULTURAL HERITAGE AND MIGRANT EXPERIENCE BUT NOT RACE

Informed by Asian American studies, the editors of *Religion and Spirituality in Korean America* name race, along with diaspora and improvisation, as "a specific category of analysis" that is "relatively muted" but still "informs each chapter."[1] This kind of

---

[1] David Yoo and Ruth H. Chung, "Introduction" in *Religion and Spirituality in Korean America*, ed. David Yoo and Ruth H. Chung (Champaign, IL: University of Illinois Press, 2008), 7. For examples of other works on Korean American Christianity that engage race, see Choi Hee An, *A Postcolonial Self: Korean Immigrant Theology and Church* (Albany, NY: SUNY Press, 2015), 72–76. Sharon Kim, *A Faith of Our Own: Second-generation Spirituality in Korean American Churches* (New Brunswick, NJ: Rutgers University Press, 2010). For a study of race and Asian American churches of later generation, see Russell Jeung, *Faithful Generation: Race and New Asian American Churches* (New Brunswick, NJ: Rutgers University Press, 2005). For Korean American theologians engaging race, see Jung Young Lee, *Marginality: The Key to Multicultural Theology* (Minneapolis: Fortress, 1995), Andrew Sung Park, *Racial Conflict and Healing: An Asian–American Theological Perspective* (Maryknoll, NY: Orbis,

critical racial awareness, formed out of the broader framework of Asian American studies with its one hundred and seventy years of history, situates Korean Americans in the historical narrative of Asian America. Asian American studies uses a panethnic interpretative paradigm that arose out of the Third World Liberation Front strikes of 1968 and the related Asian American movement. Outside of the academic guild, for many Korean Americans who lack this critical awareness of history and structures of race, this panethnic coalitional identity can be challenging to grasp.

If assimilation and migration become the primary category of analysis for Korean American churches, race easily becomes marginal, as something only impactful for the Black community, for example. R. Stephen Warner, noting the process of white acceptance of Jews and the Irish, states that while race must be "one of the basic categories" of analysis for the post-1965 immigration churches, its continual place and meaning are debatable.[2] Various works display this ambivalent perspective on race regarding the Korean American church. Discussing the context, experience, and ministry of these immigrant churches, the rubrics that are often used are that of cultural heritages, migration experience, and dynamics of assimilation or acculturation, but not so much race. For example, the edited volume *Korean Americans and Their Religions*, one of the early academic works on the post-1965 Korean American religions, uses mainly cultural or migration themes for analysis and reflection.[3] Race is mentioned in two of the chapters

---

1996), Sang Hyun Lee, *From A Liminal Place: An Asian American Theology* (Minneapolis: Fortress, 2010).

2   R. Stephen Warner, "Immigration and Religious Communities in the United States" in *Gathering in Diaspora: Religious Communities and the New Immigration*, ed. R. Stephen Warner and Judith G. Wittner (Philadelphia: Temple University Press, 1998), 14.

3   See Ho-Young Kwon, Kwang Chung Kim, and R. Stephen Warner, eds, *Korean Americans and Their Religions Pilgrims and Missionaries*

but not in any substantial manner. With the later migration generations are included, generational differences and tensions, and bicultural or bilingual competency, might be included as well, but again engagement of race is peripheral.[4]

When race is taken up, the concern is the experience of racism, discrimination, and marginalization. For example, a number of works that address race for Korean American Christianity mention that external force of racism that presses Korean Americans toward their own ethnic churches to avoid racial marginalization and invisibility in white churches. Jung Young Lee and Sang Hyun Lee in early Korean American theology grounds their theologies on the marginality and liminality, respectively, as external forces that press upon Asian Americans.[5] Sharon Kim shows how race is "a key variable in understudying why second-generation Korean Americans . . . choose to develop their own ethnic religious institutions."[6]

Race as an interpretative category is not just about experiences of stereotyping, discrimination, and social marginalization, which are expressions or symptoms. To take hold of race as a concept at its root means to see whiteness as "an important part of the structural 'foundation' of the U.S. 'house'" and that the ways of all of US society and people, including Asian Americans and

---

from a Different Shore (University Park, PA: Penn State University Press, 2001).

4 See Peter Cha, S. Steve Kang, and Helen Lee, eds, *Growing Healthy Asian American Churches* (Downers Grove, IL: IVP, 2006; and M. Sydney Park, Soong-Chan Rah, and Al Tizon, eds, *Honoring the Generation: Learning with Asian North American Congregations* (Valley Forge, PA: Judson, 2012). While these books are not specifically Korean American in focus, they represent the kind of ministry books read by second generation Korean Americans.

5 Jung Young Lee, *Marginality*; Sang Hyun Lee, *From A Liminal Place.*

6 Kim, *A Faith of Our Own*, 11.

other minorities, are steeped in its (de)formative influences.[7] In that sense, race is not just an external societal force pressing upon Korean Americans from the "outside" but all around them like the air they breathe. Race disciplines the ways in which invisible fumes of white normativity distort and toxify Korean American identity: intergenerational tensions, understanding of the United States as the context of discipleship, and perceptions of our racial minority neighbors, to mention some. The issue is not just about perceived incidences of racism per se, but cultural formation regarding pervasive white normativity in the minds and hearts of Korean Americans. As a caveat we must remember that even in its ubiquity, race is not always the most salient or dominant aspect of particular contexts, topics, or situations. Given the intersectional and hybrid realities of these churches, all the forementioned categories, along with race, are crucial for the analytic toolbox toward critical evaluation as well as constructive proposals. Broadly speaking, Asian heritage, migration experience, American cultural dynamics, and racialization all play indispensable roles.[8]

What this chapter seeks to do is to explain the challenges of including race as a hermeneutical category in relation to Korean American churches and to provide examples of how race can contribute to our understanding of Korean American church and ministry. I will first explain why race as a category often gets left out in the minds of those with Korean heritage, especially the immigrant generation. The mindset of ethnic nationalism, the images of white America, and Korean evangelicalism, all hinder a clear understanding of race as a core foundation of this nation. Second, for all Asian Americans, Korean Americans

---

7 Joe R. Feagin, *The White Racial Frame: Centuries of Racial Framing and Counter-Framing*, 3rd ed. (New York: Routledge, 2020), 2-3.

8 See Lee, *Doing Asian American Theology: A Contextual Framework for Faith and Practice* (Downers Grove, IL: IVP Academic, 2022).

included, there are several hinderances to a full comprehension of race. These hinderances, the perpetual foreigner trope, Black/white binary paradigm, and the erasure of Asian American history, are themselves racist forces against Asian Americans all the while remaining hidden. Lastly, I will present three examples of how using the category of race sheds insight on the pastoral care of the Korean American community, the Korean American outreach to its neighbors, and the future of the Korean American church.

KOREAN AMERICAN CHALLENGES TO GRASPING RACE

In this section, I offer three reasons for the challenges of racial conscientization for Korean Americans. While many of these reasons are not unique to Korean immigrants and Korean Americans, there are particular features of the Korean and Korean American experience that will be helpful to note, namely ethnic nationalism, acceptance of the white normative vision of the United States, and Korean evangelicalism.

First, thinking in terms of race with its phenotypical panethnic orientation contradicts ethnic-specific identities back in Asia, especially in Korea with its ethnic nationalism. The racial categories commonly used in the United States are what David Hollinger labels as the "ethno-racial pentagon" of Black, white, Native American, Asian and Latino.[9] In Korea, you are Korean, not Asian, because of the differences and historical tensions between different Asian nations, the idea of a phenotype or racial identity seems quite strange. The intra-Asian distinctions and divisions, rooted in layers of Chinese and Japanese imperialism along with European and US colonialism, still have yet to

---

9   David Hollinger, *Postethnic America: Beyond Multiculturalism* (New York: Basic, 1995), 23.

be sufficiently addressed.[10] Since phenotypical race as a concept is not something that Koreans and Korean immigrants use in common parlance, preferring the use of "ethnonationality,"[11] depending on their own accounts and descriptions can marginalize the significance of race.

According to its Japanese colonial contextual genealogy, Korean ethnic nationalism developed as an ideology of resistance and survival against imperialism and colonialism. This survivalist root is what makes Korea's ethnic nationalism seem so benign or even salutary for so many Koreans and Korean Americans. Any possible negative aspects of it are rendered invisible in the affirmation of Korea against the history of Japanese colonialism. One of Japan's reasons for annexing Korea was that the Korean people were not a separate distinction people from the Japanese. Rather than a common East Asian heritage argued by the Japanese imperialists, Sin Ch'aeho and other Korean nationalists asserted that a distinctive bloodline defined Korean people, which served to unite and define those from the Korean peninsula.[12] Later, Japanese wartime propaganda of "Asia for Asians," played against white supremacy and European imperialism, seeking to gain allies and sympathies from the Asian colonized nations.[13] Japan presented its version of imperialism under the guise of creating a "Greater East Asia Co-Prosperity Sphere," a panethnic self-sufficient coalition

---

10 See Chen Kuan-hsing, *Asia as Method: Toward Deimperialization* (Durham, NC: Duke University Press, 2010).

11 Nadia Y. Kim, *Imperial Citizens: Koreans and Race from Seoul to LA* (Stanford, CA: Stanford University Press, 2008), 31.

12 Gi-Wook Shin, *Ethnic Nationalism in Korea: Genealogy, Politics, and Legacy* (Stanford, CA: Stanford University Press, 2006), 36–37.

13 See Gerald Horne, *Race War! White Supremacy and the Japanese Attack on the British Empire* (New York: New York University Press, 2004).

to stand against the European nations.[14] In this sense, the idea of racial panethnic identity, where all Asians are brought together under one common identity, is fraught with Japanese imperial legacy for Koreans.

This Korean ethnic nationalism was reinforced by its homogenous population that lacked diversity. However, living with diversity does not and has not soften the ideological hold of this ethnic nationalism. South Korea continues to struggle with its persisting ethnocentricity and resulting racism as foreign migration and interethnic marriages have increased over last couple of decades. Gi-Wook Shin evaluates that "Korea has yet to become a multi-cultural society while it has, essentially, become a multi-ethnic nation."[15] Reflecting their immigration pattern, the Korean-ness that resides within Korean America is from the seemingly monolithic and socio-politically repressed Korea of the 1970s and 1980s before the multicultural Korea of the present. Just like Korea, Korean Americans living with diversity in the United States do not necessarily equate softened ethnic nationalism with greater awareness of prejudice, inclusivity, and acceptance. The deeply ingrained ethnic nationalism, which is broadly accepted as a fact of nature by many, blinds Koreans and Korean Americans to the significance of different identity politics and dynamics, such as the panethnic identities in our nation.

Second, since the postwar US military presence, Koreans have imbibed American TV and movies, and along with it, its white normative self-image. American Forces Korean Network (AFKN)

---

14 See Jeremy A. Yellen, *The Greater East Asia Co-Prosperity Sphere: When Total Empire Met Total War* (Ithaca, NY: Cornell University Press, 2019).

15 Gi-Wook Shin, "Racist South Korea? Diverse but Not Tolerant of Diversity," in *Race and Racism in Modern East Asia: Western and Eastern Constructions*, ed. Rotem Kowner and Walter Demel (Leiden: Brill, 2014), 370.

that broadcasted across Korea provided readily accessible US mass media for decades.[16] Because of the lack of diverse representation and the reinforcement of whiteness in its mass media, the United States propagated itself as a white nation.[17] Thus, in the minds of Koreans and recent Korean immigrants, American became synonymous with white Americans.[18] This white normativity continues to be reinforced through the mass media in the United States as well as by the educational system for the later generations. Ironically, soaking in white normativity does not lead to greater racial awareness. Unlike white supremacy, where whiteness is claimed as best, white normativity resides in the shadows "behind a screen of objectivity and colorblindness," simply assuming that white people are just normal.[19] As a cultural myth with sociopolitical implications, white normativity functions through what Roland Barthes calls the process of exnomination, not naming itself but simply doing its work.[20]

This vision of white America in light of the racial diversity in the United States results in a white assimilationist understanding of immigrants and refugees. The myth of the United States as a nation of immigrants presents a transition from immigrant to American with a lot of hard work. What is absent from this idea of a smooth transition is the liminal place of being a racial minority in the United States. Japanese American pastor and theologian Roy Sano recalls that through the 1950s and '60s, many Asian Americans "assumed that if we became like them, white would like

---

16 Kim, *Imperial Citizens*, 38.
17 See Sarah D. Nilsen and Sarah E. Turner, eds, *White Supremacy and the American Media* (New York: Routledge: 2022).
18 Kim, *Imperial Citizens*, 48.
19 Michael Morris "Standard White: Dismantling White Normativity," *California Law Review* 104, no. 4 (August 2016): 949–97.
20 Roland Barthes, "Mythology Today" in *Mythologies* (New York: Hill and Wang, 2012), 250–252.

us," believing in the American melting pot.[21] The first generation of Asian immigrants were clearly foreigners in the United States, but this foreignness was not about newness but racial difference. The Asian Americans, many of them second and third generation Japanese and Chinese Americans, were rudely awaked to the fact that instead of white American, they were categorized as a racial minority, an "Oriental." This disappointment with white assimilation and seeking a new identity beyond the racist "Oriental" label, catalyzed the Asian American movement. Mentored by the Black liberation movement, Asian American panethnic, political, and activist identity was born.[22]

Second- and third-generation Korean Americans find themselves in a similar place as the second- and third-generation Japanese and Chinese Americans of the 1970s: seeing if they are accepted as just Americans alongside white Americans. Unlike their predecessors, however, Korean Americans must deal with, on the one hand, the model minority myth, which promises honorary whiteness as long as white normativity is accepted, and on the other, a reinvigorated Asian American movement as a result of Black Lives Matters, the Trump presidency, and AAPI hate connected to COVID-19.

Third, Korean and Korean American evangelicalism also hinders racial awareness. Unlike expressions of Christianity in other parts of Asia, where Christianity and Western imperialism intertwined, Korean Christianity historically represented an anti-imperial and anti-colonial force. In Korea and Korean America, colonialism and imperialism primarily imply Japanese occupation and oppression and not a Western one. Also, the

---

21 Roy I. Sano, "Shifts in reading the Bible: hermeneutical moves among Asian Americans" in *Semeia* 90/91: *The Bible in Asian America*, ed. Tat-siong Benny Liew and Gale A. Yee (2002), 109.
22 See Daryl J. Maeda, *Chains of Babylon: The Rise of Asian America* (Minneapolis: University of Minnesota Press, 2009).

successful indigenization of Christianity into Korean religious heritage of Shamanism and Daoism has made it a Korean religion.[23] As a result, Korean Christianity aligns well with its ethnic nationalism noted above.

As Korean Christianity turned more toward conservative evangelicalism coming to its apex in the 1980s, its features also indirectly made it vulnerable to racism. The evangelical turn away from Korean Christianity's political heritage—first against Japanese colonialism and later against the oppressive dictatorship of Park Chung-hee—became quietist, moralistic, and over-spiritualized, focusing on personal "health, wealth, power and honor."[24] This version of Christianity with its rapid growth became prominent in Korea, especially when post-1965 immigration to the United States was at its height.

Reflecting upon its cultural currents, Korean American church exists at the intersection of ethnic nationalism, evangelicalism, and an idealized picture of the United States. From the very beginning of Korean American immigration, Christianity has played a significant role. Dr. Horace Allen, missionary, medical doctor, and ambassador, was instrumental in helping the first group of Koreans in the United States. Allen and other missionaries not only shared their view of the United States as a Promised Land of fortune, better life, education, and political and religious freedom.[25] As a result, the many Koreans who arrived in Hawai'i shared the Christian faith or converted after their migration to

---

23 See Sung-Deuk Oak, *The Making of Korean Christianity: Protestant Encounters with Korean Religions, 1876–1915.* (Waco, TX: Baylor University Press, 2013).

24 Timothy S. Lee, *Born Again: Evangelicalism in Korea* (Honolulu: University of Hawaii Press, 2009), 123.

25 Edward T. Chang and Carol K. Park, *Korean Americans: A Concise History* (Riverside, CA: Young Oak Kim Center for Korean American Studies at the University of California Riverside, 2019), 4.

the "beautiful country," the meaning of the Korean name for the United States, *Mi-guk*.

This confluence of evangelical Christianity, ethnic nationalism, and an idealized image of the United States comprise the heart of Korean American culture. Unlike South Korea, which is around 15 percent Protestant, Korean America is close to 70 percent Protestant, or at least culturally so with Korean American church attendance. Korean America experienced a double miss to gain a sober perspective of the United States.[26] On the one hand, because of their immigration timeline Korean Americans missed the civil rights movement and the tremendous cost of racial justice, merely taking hard earned rights for granted. The Ronald Reagan and George H. W. Bush eras busily propagated "Colorblind White Dominance" and naive multiculturalism as Korean America took shape and matured.[27] On the other hand, whereas South Korea has become more progressive, moving away from the right-wing dictatorships of the 1970s and 1980s and more critical of the United States and also of fundamentalist Christianity, Korean America missed the progressive development and continued its idealistic view of the United States. South Korea has come to soften its understanding of North Korea, recovering from the bitter and ugly history around the Korean War with guilt and atrocities from all sides, moving beyond a simplistic Cold War binary and Red Scare ideology. Korean America on the other hand, still suffers from much ignorance, formed by American education and its own propaganda about its military actions in Korea and its political agendas and global evaluations, such as regarding the

---

26 For a similar argument about the South Asian American community, see Vijay Prashad, *Uncle Swami: South Asians in America Today* (New York: The New Press, 2012), 9–13.

27 Ian Haney López, *White by Law: The Legal Construction of Race*, 2nd ed. (New York: New York University Press, 2006), 147–148.

"axis of evil" that stands in the way of the "beautiful" and righteous United States.

Amos Yong explains that "methodologically and materially, evangelical theology has been understood to be a-historical, a-contextual and even a-contextual."[28] Internalizing this theology, many Korean and Korean American pastors trained in evangelical seminaries do not possess theological or spiritual categories to clearly perceive the historical and structural realities of race in the United States. Soong-Chan Rah notes that US evangelicalism is captive to white culture and racism.[29] In this sense, colorblind evangelical theology enforces the unnamed white normativity in American society. Then the Korean American church, serving as a community center for the majority of Korean Americans, propagates this colorblind white normativity.

ASIAN AMERICAN STRUGGLES TO GRASPING RACE

Along with their particular hindrances in deciphering the nature of race in the United States, Korean and Korean Americans face challenges that all Asian Americans must deal with. The exclusion of race as a hermeneutical category in the mind of Asian Americans occurs through the perpetual foreigner and similar tropes, the Black/white binary paradigm, and erasure of Asian American history in the American education system and society.

First, the perpetual foreigner trope, and others like honorary white or model minority myth, in their own ways make the category of race seemingly irrelevant for Asian Americans. With the

---

28   Amos Yong, *The Future of Evangelical Theology: Soundings from the Asian American Diaspora* (Downers Grove, IL: IVP Academic, 2014), 114.

29   See Soong-Chan Rah, *The Next Evangelicalism: Freeing the Church from Western Cultural Captivity* (Downers Grove, IL: IVP, 2009).

perpetual foreigner trope, which puts Asian Americans as Asians living in America, but never American, stresses the cultural differences, not race. In her paper on the racial triangulation of Asian Americans, Claire Kim explains how Asian Americans primarily experience racism through exclusion, being labeled as outsiders, and as perpetual foreigners.[30] As foreigners in the United States, they are excluded from the great drama of America's original sin of race. This exclusion, of course, is how Asian Americans experience race and racism, but because it assaults indirectly, it covers its steps, hiding its moves.

If Asian Americans are included as part of a racial grouping, they are often cast as "honorary whites," enveloped into a pseudo-white identity. In this framing, Asian Americans enjoy the privilege of white proximity and avoid systemic racist repercussions. As such "model minorities," able to succeed in the United States despite their status as racial minorities, Asian Americans are held up as proof of contemporary post-racial reality. The model minority myth is a social contract that allows Asian Americans to succeed academically and financially, but not culturally or politically. This myth functions as a filter that excludes any narratives of experiences that challenge the "Promised Land" vision of the United States with its American Dream and individualistic bootstrapping ethics. Because this self-reliance and independence resonates with certain Asian cultural values, such as Confucian ethics of self-cultivation and discipline, its more pernicious and erroneous aspects are not often clear even to many Asian Americans simply relieved to escape the fate of yellow peril. In this misrepresentative honorary white, or model minority, inclusion into American society, Asian Americans are not afforded their particular racial identity as Asian Americans, thus experiencing a different kind of exclusion: invisibility.

---

30 Claire Jean Kim, "The Racial Triangulation of Asian Americans," *Politics & Society* 27, no. 1 (1999): 105–138.

In this sense, the idea of an immigrant church easily fits into this mode of foreigners living in the United States, experiencing cultural differences, but not a part of the racial drama of the nation. For example, writing about Asian churches in relation to the need for multiethnic churches, the authors of *United by Faith*, fail to fully take into account the impact of whiteness upon Asian American communities, only stressing their assimilation over time.[31] In this sense, the categories of immigrant and of white America can make sense as ethnic identities. As Viet Nguyen quips the "ethnic is what America can assimilate, while racial is what America cannot digest."[32] As long as Asian Americans assimilate to white America, accepting the selective erasure and redaction of themselves, and protecting the white structures, there would be no trouble.

Second, closely connected to this exclusion of Asian Americans from the racial map of the United States is the Black/white binary paradigm. Basically, Asian Americans are seen as not American enough to experience racism, a racism mostly and narrowly defined within the Black/white binary paradigm. In his article "Black/White Binary Paradigm of Race," Juan Perea explains how those who are not Black or white are erased from the racial history of the United States.[33] Under this ubiquitous paradigm, Asian Americans do not experience racism, nor do they resist racism.

---

31   Curtiss Paul DeYoung, Michael O. Emerson, George Yancey, and Karen Chai Kim, *United by Faith: The Multiracial Congregation as an Answer to the Problem of Race* (New York: Oxford University Press, 2003), 127.

32   Viet Thanh Nguyen, *Nothing Ever Dies: Vietnam and the Memory of War* (Cambridge: Harvard University Press, 2016), 199.

33   Juan F. Perea, "The Black/White Binary Paradigm of Race: The 'Normal Science' of American Racial Thought," *California Law Review* 85, no. 5 (October 1997): 1213–1258.

They are merely passive spectators to the great drama and struggle of white oppression and Black resistance.

In its workings as a paradigm that organizes and accepts relevant data, whatever does not fit the grand narrative of white oppression against Black bodies, and of Black resistance and struggle simply ends up inadmissible. Because other stories of oppression and resistance do not fit the narrative, they are simply excised from history. Consider that most lynchings in the West Coast occurred against Latinx and Asian bodies. The Los Angeles Chinese massacre of 1871, considered one of the worst lynchings in the United States; the Hells Canyon Massacre of 1887 in Oregon; the Rock Springs Massacre of 1885 in Wyoming; Denver's 1880 Race Riot; the 1907 Bellingham Riots in Washington; and the Watsonville Riots of 1930 in California all attest to white violence upon Asian bodies. The California Supreme Court case *People v. Hall* (1854) ruled that Chinese Americans cannot testify against white citizens, which created an open season for anti-Asian violence with impunity.

Not only the sufferings of Asian Americans through history, but also the long struggle of Asian American activism ends up outside its parameters. The Black/white binary paradigm renders invisible the legal challenges of Wong Kim Ark for *jus soli* citizenship of those with Chinese parents, of Mamie Tape for California public school desegregation, of Takao Ozawa and Bhagat Singh Thind for naturalization and citizenship, of Fred Korematsu against Japanese American incarceration, and the activism of Larry Itliong, Grace Lee Boggs, and Yuri Kochiyama and so many others, making Asian Americans passive observers and beneficiaries to the Black struggle for civil rights.

This historically prevalent Black/white binary paradigm about the problem of race and struggle for racial justice continues to the present day where a race expert such as Ibram X. Kendi writing a "definitive history of racist ideas in America" can easily ignore everyone other than Black and white.³⁴ Even Kendi's *How to be an Antiracist* ignores the complexities of race and racism beyond the Black/white binary.³⁵ To be sure, the Black/white narrative is formative for the racial history of the United States, however it ends up oppressive to other people of color, who experience whiteness and racism in different expressions and manifestations. When Asian Americans internalize the Black/white binary paradigm as definitive and complete, they cannot clearly make sense of what racism or antiracism means.

Around the time of the Third World Liberation Front and the coinage of "Asian American" as a new political, racial, and activist identity, Asian Americans moved through a number of developments starting from rejecting white as their racial identity. To be exact, what they rejected was the idea that they were ethnically of Asian heritage but rather are, or at least are on their way to becoming, racially white, like European immigrants of the past. Daryl Maeda shows how as the white racial identity was rejected, these activists tried Black racial identity as a possibility, before forming their own distinct Asian American identity.³⁶ Even though they realized that Black racial identity was not going to work for them, these early "Asian Americans" were nevertheless mentored and influenced by Black activists. They created a new space that did not easily fit the Black/white binary paradigm that was afforded to them.

Third, the ubiquitous Black/white Binary paradigm results in the erasure of Asian American history, which of course, itself is racist. Asian Americans are not better informed than non-Asian Americans in these racial matters. In fact, the influence of Asian

---

34   Ibram X. Kendi, *Stamped from the Beginning: The Definitive History of Racist Ideas in America* (New York: Bold Type, 2017).
35   Ibram X. Kendi, *How to be an Antiracist* (New York: One World, 2019).
36   Maeda, *Chains of Babylon*, 75.

American studies "remain limited and tenuous. Its impact on the broad public consciousness has been modest at best."[37] In their book *Myth of Model Minority*, Chou and Feagin argue that the "lack of knowledge appears to add to the identity struggles and related stresses involved in having an Asian heritage in a racist country" and that "gaining accurate knowledge of this history [of Asian Americans and of anti-Asian discrimination] has frequently served as an important turning point in their lives."[38]

As part of their racial formation and socialization, Asian Americans themselves in turn can exclude race as an interpretative category for their experiences. Whereas relevance of race for Asian Americans is questioned, mainstream society readily offers Asian culture as an essential core of Asian Americanness. As Asian Americans experience racism that remains invisible and unrecognized as racism by mainstream society, the blame for their troubles can often be directed toward the Asian values tethered to their visibly and explicitly distinguishing features. While Asian values and even shame can be a source of pain, conflict, and struggle for Asian Americans, the erasure of racial dynamics leads to almost an exclusive pathologizing and scapegoating of these Asian values. More generally speaking, interpreting Asian American experiences while suffering from lack of adequate contextual literacy, or using a white normative one, will result in internalized racism, in this case, imagining one's Asian cultural values as the primary sources of one's racism woes.

As noted above for Asian American evangelicals, these aspects of erasure and invisibility are further aggravated through white normative theological education at evangelical seminaries

---

37 Shelley Sang-Hee Lee, *A New History of Asian America* (New York: Routledge, 2013), 2–3.
38 Rosalind S. Chou and Joe R. Feagin, *The Myth of the Model Minority: Asian Americans Facing Racism* (Boulder, CO: Paradigm, 2010), 193–194.

and the corresponding colorblind spirituality that is propagated. When evangelical seminaries assign Asian American ministry to the field of missiology, they also affirm the foreignness of Asian Americans, overemphasizing cultural differences and ignoring race. For second-generation Asian Americans, evangelicalism can also make them "trade" the painful and problematic ethnic or racial identity for a spiritual one, thinking that the former no longer matters as Christians.[39] Many Asian American churches can teeter between white approval or respectability and confusion by the Black/white binary paradigm to properly situate themselves.

In these ways, Korean Americans who are formed by American educational and cultural forces are up against strong currents that make themselves racially invisible. I have spent most of the discussion above on stumbling blocks and hindrances to Korean American racial conscientization, which is crucial to simply make sense of their lives in the United States, its culture, politics, and economics. Like water that envelopes our lives, the race issue is not only limited to the racism and marginalization experienced from without, but also includes white normative ideals and the internalizing of that white framework within Korean American communities and individuals.

RACE AND THE KOREAN AMERICAN MINISTRY

In this final section I offer three examples of how using racial awareness is crucial to the Korean American church in terms of its ministry, pastoral care, neighborhood outreach and public

---

39   Rudy Busto, "The Gospel According to the Model Minority? Hazarding an Interpretation of Asian American Evangelical College Students" in *New Spiritual Homes: Religion and Asian Americans*, ed. David K. Yoo (Honolulu: University of Hawai'i Press, 1999), 169-187.

witness, and envisioning its future. By race, I am referring to the impact of racism, and racial formation, external to and internalize within the Korean American community. The racism that concerns us is not coming from outside the family or the church, rather inside, in the minds of every family and church member.

First, race is crucial in understanding the dynamics of intergenerational relations in the Korean American community. Sumie Okazaki and Nancy Abelmann point out that "both the psychological literature and public discourse on Asian American immigrant families . . . have long [been] fixated on intergeneration cultural conflict between "Asian" (to indicate old-fashioned, "traditional") parents and "American" (to indicate modern, individualistic youth)."[40] Ministry books have often followed suit in this narrow cultural conflict narrative framing.[41] This rubric of "acculturation gap" uses a white normative perspective on immigrant family dynamics ignoring the complications that race brings as well as taking for granted Orientalized assumptions about the East (backwards) versus the West (modern). There are indeed intercultural dynamics at play, however, the psychological stress and trauma from racism and racialization upon both generations complicates and aggravates these dynamics. Thus, intergenerational conflict is not simply cross-cultural or cross-generational concerns.

David Eng and Shinhee Han explain that for the Asian American immigrant generation, the visible and invisible losses that they experience in their transition cannot be replace by

---

[40] Sumie Okazaki and Nancy Abelmann, *Korean American Families in Immigrant America: How Teens and Parents Navigate Race* (New York: New York University Press, 2018), 4.

[41] While very helpful in many regards, this narrow intercultural view of the generational tension is the chief limitation of Jeanette Yep, Peter Cha, Susan Cho Van Riesen, Greg Jao, and Paul Tokunaga, *Following Jesus without Dishonoring Your Parents* (Downers Grove, IL: InterVarsity, 1998).

their counterparts in the new country because of racial marginalization and suspended assimilation.[42] Using Freudian terminology, they label this experience of suffering the loss without a suitable replacement "racial melancholia" of Asian Americans, "a mourning without end." They note that this racial melancholia can lead to transgenerational tensions and pressures as the second generation seeks to alleviate the mourning to their own striving, seeking to replace that loss, putting an end to the grieving. The pathological burden placed upon both generations in this sense is racial, not just cultural. Of course, the cultural values such of familialism and collectivism are without a doubt presence, but the toxicity of this suspended assimilation cannot be ignored.

Put differently, Won Moo Hurh and Kwang Chung Kim, focusing on the loss of social or sociological (*gesellschaft*) status of the immigrant generation, show the fraught weight of ecclesial or communal (*gemeinschaft*) roles, making church politics ever more dysfunctional.[43] Experiencing dislocation, indignities, and disrespect in the racialized society can also laden their relationships at home as well, making the need for affirmation and respect by the children and younger generation acute and their lack especially bitter.

While racial marginalization impacts the second generation as well, for them the racial formation that they internalized through their white normative education and the Orientalized representation of their Asianness color their relationship with the first generation. One of the themes of microaggressive messages that Asian Americans encounter is the pathologizing of Asian values, meaning compared to the "normal" white American values,

---

42 David L. Eng and Shinhee Han, "A Dialogue on Racial Melancholia," *Psychoanalytic Dialogues* 10, no. 4 (2000): 667–700.

43 See Won Moo Hurh and Kwang Chung Kim, "Religious Participation of Korean Immigrants in the United States," *Journal for the Scientific Study of Religion* 29, no. 1 (1990): 19–34.

something is wrong with Asian ones. They are either too indirect, too quiet, too diligent, too thoughtful, etc.[44] While all Asian Americans are fed these messages, the first generation, who have their social and cultural formation from Asia, can more readily know that they are being attacked for something that people back in Asia find perfectly normal. However, the second generation, who have no such reference point and are surrounded by white normative ideals, stand more vulnerable to internalizing these racist evaluations.

The long history of Orientalism in representation in the United States, which conceptualizes Asianness by "its strangeness, difference, exotic sensuousness, eccentricity, backwardness, silence indifference, feminine penetrability, uncivilized nature, and the like," shows up in various places in pop culture.[45] While Asian American representation has improved significantly in the last decade, the recent advances are still limited in scope and impact given the long history of wide distortion and pervasive erasure.[46] The second generation projects this Orientalized view of Asianness upon their first generation parents, who end up as symbolic representation of Asia, presenting an extremely

---

44 Derald Wing Sue, Jennifer Bucceri, Annie I. Lin, Kevin L. Nadal, and Gina C. Torino, "Racial Microaggressions and the Asian American Experience," *Cultural Diversity and Ethnic Minority Psychology* 13, no. 1 (2007): 72–81.

45 Namsoon Kang, "Who/What is Asian? A Postcolonial Theological Reading of Orientalism and Neo-Orientalism" in *Postcolonial Theologies: Divinity and Empire*, eds. Catharine Keller, Michael Nausner, and Mayra Rivera (St. Louis: Chalice, 2004), 102. Also, see Edward Said, *Orientalism* (New York: Vintage, 1994), 206–7.

46 On lack of Asian American representation or misrepresentation in popular media, see Nancy Wang Yuen, *Reel Inequality: Hollywood Actors and Racism* (New Brunswick, NJ: Rutgers University Press, 2016) and Kent A. Ono and Vincent N. Pham, *Asian Americans and the Media* (Malden, MA: Polity, 2009).

narrow view of what it means to be Asian.⁴⁷ The first generation as symbols of Asian heritage are problematic because they often have a time capsule view of their Asian heritage, for example, referring to Korea of their immigration days as *de facto* Korea in their minds.

All this means that in terms of pastoral care, the culprit that deserves our attention is not only better intercultural understanding and appreciation. There must also be an unveiling of the diabolical forces of white supremacy and white normativity that poison our minds and hearts against each other. Properly naming the demon that must be cast out is an essential part of the healing process. Ministry toward healing of racial trauma in all generations would have to be a vital part of mending intergenerational relationships within families and congregations.⁴⁸

Second, racial awareness enhances the mission of the Korean American church with sharper eyes to see our neighbors. Without considering the history of race and racism in the United States, it is impossible to actually see our neighbors who are, like us, categorized, formed, and impacted by historical and structural racism, whether they be Asian American, Latinx, Black, white, or Native American. Race obviously is not the sole or even always the most salient formative influence. However, without being critically racially aware, the why and how of our neighbors will be merely left to individualistic or cultural explanations.

When reflecting upon the Los Angeles Riots of 1992, what would it have been like if Korean Americans understood the

---

47 Daniel D. Lee, "Parents," in *Intersecting Realities: Race, Identity, and Culture in the Spiritual–Moral Life of Young Asian Americans*, ed. Hak Joon Lee (Eugene: Cascade, 2018).

48 For an example of discipleship formation regarding racial trauma, see Daniel D. Lee, "God's Shalom to All of Ourselves: Integrating the Asian American Double Self," *Christianity Next Journal* 5 (2021): 53–74.

history and structures of racism that brought about the Black communities to be in these impoverished neighborhoods, beyond the "culture" stereotypes of laziness, addictions, violence, and lack of family systems or values. The idea of "culture" in this context has no knowledge of chattel slavery, Jim Crow laws, lynching, segregation, civil rights movement, redlining, police brutality, and other dehumanizing struggles. Racial awareness makes this racial history available, to think other than in cultural terms. To properly see the Black neighbors, their present struggles, travails, and longings, this longer history must be taken up. The racial imaginary opens a way to connect with Black Americans as those who share a common experience as racial minorities, even if this commonality is perceived by them. Accepting a racial identity with its panethnicity has its limitations in the ways that it flattens the ethnic differences and also fronting privileged narratives over others. However, it is not an either/or proposition of accepting or rejecting racial coalitional identity, but a negotiation of identificational multiplicity.[49] Whereas ethnicity provides the cultural resources, the racial identity provides an understanding of US history and a way to situate yourself in its racial drama and tragedies.[50]

To see and, furthermore, to love Latinx Americans as our neighbors, the American imperial narrative of manifest destiny opens up a different lens for contemporary political interpretation. The racial history of the Chinese Exclusion Act guides Korean Americans to see the issue of undocumented immigration as a structural problem of a broken system, rather than simply

---

49   Yen Le Espiritu, *Asian American Panethnicity: Bridging Institutions and Identities* (Philadelphia: Temple University Press, 1992), 161.
50   See Daniel D. Lee, "Diaspora, Origins, and Asian American Theology" in *Reflections of Asian Diaspora: Mapping Theologies and Ministries, Asian Diaspora Christianity* Vol. 3., ed. Sam George (Minneapolis: Fortress, 2022).

lawbreaking. If they were not acknowledged already, this new purview can note the undocumented within the Korean American and the broader Asian American community.

Loving these neighbors means working at an interpersonal level toward service and mutual understanding as many Korean Americans did to close the gulf between them and their Black neighbors.[51] However, as the root of the problems resides at the structural and societal level, Korean American civic activism and engagement will be an important aspect as well. Whether Korean American immigrants are here in the United States as missionaries, exiles, or sojourners, God calls us to seek the peace and welfare of this nation, in the cities and neighborhoods that we found ourselves in (Jer 29:7). This vocation means among many other things that Korean Americans are tasked along with all those seeking the shalom in this nation to works toward the uprooting and the eradication of white supremacy and racism which lie at the very foundation of this nation. This call requires that Korean American abandon the siren call to be a model minority and to fully participate in the antiracist work that must continue at every level of our society, not only for our communities and the broader Asian America, but for all people of color and further to everyone living in the United States and also impacted by this nation's reach.

Third, racial awareness will be crucial for the future of the Korean American Church. The Korean American immigrant church faces declining membership, first, due to the aging demographic, and second, because new immigrants from Korea are not joining their ecclesial communities.[52] This latter point is a

---

51 For examples, see Pyong Gap Min, *Caught in the Middle: Korean Communities in New York and Los Angeles* (Los Angeles: University of California Press, 1996), 126–145.

52 John J. Oh, "From Silent Exodus to Silent Divergence: Changing Immigrant Society Unchanging Immigrant Church," *Journal of Language, Culture, and Religion* 2, no. 2 (2021): 51–74.

departure from historical precedence, where many Korean immigrants were Christians or converted once arriving. This disconnection to the Korean American church could be due to the decline and low public perception of the Protestant church in Korea for being self-adsorbed and corrupt.[53] Also, given the large Korean American presence in many metropolitan areas, Korean immigrants might not feel the need to join a congregation for social and relational support as they had in the past. If this trend continues the Korean speaking ministries will eventually become stewarded under the second generation and the English ministry, or some sort. For the second-generation churches or ministries, whether they be English ministry within a Korean ministry, recently independent English ministry, or a predominately Korean American church seeking to become multiethnic, racial awareness will provide not only a way to develop the appropriate theology, especially ecclesiology for their being and mission at hand.

I have argued elsewhere that Asian American churches must be not only culturally and socially Asian American, but also theologically so.[54] This theologically owning yourself and your community requires that Korean Americans function out of a white normative theology that ill suits their ministry. As the next generation envisions ministry, along with insights from cultural heritage and migration studies, racial awareness will inform them about the particular pains, sins, and gifts that they must attend to within their community as well as the those of their neighbors.

Especially for those Korean American ministries seeking to move toward a multicultural congregation, they must see through the diversity propaganda that prioritizes optics while ignoring the complexity and challenges around discipleship and pastoral care. The multiethnic church bubble of the past decades

---

53 K Kale Yu, *Understanding Korean Christianity: Grassroot Perspectives on Causes, Culture, and Responses* (Eugene: Pickwick, 2019), 230–231.

54 See Lee, *Doing Asian American Theology*.

is bursting because the problem of white hegemony is real and that structural racism is toxic for people of color including Asian Americans.[55] While we might assume that a multiethnic church led by a person of color like a Korean American fairs better, Korie Edwards' research shows that the power of white hegemony is far stronger than assumed even with such leadership. Becoming a church that sees the particular narratives, histories, and identities of the diverse peoples will require a multidimensional interpersonal hermeneutic that includes race along with many other parameters. Of course, a theological apparatus to engage these parameters will be invaluable as well.

CONCLUSION

While there are a number of challenges and obstacles on various fronts, racial conscientization will be an integral aspect of Korean American identity and Christian ministry. Among Korean Americans such awareness is growing, along with other Asian Americans racially and politically catalyzed by Donald Trump's presidency and the anti-AAPI hate related to the COVID-19 epidemic. Cathy Park Hong's *Minor Feelings*, while lacking in an Asian American studies background, nevertheless, deftly expresses the racial angst that Asian American experience in between the Black/white binary.[56] On the other hand, Jay Caspian Kang's *The Loneliest Americans* display a failure to comprehend the place and significance of the Asian American movement in Korean American lives.[57] Thus, the struggle continues for the Korean American community.

---

55 See Korie Edwards, *The Elusive Dream: The Power of Race in Interracial Churches* (New York: Oxford University Press, 2021).
56 Cathy Park Hong, *Minor Feelings: An Asian American Reckoning* (New York: One World, 2020).
57 Jay Caspian Kang, *The Loneliest Americans* (New York: Crown, 2021).

Many Korean American Christian leaders are rising to prominent positions within evangelical Christianity, such as Walter Kim of the National Association of Evangelicals, Julius Kim of The Gospel Coalition, Eugene Cho of Bread for the World, and others. But are they making a significant contribution that is better or different from what a white leader would have done, especially regarding the area of race and diversity?[58] Their Korean American identity alone would not necessarily mean that they have any better insights than a model minority seeking to be an honorary white, since that is the role that Asian American Christians play regarding diversity: being benign decorations.[59]

If they do bring insights regarding race, would it be something beyond the Black/white binary paradigm that tends to erase others who do not fit? Critical knowledge is something beyond personal experiences. It requires a sophisticated racial awareness from an Asian American perspective and for these leaders to see themselves as Asian American as well as Korean American. Using missiological and assimilationist reasoning, evangelicalism encourages and affirms ethnic narratives, but often fails to see race clearly. When race is acknowledged, the current state of evangelicalism struggles to go beyond the Black/white binary paradigm to be fully inclusive. Thus, these Asian American leaders must swim against strong currents if they are going to contribute as Asian Americans.

For Korean American Christians to witness to God who has called and sends them for kingdom work embodied and

---

58 Morgan Lee, "Historically White Christian Ministries Now Have Korean American Male Leaders," *Quick to Listen Podcast*, March 11, 2020, https://www.christianitytoday.com/ct/podcasts/quick-to-listen/korean-evangelicals-eugene-cho-walter-kim-julius.html.

59 See K. Kale Yu, "Christian Model Minority: Racial and Ethnic Formation in Asian American Evangelicalism," *Journal of Race, Ethnicity, and Religion* 7, issue 6 (November 2016): 1–24.

encultured as Korean Americans, our journey of discipleship goes through the process of taking up all of ourselves, which inevitably includes our racial identities, along with our ethnic, gender, class, familial, and many other identities. The task of guiding Korean American Christians through this journey falls upon Korean American churches and ministers.

BIBLIOGRAPHY

An, Choi Hee. *A Postcolonial Self: Korean Immigrant Theology and Church.* Albany, NY: SUNY Press, 2015.

Barthes, Roland. *Mythologies.* New York: Hill and Wang, 2012.

Busto, Rudy. "The Gospel According to the Model Minority? Hazarding an Interpretation of Asian American Evangelical College Students." In *New Spiritual Homes: Religion and Asian Americans*, edited by David K. Yoo, 169–187. Honolulu: University of Hawai'i Press, 1999.

Cha, Peter, S. Steve Kang, and Helen Lee, eds. *Growing Healthy Asian American Churches.* Downers Grove, IL: IVP, 2006.

Chang, Edward T., and Carol K. Park. *Korean Americans: A Concise History.* Riverside, CA: Young Oak Kim Center for Korean American Studies at the University of California Riverside, 2019.

Chen, Kuan-hsing. *Asia as Method: Toward Deimperialization.* Durham, NC: Duke University Press, 2010.

Chou, Rosalind S., and Joe R. Feagin. *The Myth of the Model Minority: Asian Americans Facing Racism.* Boulder, CO: Paradigm, 2010.

DeYoung, Curtiss Paul, Michael O. Emerson, George Yancey, and Karen Chai Kim. *United by Faith: The Multiracial Congregation as an Answer to the Problem of Race.* New York: Oxford University Press, 2003.

Edwards, Korie. *The Elusive Dream: The Power of Race in Interracial Churches.* New York: Oxford University Press, 2021.

Eng, David L., and Shinhee Han. "A Dialogue on Racial Melancholia." *Psychoanalytic Dialogues* 10, no. 4 (2000): 667–700.

Espiritu, Yen Le. *Asian American Panethnicity: Bridging Institutions and Identities.* Philadelphia: Temple University Press, 1992.

Feagin, Joe R. *The White Racial Frame: Centuries of Racial Framing and Counter-Framing*, 3rd ed. New York: Routledge, 2020.

Hollinger, David. *Postethnic America: Beyond Multiculturalism.* New York: Basic, 1995.
Hong, Cathy Park. *Minor Feelings: An Asian American Reckoning.* New York: One World, 2020.
Horne, Gerald. *Race War! White Supremacy and the Japanese Attack on the British Empire.* New York: New York University Press, 2004.
Hurh, Won Moo, and Kwang Chung Kim. "Religious Participation of Korean Immigrants in the United States." *Journal for the Scientific Study of Religion* 29, no. 1 (1990): 19–34.
Jeung, Russell. *Faithful Generation: Race and New Asian American Churches.* New Brunswick, NJ: Rutgers University Press, 2005.
Kang, Jay Caspian. *The Loneliest Americans.* New York: Crown, 2021.
Kang, Namsoon. "Who/What Is Asian? A Postcolonial Theological Reading of Orientalism and Neo-Orientalism" in *Postcolonial Theologies: Divinity and Empire* edited by Catharine Keller, Michael Nausner, and Mayra Rivera, 100–117. St. Louis: Chalice, 2004.
Kendi, Ibram X. *How to be an Antiracist.* New York: One World, 2019.
Kendi, Ibram X. *Stamped from the Beginning: The Definitive History of Racist Ideas in America.* New York: Bold Type, 2017.
Kim, Claire Jean. "The Racial Triangulation of Asian Americans." *Politics & Society* 27, no. 1 (1999): 105–138.
Kim, Nadia Y. *Imperial Citizens: Koreans and Race from Seoul to LA.* Stanford, CA: Stanford University Press, 2008.
Kim, Sharon. *A Faith of Our Own: Second-generation Spirituality in Korean American Churches.* New Brunswick, NJ: Rutgers University Press, 2010.
Kwon, Ho-Young, Kwang Chung Kim, and R. Stephen Warner, eds. *Korean Americans and Their Religions Pilgrims and Missionaries from a Different Shore.* University Park, PA: Penn State University Press, 2001.
Lee, Daniel D. "Diaspora, Origins, and Asian American Theology," in *Reflections of Asian Diaspora: Mapping Theologies and Ministries, Asian Diaspora Christianity* Vol. 3., edited by Sam George, 123–139. Minneapolis: Fortress, 2022.
———. "God's Shalom to All of Ourselves: Integrating the Asian American Double Self." *Christianity Next Journal* 5(2021): 53–74.
———. "Parents," in *Intersecting Realities: Race, Identity, and Culture in the Spiritual-Moral Life of Young Asian Americans,* edited by Hak Joon Lee, 27–38. Eugene: Cascade, 2018.

———. *Doing Asian American Theology: A Contextual Framework for Faith and Practice*. Downers Grove, IL: IVP Academic, 2022.

Lee, Jung Young. *Marginality: The Key to Multicultural Theology*. Minneapolis: Fortress, 1995.

Lee, Morgan. "Historically White Christian Ministries Now Have Korean American Male Leaders." *Quick to Listen Podcast*, March 11, 2020, https://www.christianitytoday.com/ct/podcasts/quick-to-listen/korean-evangelicals-eugene-cho-walter-kim-julius.html.

Lee, Sang Hyun. *From A Liminal Place: An Asian American Theology*. Minneapolis: Fortress, 2010.

Lee, Shelley Sang-Hee. *A New History of Asian America*. New York: Routledge, 2013.

Lee, Timothy S. *Born Again: Evangelicalism in Korea*. Honolulu: University of Hawai'i Press, 2009.

López, Ian Haney. *White by Law: The Legal Construction of Race*, 2nd ed. New York: New York University Press, 2006.

Maeda, Daryl J. *Chains of Babylon: The Rise of Asian America*. Minneapolis: University of Minnesota Press, 2009.

Min, Pyong Gap. *Caught in the Middle: Korean Communities in New York and Los Angeles*. Los Angeles: University of California Press, 1996.

Morris, Michael. "Standard White Standard White: Dismantling White Normativity." *California Law Review* 104, no. 4 (August 2016): 949–97.

Nguyen, Viet Thanh. *Nothing Ever Dies: Vietnam and the Memory of War*. Cambridge: Harvard University Press, 2016.

Nilsen, Sarah D., and Sarah E. Turner, eds. *White Supremacy and the American Media*. New York: Routledge: 2022.

Oak, Sung-Deuk. *The Making of Korean Christianity: Protestant Encounters with Korean Religions, 1876–1915*. Waco, TX: Baylor University Press, 2013.

Oh, John J. "From Silent Exodus to Silent Divergence: Changing Immigrant Society Unchanging Immigrant Church." *Journal of Language, Culture, and Religion* 2, no. 2 (2021): 51–74.

Okazaki, Sumie, and Nancy Abelmann. *Korean American Families in Immigrant America: How Teens and Parents Navigate Race*. New York: New York University Press, 2018.

Ono, Kent A., and Vincent N. Pham, *Asian Americans and the Media*. Malden, MA: Polity, 2009.

Park, Andrew Sung. *Racial Conflict and Healing: An Asian–American Theological Perspective.* Maryknoll, NY: Orbis, 1996.

Park, M. Sydney, Soong-Chan Rah, and Al Tizon, eds. *Honoring the Generation: Learning with Asian North American Congregations.* Valley Forge, PA: Judson, 2012.

Perea, Juan F. "The Black/White Binary Paradigm of Race: The 'Normal Science' of American Racial Thought." *California Law Review* 85, no. 5 (October 1997): 1213–1258.

Prashad, Vijay. *Uncle Swami: South Asians in America Today.* New York: The New Press, 2012.

Rah, Soong-Chan. *The Next Evangelicalism: Freeing the Church from Western Cultural Captivity.* Downers Grove, IL: IVP, 2009.

Said, Edward. *Orientalism.* New York: Vintage, 1994.

Sano, Roy I. "Shifts in reading the Bible: hermeneutical moves among Asian Americans." In *Semeia* 90–91: *The Bible in Asian America*, edited by Tat-siong Benny Liew and Gale A. Yee, 105–118. Atlanta: The Society of Biblical Literature, 2002.

Shin, Gi-Wook. "Racist South Korea? Diverse but Not Tolerant of Diversity," in *Race and Racism in Modern East Asia: Western and Eastern Constructions*, edited by Rotem Kowner and Walter Demel, 369–390. Leiden: Brill, 2014.

Shin, Gi-Wook. *Ethnic Nationalism in Korea: Genealogy, Politics, and Legacy.* Stanford, CA: Stanford University Press, 2006.

Sue, Derald Wing, Jennifer Bucceri, Annie I. Lin, Kevin L. Nadal, and Gina C. Torino. "Racial Microaggressions and the Asian American Experience." *Cultural Diversity and Ethnic Minority Psychology* 13, no. 1 (2007): 72–81.

Warner, R. Stephen. "Immigration and Religious Communities in the United States," in *Gathering in Diaspora: Religious Communities and the New Immigration*, edited by R. Stephen Warner and Judith G. Wittner, 3–34. Philadelphia: Temple University Press, 1998.

Yellen, Jeremy A. *The Greater East Asia Co-Prosperity Sphere: When Total Empire Met Total War.* Ithaca, NY: Cornell University Press, 2019.

Yep, Jeanette, Peter Cha, Susan Cho Van Riesen, Greg Jao, and Paul Tokunaga. *Following Jesus without Dishonoring Your Parents.* Downers Grove, IL: InterVarsity, 1998.

Yong, Amos. *The Future of Evangelical Theology: Soundings from the Asian American Diaspora.* Downers Grove, IL: IVP Academic, 2014.

Yoo, David and Ruth H. Chung, "Introduction," in *Religion and Spirituality in Korean America*, edited by David Yoo and Ruth H. Chung, 1–19. Champaign, IL: University of Illinois Press, 2008.

Yu, K. Kale. "Christian Model Minority: Racial and Ethnic Formation in Asian American Evangelicalism." *Journal of Race, Ethnicity, and Religion* 7, issue 6 (November 2016): 1–24.

Yu, K. Kale. *Understanding Korean Christianity: Grassroot Perspectives on Causes, Culture, and Responses.* Eugene: Pickwick, 2019.

Yuen, Nancy Wang. *Reel Inequality: Hollywood Actors and Racism.* New Brunswick, NJ: Rutgers University Press, 2016.

8

IMMIGRATION AND US CONGREGATIONS
Contemporary Trends and Issues

Allison L. Norton

INTRODUCTION

In this chapter, I briefly overview the major trends and issues related to immigration and congregational life in the United States. Today, nearly 14 percent of US residents are immigrants, a figure that rises to one-quarter of the US population when including the second generation.[1] No exploration of the US religious landscape can ignore this reality. This chapter considers migrant churches and the figure of the Christian migrant as embedded in migratory processes and the complex social transformations that shape our world. In other words, I take as a starting point that the mission of migrants and their communities cannot be understood apart from broader social processes marked by considerable flux and dynamism. This is rooted in an essential sociological proposition: that behavior is shaped by the overarching social structures in which people are embedded. Additionally, the relationship

---

1 Cecilia Esterline and Jeanne Batlova, "Frequently Requested Statistics on Immigrants and Immigration in the United States." Migration Policy Institute, 2022, https://tinyurl.com/4bc3fp32.

between these social structures and human agency is a key overarching project of the sociology of migration.[2] Stephen Castles promotes what he calls the "social transformation perspective" in migration studies—the need to embed migration research in forms of inquiry within processes of rapid social transformation that further discussion on "the complexity, interconnectedness, variability, contextuality, and multi-level mediations of global change."[3] Studies about mission and migration, I argue, should do the same: further our understanding of migrant Christianity and migrant ecclesiology as embedded within, not distinct from, broader social relationships and change processes.

In particular, I focus on three intertwining topics from this perspective of social transformation in the study of immigration and religion that contribute to bringing new light to long-standing questions posed by pastors, religious leaders, and scholars: (1) the role of immigration on the changing composition of US congregations and their membership, (2) the capacity of transnational religious faith and institutions to contribute to both immigrant resilience and a global outlook, and (3) the processes of reinvention in community, faith, and culture that occur as second and third generation descendants of immigrants create their own religious spaces of belonging. I do this from my position as a white, American, Pentecostal woman who spent the early years of adulthood living as an immigrant in Ghana. Additionally, both my research and personal religious life is deeply tied with Pentecostal Ghanaian communities of faith in the United States, and these experiences and relationships impact and influence my

---

[2] Stephen Castles, "Twenty-First-Century Migration as a Challenge to Sociology," *Journal of Ethnic and Migration Studies* 33, no. 3 (2007): 351–371.

[3] Stephen Castles, "Understanding Global Migration: A Social Transformation Perspective," *Journal of Ethnic and Migration Studies* 36, no. 10 (2010): 1566.

foundations and starting points for refection, providing the background to identifying what I consider the most important connections between migration theories and ecclesial communities in the US.

Although there is growing evidence that post-1965 immigrant Christianity is (again—as it has through the history of this nation) reshaping the American religious landscape in lasting and consequential ways, this narrative is often lost in the preoccupation by religious scholars and theologians alike in the decline of Christianity that the United States has witnessed over the past sixty years. It is true that, judging from the recent survey data, the future of Christianity in the United States does not look too bright.[4] However, alongside Harvey Kwiyani, I propose that although this decline raises valid issues and concerns, attention to the ways in which migrant Christians and their descendants disproportionately "keep Christianity going" in Western contexts is perhaps of even greater, or at least equal, importance when considering the future of the Western religious landscape.[5]

IMMIGRATION AND THE CHANGING COMPOSITION OF US CONGREGATIONS

In her introduction to *Church in an Age of Global Migration*, Susanna Snyder points out that contemporary ecclesiological responses to global migration have focused on the ethical role of churches and religious organizations in moral and practical responses to migration. However, she states the need for more

---

4   Mark Silk and Andrew H. Walsh, "Series Editors' Introduction: The Future of Religion in America," in *The Future of Evangelicalism in America*, ed. Candy Brown and Mark Silk (New York: Colombia University Press, 2016), vvi

5   Harvey C. Kwiyani, *Multicultural Kingdom: Ethnic Diversity, Mission and the Church* (London: SCM Press, 2020), 19.

reflection "where ecclesial identities and futures and migration intersect—or, in other words, the ways in which migration is changing the church."[6] More pointedly, she calls out the narrative promoted by pastors and theologians in the global North to "think of the church as responding to migrants—as if migrants were outside it and recipients of Christian welfare—rather than migrants being part of the Christian 'we'."[7]

Exploring the impact of post-1965 immigration on changing American religious institutions calls us to shed nationalistic or Eurocentric notions of the American church. In their series on the future of religion in America, Mark Silk and Andrew Walsh identify post-1965 and ongoing immigration as one of the most salient phenomena reconfiguring American religious life the past twenty-five years, alongside the rise of the "Nones" and the rise of evangelicalism as the now "normative form of non-Catholic American Christianity." Of course, post-1965 immigration has introduced adherents of world religions previously little known in the United States, but "more significantly, [it has] changed the face of American Christianity."[8] As demonstrated by Jehu Hanciles, "one of the most striking coincidences of contemporary globalization [is] that the decline of the Christian faith in North America has corresponded with a phenomenal influx of Christian migrants."[9] While much of white mainline Protestantism has not seen growth in decades, Korean Methodists and Presbyterians, Salvadoran

---

6   Susanna Snyder, "Introduction," in *Church in an Age of Global Migration: A Moving Body*, ed. Susanna Snyder, Joshua Ralston, and Agnes M. Brazal (Hampshire, UK: Palgrave Macmillan, 2016), 5.
7   Susanna Snyder, *Church in an Age of Global Migration*, 5.
8   Silk and Walsh, *The Future of Evangelicalism*, x.
9   Jehu Hanciles, *Beyond Christendom: Globalization, African Migration, and the Transformation of the West*, (Maryknoll, NY: Orbis Books, 2008), 85.

Pentecostals, and Mexican Catholics represent some of the fastest growing segments of American religion.[10]

Since the 1965 Immigration Reform Act, which discontinued previous patterns of overwhelmingly European-centric quotas, the United States has become more racially, ethnically, and religiously diverse. Post-1965 immigrants and their descendants have contributed substantially to the redefinition and expansion of racial categories in the United States. In the last fifty years, both the patterns and pace of immigration have shifted. Also, since 1990, one-third of the overall population growth in the United States is attributed to immigration.[11] The increasing racial and ethnic diversity in the US population is seen in US congregations as well. Denominations across the Christian family have become increasingly diverse and nondenominational churches have similarly experienced increased racial and ethnic diversity. The substantial rise in the percentage of congregations which are multiracial, from only 8 percent in 2000 to 25 percent in 2020 according to the Faith Communities Today data, is driven both by immigration and growing African American presence within multiracial churches.[12]

We see this shift, perhaps most obviously, in the changing ethnic and geographic shifts within American Catholicism. This is

---

10 Nancy T. Ammerman, "America's Changing Religious and Cultural Landscape and Its Implications for Theological Education" in *Looking Forward with Hope: Reflections on the Present State and Future of Theological Education*, ed. Benjamin Valentin (Eugene, OR: Cascade Books, 2019), 38.

11 Barry A. Kosmin and Ariela Keysar, *American Religious Identification Survey (Aris 2008) Summary Report*. (Hartford, CT: Trinity College, 2009).

12 Twenty Years of Congregational Change: The 2020 Faith Communities Today Overview. Faith Communities Today. https://faith-communitiestoday.org/fact-2020-survey/.

due, in large part, to an increase in Latinx members of the church who represent almost 40 percent of the American Catholic population today and account for over 70 percent of the US Catholic population growth since 1960.[13] When compared across generations, it is clear that future cohorts of Catholics will be increasingly Latinx, as they make up almost half of Catholics under the age of forty.[14] Without the influx of immigrant Catholics, the Catholic Church in the United States would face a story of decline rivaling that within mainline Protestantism, which no longer serves as the "religion of choice of immigrants."[15] As Carmen Nanko-Fernández states, "We are not your diversity, we are the church!"[16] However, alongside the Catholic Church, we also see this shift in the growth of ethnic and racial diversity across nearly all spaces of Christian life in America—in the immigrant-led storefront churches nearly hidden away in shopping centers and industrial spaces, in the immigrant-majority mainline congregations, and in the tremendous growth of multiracial congregations over the past twenty years. As such, migrant Christians and their growing religious institutions represent not merely the future of American Christianity, but also its present.

Korean immigrant churches additionally contribute to changing the US congregational landscape in meaningful ways. As exemplified in the work of Choi Hee An, the practice of communal

---

13 Carmen M. Nanko-Fernández, "We Are Not Your Diversity, We Are the Church! Ecclesiological Reflections from the Marginalized Many," *Perspectives: Hispanic Theological Initiative Occasional Paper Series*, no. 10 (2006): 83.

14 Luis Lugo, "A Land of Immigrants, a Shifting Religious Marketplace." *Reflections* 95, no.2. (Fall 2008): 15.

15 Graham Reside, "The State of Contemporary Mainline Protestantism" in *The Future of Mainline Protestantism in America*, ed. James Hudnut-Beumler, Mark Silk, and Andrew Walsh (New York: Columbia University Press, 2019), 36.

16 Nanko-Fernández, "We Are Not Your Diversity," 81.

transformational leadership is exercised in the agency of women lay leaders within Korean churches in the immigrant context.[17] These churches form a protective barrier against the threats of a predominately white society, and provide a space to exercise a strong sense of "we," of *Woori* that prioritizes the needs of the community. This style of leadership in the United States extends toward recognizing the existence and needs of other marginalized communities, leading toward theologies that recognize and include other immigrant communities within the sense of the "we." This theology of respect for and inclusion of the "other" is an approach to leadership and community that seeks to redefine the contours of belonging in religious communities in the US landscape. Additionally, we cannot ignore the ways in which Korean immigrants have transformed the denominational life within Presbyterian and Methodist communities in the United States, through establishing both independent Korean denominations and dramatically contributing to the growth and witness of these denominations in the United States.

So first, we witness the ways in which America's changing ethnic and racial landscape intersects with changes in its religious character and composition. The American religious landscape has always been a lively one, characterized by change. However, we are witnessing a dynamic redrawing of the contours of American Christianity, away from what Snyder calls "monochrome Christianity" toward "multireligious transnational diversity," due in part, to the agency and presence of the Christian migrant.[18]

Secondly, data from multiple survey sources and case studies suggests that on several general markers of religiosity, especially church attendance, immigrants to the United States are more

---

17   Choi Hee An, "Challenges of Korean Immigrant Leadership in the Church," *International Journal of Practical Theology* 23, no. 2 (2019): 224–241.

18   Snyder, *Church in an Age of Global Migration*, 6.

religious than the native-born population.[19] Those studying immigrant religion have observed over and over again that "immigrants are religious—by all counts more religious than they were before they left home."[20] Timothy Smith explains this in describing the act of migration as a "theologizing experience."[21] José Casanova contends that it is not the specific act of migration but rather the "uprootedness" and experiences of "being strangers in a new land" that migration entails that "calls forth such a religious response."[22] But in any case, religion is highly salient to many migrants, and religious immigrants tend to exhibit a higher level of religious intensity compared with the native-born population.[23] Of course, not all immigrants are highly religious—although the proportion of Christians among Asian immigrants in the United States is generally much higher than in their countries of origin. For example, there are substantially more Korean Americans that identify as Christian in the United States compared to the population in Korea, while Asian Americans overall are less likely to

---

19 For example, see Teresa Garcia-Muñoz and Shoshana Neuman, "Bridges or Buffers? Motives Behind Immigrants' Religiosity," *IZA Journal of Migration* 2, no. 23 (2013): 1–23 and Nancy Foner and Richard D. Alba, "Immigrant Religion in the U.S. And Western Europe: Bridge or Barrier to Inclusion?" *International Migration Review* 42, no. 2 (2008): 360–392.

20 Raymond Brady Williams, *Religions of Immigrants from India and Pakistan: New Threads in American Tapestry* (New York: Cambridge University Press, 1988): 29.

21 Timothy L. Smith, "Religion and Ethnicity in America," *The American Historical Review* 83, no. 5 (1978): 1155–1185.

22 Casanova, José, "Immigration and the New Religious Pluralism: A EU/US Comparison," *The New Religious Pluralism and Democracy* (April 2007): 13.

23 R. Stephen Warner, "Religion and New (Post-1965) Immigrants: Some Principles Drawn from Field Research," *American Studies* 41, no. 3 (2000): 273.

be religiously unaffiliated than other racial or ethnic groups in the United States.[24] Similarly, a recent Pew Research Center study shows that while immigrants from the Caribbean largely mirror the religious lives of the US-born Black population, who already tend to be more religious than Americans of other races, immigrants from sub-Saharan Africa tend to be *more* religious than their US-born or Caribbean immigrant counterparts.[25] However, it is true that the Christian migrant impact on American Christianity, at least among some populations, results in expressions of religious intensity (such as service attendance, prayer, scripture reading, and salience of religion in their daily lives) that vastly outpace that of the native-born Christian population.

In summary, the accelerated social transformation processes in the United States as a consequence of post-1965 immigration have a clear and direct relationship with the changing American religious landscape. As Stephen Warner, Jehu Hanciles, Kirsteen Kim and others have argued, an important consequence of immigration to the United States has been the "de-Europeanization of Christianity" rather than simply the pluralization of American religion.[26] In particular, American Christianity is not only becoming more racially and ethnically diverse, but is influenced

---

24 Barry A. Kosmin and Ariela Keysar, *American Religious Identification Survey (Aris 2008) Summary Report* (Hartford, CT: Trinity College, 2009), 15.

25 Jeff Diamant, "African Immigrants in U.S. More Religious Than Other Black Americans, and More Likely to Be Catholic," Pew Research Center (2021). https://tinyurl.com/4ap9pds7.

26 See the following works: R. Stephen Warner, "Religion and New (Post-1965) Immigrants: Some Principles Drawn from Field Research," *American Studies* 41, no. 3 (2000); Jehu Hanciles, *Beyond Christendom: Globalization, African Migration, and the Transformation of the West* (Maryknoll, NY: Orbis Books, 2008); Kim, Kirsteen. "Mission's Changing Landscape: Global Flows and Christian Movements." *International Review of Mission* 100, no. 2 (2011): 244–267.

by the importance of religion for many immigrants and their descendants, alongside the importance of understanding migrant faith with a transnational lens.

TRANSNATIONAL RELIGIOUS FAITH: IMMIGRANT RESILIENCE AND GLOBAL OUTLOOK

The literature from social scientists on immigration and congregations has traditionally emphasized the ways in which religion has promoted the incorporation of immigrants into new societies and has served to facilitate coping and adaptation to new contexts.[27] Immigrant congregations have stood as buffers to the hostility, racism, and discrimination often experienced within the United States' racialized society while also embedding immigrants within networks facilitating economic mobility and the promotion of social recognition. Charles Hirschman has stressed this functionalist approach to understanding the role of religion through the formula of the "three R's": refuge, respectability, and resources.[28] Additionally, immigrant-led congregations meet the spiritual needs of immigrants by incorporating worship practices and theologies that draw from the origin country's religious practices and languages. As such, this theme suggests that migrant congregations contribute to immigrant resilience while also seeing religion as key to the incorporation of minorities groups in America.

However, no meaningful understanding of the intersection of the Christian migrant in the United States and social transformations can ignore the centrality of transnationalism. Starting

---

27   Foner and Alba, "Immigrant Religion in the U.S," 361.
28   Charles Hirschman, "The Role of Religion in the Origins and Adaptations of Immigrant Groups in the United States," *International Migration Review* 38 (2004): 1228.

in the 1990s, a transnational lens became increasingly associated with the economic, social, religious, and political cross-border activities of migrants. The creation of a transnational framework represented a conscious epistemic move away from methodological nationalism—the assumption that the nation-state and its boundaries represent a given in social analysis.[29] In response, theories of transnational migration "are interested in analyzing the formation of new social contexts which are simultaneously situated within two or even more nation state frames."[30]

Perhaps the most useful methodological concept for understanding the domain created by social relationships that extend across borders is the transnational social field. Glick Schiller and Levitt put forward a notion of society based on the concept of the transnational social field that connects actors through cross-border relations.[31] According to Thomas Faist's definition, transnational social spaces "consist of combinations of sustained social and symbolic ties, their contents, positions in networks and organizations, and networks of organizations that can be found in multiple states."[32]

---

29 Andreas Wimmer and Nina Glick Schiller, "Methodological Nationalism, the Social Sciences, and the Study of Migration: An Essay in Historical Epistemology," in *The Transnational Studies Reader: Intersections and Innovations*, ed. Sanjeev Khagram and Peggy Levitt (New York: Routledge, 2008).

30 Anna Amelina, "Searching for an Appropriate Research Strategy on Transnational Migration: The Logic of Multi-Sited Research and the Advantage of the Cultural Interferences Approach," *Forum: Qualitative Social Research* 11, no. 1 (2010): 2.

31 Peggy Levitt and Nina Glick Schiller, "Conceptualizing Simultaneity: A Transnational Social Field Perspective on Society," *The International Migration Review* (2004).

32 Thomas Faist. *The Volume and Dynamics of International Migration and Transnational Social Spaces* (Oxford: Oxford University Press, 2000):199.

Instead of conceptualizing international migration as mere linkages between the sending and receiving regions, the concept of the transnational social field recognizes the connections between both worlds and the ways migrants build ties "by maintaining multiple and border-transgressing familial, economic, social, religious, cultural, and political relationships."[33] A transnational social field perspective provides a reformulation of the concept of society, no longer automatically equating it with, or confining it to, the boundaries of the nation-state.[34] This approach also implies continued transactions and repeated movements, and broadens the scope to include not just the movement of people, but also as goods, ideas, information, and symbols that are exchanged transnationally within the social field. The recent transnational turn in the literature has begun to theorize how religion is lived across borders, particularly with respect to congregational life. This has led scholars to conceptualize social fields as religious social spaces and social remittances as spiritual remittances.[35]

The studies of immigrant religion and ethnic churches in the United States have often focused on the role of immigrant congregations in facilitating simultaneous incorporation into both American life and society and the traditions and values of

---

33 Thomas Faist, "Transnationalization in International Migration: Implications for the Study of Citizenship and Culture," *Ethnic and Racial Studies* 23 (2000): 212.

34 Levitt and Glick Schiller, "Conceptualizing Simultaneity."

35 See, in particular, the works of Afe Adogame, *The African Christian Diaspora: New Currents and Emerging Trends in World Christianity* (London: Bloomsbury, 2013) and Olivia Sheringham, "Transnational Faith, Families and Belonging: Brazilians in London and "Back Home," in *Rescripting Religion in the City: Migration and Religious Identity in the Modern Metropolis*, ed. Jane Garnett and Alana Harris (Farnham, Surrey: Ashgate, 2013).

the homeland.[36] Congregations that exhibit high transnationality through sustained and regular flows of people, money, and ideas across borders are situated to become sites that facilitate both the maintenance and redefinition of ethnic identities across generations. Congregations provide communal sites where the complex relationships between ethnicity, identity, and adaptation are enacted within transnational social fields that link migrants with their homeland and facilitate incorporation into destination communities. Therefore, religious communities themselves cannot be considered confined to nation-state borders, especially in contexts characterized by migration.

Thus, the role of religious identities and institutions in forging and sustaining transnational ties is a considerable emerging topic that is beginning to gain traction among scholars of transnational studies.[37] In many immigrant congregations, the frequent travel of religious leaders and church members facilitates the flow of information and communication between destination countries and the homeland.[38] Afe Adogame has called this

---

36 In particular, see the following scholars' books: Peggy Levitt and B. Nadya Jaworsky, "Transnational Migration Studies: Past Developments and Future Trends," *Annual Review of Sociology* 33: 129–156; R. Stephen Warner and Judith G. Wittner, *Gatherings in Diaspora: Religious Communities and the New Immigration* (Philadelphia: Temple University Press, 1998); Peggy Levitt. *The Transnational Villagers* (Berkeley: University of California Press, 2001).

37 Levitt and Jaworsky, "Transnational Migration Studies"; Helen Rose Ebaugh and Janet Saltzman Chafetz, eds, *Religion Across Borders: Transnational Immigrant Networks* (Walnut Creek, CA: AltaMira Press, 2002); Peter Kivisto, *Religion and Immigration: Migrant Faiths in North America and Western Europe* (Cambridge, MA: Polity Press, 2014).

38 Moses O. Biney, *From Africa to America: Religion and Adaptation among Ghanaian Immigrants in New York* (New York: New York University Press, 2011); Kenneth J. Guest, *God in Chinatown:*

a type of "spiritual remittance" system, in which the international travel of church leaders facilitates transnational connections and networks between churches located around the world.[39] Beyond solely remitting spiritual ideas and beliefs, there is also reciprocity (if not always symmetry) in these transnational flows.

Considering the migrant church in the American context, a transnational lens implies looking beyond the nation-state as the main unit of analysis and recognizing the ways migrants and local congregations are also part of a larger transnational religious community. Building on the work of Jehu Hanciles, my own research into faith transmission in African-led communities of faith proposes that being socialized within a milieu of transnational orientations and practices will have a substantial influence on the longer-term configurations of religious identity and belonging not just for the immigrant generation, but for subsequent generations.[40] In the Korean immigrant setting, as Korean immigrants have increasingly established strong transnational ties to their homeland—ties that have been particularly strengthened

---

Religion and Survival in New York's Evolving Immigrant Community (New York: New York University Press, 2003); Patricia Fortuny-Loret de Mola, "The Santa Cena of the Luz Del Mundo Church: A Case of Contemporary Transnationalism," in *Religion across Borders: Transnational Immigrant Networks*, ed. Janet Saltzman Chafetz and Helen Rose Ebaugh (Walnut Creek, CA: AltaMira Press, 2002), 15–50; Kristine Krause, "Spiritual Spaces in Post-Industrial Places: Transnational Churches in North East London," in *Transnational Ties: Cities, Migrations, and Identities*, ed. Michael Peter Smith and John Eade (New Brunswick, NJ: Transaction Publishers, 2008).

39 Afe Adogame, "Transnational Migration and Pentecostalism in Europe," (paper presented at the GloPent: Transnational Pentecostalism in Europe Conference, University of Birmingham, 2009).

40 Allison L. Norton, "Fanning the Pentecostal Fire: Faith Transmission and the Second Generation in African Immigrant Churches," in *African Pentecostal Missions Maturing: Essays in Honor of Apostle Opoku Onyinah*, ed. Elorm Donkor and Clifton Clarke (Eugene, OR: Wipf and Stock, 2018).

by technological advances beginning in the mid-2000s—they have been able to preserve Korean cultural practices in church and in community life.[41] As such, religious impulses flow along transnational ties that encourage a vibrancy of faith and witness that transcends nation-state borders and provides the resources to nurture and sustain spiritual life in diaspora settings.

Rather than serving as a liability, the transnational nature of immigrant congregations makes them one of the most important spaces within which religion travels. My research confirms the work of Peggy Levitt, who argues that "religion lends itself particularly well to expressions of transnational belonging... If transnational belonging is the wave of the future, religion is likely to be its principal stage."[42] Because transnational religious spaces exist within transnational social fields, and as such are situated in such a way that religion is lived across borders, that the opportunities for institutional innovation and change are enhanced. Immigrant congregations, already centers of resilience, adaptation, and change, can selectively draw on religious sources from multiple contexts positioning them at the forefront of potential adaptation in response to changing circumstances.

PROCESSES OF REINVENTION: FAITH ACROSS GENERATIONS

For missiologists, understanding the transmission and travel of faith is of prime importance. The crossing of boundaries—be they generational or national—has always been a vital part of the Christian story, but immigration and transnationalism have

---

41 Pyong Gap Min, *Transnational Culture Flow from Home: Korean Community in Greater New York* (New York: Rutgers University Press), 2022.

42 Peggy Levitt, "Redefining the Boundaries of Belonging: The Transnationalization of Religious Life," in *Everyday Religion: Observing Modern Religious Lives*, ed. Nancy Tatom Ammerman (Oxford: Oxford University Press, 2007).

made it even more central to that story. Concerns regarding intergenerational religious transmission and socialization are at the heart of most religious institutions, as religious continuity across generations is essential for the viability and maintenance of faith communities. However, processes of faith transmission are further complicated in migrant-led congregations that operate within transnational religious fields. Some first-generation parents come from contexts of deep religious and spiritual fervor and thus find that the successful transmission of their most cherished cultural and religious values is complicated in the United States. What may have occurred seemingly by osmosis in the homeland now requires more purposeful packaging and communication in the host land. Others wrestle with the paradox that the very packaging of faith that makes it especially desirable to the first generation can raise the most resistance from future generations.

Most of the literature on immigrant religious identities explores the intersection of ethnic and religious identities, focusing on the ways immigrant religious organizations act to preserve and sustain ethnicity over generations.[43] Sociologists and historians have long been interested in analyzing the intersection of religion and the maintenance of ethnic identities within immigrant communities in the United States. Scholars of the earlier European Christian immigrant groups, such as Will Herberg, emphasized that participation in religious congregations served as a primary mechanism for the expression of ethnic identities.[44] Drawing on the classic assimilation theories of the time, Herberg argued that religion and ethnicity are closely connected in the immigrant generation, but become successively detangled with successive generation. He maintained that while the immigrant

---

43 Helen Rose Ebaugh and Janet Saltzman Chafetz, *Religion Across Borders*; Warner and Wittner, *Gatherings in Diaspora*.

44 Will Herberg, *Protestant, Catholic, Jew: An Essay in American Religious Sociology* (Chicago: The University of Chicago Press, 1955).

generation was expected to shed their language and national identities, their religious affiliations and institutions—as Protestants, Catholics, or Jews—would become the primary source of identity for future generations. According to Herberg, becoming "American" did not require putting aside or changing religious affiliation:

> The newcomer is expected to change many things about him as he becomes American—nationality, language, culture. One thing, however, he is not expected to change— and that is his religion. And so, it is religion that with the third generation has become the differentiating element and the context of self-identification and social location.[45]

More recent studies on the intersection of race, ethnicity, and religion among post-1965 immigrants and their descendants have affirmed Herberg's insightful thesis regarding the continued salience of religious identities across generations, but have rightly critiqued his assumptions regarding Anglo-conformity. While they largely affirm Herberg's thesis regarding the continued salience of religious identities across generations, they have critiqued the application of his thesis to post-1965 immigrants and their children, arguing that changes within American society and the composition of international migrants means that racial and ethnic identities are not simply eclipsed by religion, but instead that "race and religion matter enormously for the new second generation, the children of post-1965 immigrants."[46]

---

45 Herberg, *Protestant, Catholic, Jew*, 23.
46 Carolyn Chen and Russell Jeung, *Sustaining Faith Traditions: Race, Ethnicity, and Religion among the Latino and Asian American Second Generation* (New York: New York University Press, 2012).

Studies of Asian communities and religion in the United States has stood at the forefront of understanding intersecting racial, ethnic, and religious identities of the "new" second generation, the US-born children of post-1965 immigrants. In their research on religion and adaptation among Vietnamese immigrants, Carl Bankston and Russell Zhou indicate that religious participation has a major impact on ethnic identification, even greater than that of family or individual characteristics.[47] Religious activity thus serves to reinforce ethnicity, binding immigrant adolescents and the young second generation to their ethnic group identities. Kelly Chong's ethnographic study of Korean American Christians in Chicago also supports the intersectionality of religion and ethnicity for the next generation.[48] Focused specifically on congregations, she has argued that the Korean ethnic church is the primary site of cultural reproduction, playing a powerful role in the construction and maintenance of Korean ethnic identities through the "sacralization" of traditional Korean culture and values within a Christian worldview.

Similarly, Rebecca Kim's research on Christian Korean American college students demonstrates how students link ethnicity and religion by opting to participate in ethnic-specific religious organizations rather than joining multicultural groups.[49] In Kim's study, the second generation does not generally maintain participation in their parent's religious organizations—rather, they selectively combine the religious practices of their parents with those

[47] Carl L. Bankston III, and Min Zhou, "Religious Participation, Ethnic Identification, and Adaptation of Vietnamese Adolescents in an Immigrant Community" The Sociological Quarterly 36, no. 3 (1995): 523–34.

[48] Kelly H. Chong, "What It Means to Be Christian: The Role of Religion in the Construction of Ethnic Identity and Boundary among Second-Generation Korean Americans" Sociology of Religion 59, no. 3 (1998): 259–86.

[49] Rebecca Y. Kim, *God's New Whiz Kids: Korean American Evangelicals on Campus* (New York: New York University Press, 2006).

of their white, evangelical peers. Kim argues that this is not an inherited reproduction of first-generation ethnicity and religion, but a "made in the USA" relationship forged in the shared experience of intergenerational and intercultural strife. Sharon Kim's research also supports the link between religion and ethnicity: her study on Korean American Christian congregations in Los Angeles asserts that Korean Americans form their own second generation congregations as "hybrid third spaces" in the selective fusion of mainstream evangelical culture with Korean spirituality, resulting in congregations that express a uniquely second generation spirituality.[50] Consequently, these scholars see ethnic religion as playing a far greater role in the lives of the new second generation than Will Herberg argued regarding earlier generations of European-origin migrants and their descendants. The second generation has also often critiqued the faith of their immigrant parents as too ethnically and culturally focused, resulting in generational disagreements around gender roles and leadership in religious institutions.[51] Prema Kurien has made similar observations in her study of Indian American Christians: she discovered that although ethnic identities are maintained by the second generation, religion is viewed as a personal, individual quest, and is thus held distinct from ethnic markers.[52]

---

50 Sharon Kim, *A Faith of Our Own: Second-Generation Spirituality in Korean American Churches* (New Brunswick, NJ: Rutgers University Press, 2010).

51 Peter T. Cha, "Ethnic Identity Formation and Participation in Immigrant Churches: Second Generation Korean American Experiences," in *Korean Americans and Their Religions: Pilgrims and Missionaries from a Different Shore*, ed. Ho-Youn Kwon, Kwang Chung Kim and R. Stephen Warner (University Park, PA: Pennsylvania State University Press, 2001) 141–56.

52 Prema Kurien, "Decoupling Religion and Ethnicity: Second-Generation Indian American Christians" *Qualitative Sociology* 35, no. 4 (2012): 447–468.

What these various cases and contexts reveal is that the act of passing on the faith to a new generation is a tremendous source of innovation, change, and expansion. Immigrant churches and families are doing the hard work of "taking their inherited faith traditions and reshaping them so that they make sense in the context of their families' daily lives now.".[53] While not all of the second generation will remain in the congregations of their parents, the very act of working out their religious identities and trajectories serves to reinvent religious communities that grapple with sustaining relevance across generations. Thus, immigrant communities of faith in the United States regularly discern the means by which to facilitate effective transference of religious ritual and belief from one generation to the next and do so within a highly racialized society. They do not always succeed in building spaces of belonging across generations, but they face the challenges of creating "chains of memory" that preserve continuities with the past, while constructing porous boundaries that will allow for non-threatening intergenerational negotiation and change.[54]

The emergence of multi-generational churches in diaspora is a story of boundary crossing and generational change. Although it is too early to say whether the transnational ties of the first and second generations will endure for future generations, what is certain is that religious transnational spaces populated by migrants and the next generation is part of the larger phenomenon of boundary-crossing religion. Immigrant congregations must be willing to redraw the boundaries of belonging to include their American-born or raised children, creating a youth-oriented and American-inflected version of a transnationally constituted

---

53 Peggy Levitt, "Crossing Boundaries of Religious Tradition," *Reflections* (Fall 2008).

54 Danièle Hervieu-Léger, *Religion as a Chain of Memory* (New Brunswick, NJ: Rutgers University Press, 2000).

religious experience. Additionally, the content of religious programs and the theological concerns of the church must be relevant to the needs of a generation growing up in a racialized society. Otherwise, immigrant churches act more as prisons than as sources of religious vitality for future generations. This is both the challenge and the great strength inherent in the processes of immigrant faith transmission: when traditions of the faith are maintained unchanged, they are likely to become irrelevant to future generations. Yet, immigrant congregations can be important workshops for processes of intergenerational transmission, where practices are likely to be translated, invented, and reinvented in a new land. What may have been taken for granted now requires hard work and negotiation—the processes of contextualization and reinvention must continue.[55] As such, these transnational religious communities have much to offer to non-migrant faith communities in the West who also struggle with passing on the faith to their own children and grandchildren. This is a lesson the whole Christian church must learn.

CONCLUSION

Finally, I close with a few thoughts on how a deeper exploration of the social transformation perspective alongside perspectives from racial/ethnic studies expand our understandings of the Christian migrant and their institutions.

First, the nature of the American religious landscape is better understood *from the perspective of mobility* than it is from the stance of stasis. As Thomas Nail identifies, a major problem plaguing our understanding of the figure of the migrant is that "the migrant has been predominately understood from the perspective of stasis and perceived as a secondary or derivative figure with

---

55   R. Stephen Warner, "Religion and New (Post-1965) Immigrants."

respect to place-bound social membership."⁵⁶ He further argues that "the figure of the migrant exposes an important truth . . . the figure of the migrant has always been the true motivating force of social history." Indeed, the movement of people across boundaries and borders is a permanent condition of modern life. Migration is self-perpetuating, transforming, and systemic. This does not mean that mobility itself is not selective and class-specific or that the ability to move does not remain governed by extension restrictions by nation-states.⁵⁷ However, not only are there more people on the move today than at any other point in human history, but also migration "has been a constant feature of human existence, embedded in the complex transformations that shape our world."⁵⁸ This perspective should not simply valorize movement, but it does call us to understand society, and in particular, its religious character, without a sedentary bias. Human movement and international migration represents one of the most important factors in global change of the modern world not only in political and economic spheres, but also in the world's religious contours. Christian migrants have created their own forms of religious social organizations and have breathed life into existing forms. Making mobility a guiding framework creates options for analyzing the capacity of Christian migrants and their descendants that create alternatives to stories of religious decline and to pay attention to sources of religious vitality

---

56　Thomas Nail, *The Figure of the Migrant* (Stanford, California: Stanford University Press, 2015), 3.

57　Zygmunt Bauman "On Glocalization: Or Globalization for Some, Localization for Some Others" *Thesis Eleven* 54, no. 1 (1998): 37–49; Jennifer B. Saunders, Elena Fiddian-Qasmiyeh, and Susanna Snyder, *Intersections of Religion and Migration: Issues at the Global Crossroads* (New York, Palgrave Macmillan, 2016).

58　Jehu Hanciles, *Migration and the Making of Global Christianity* (Grand Rapids, Michigan: William. B. Eerdmans, 2021), 14.

and major social transformations that stand outside explanations centered on structures of dominance.

Secondly, the Christian migrant as the racial, ethnic, or religious "outsider" within the American Christian landscape profoundly impacts both the nature and mission of the migrant church. As Jehu Hanciles has argued, "the inextricable link between migration and the propagation of the Christian faith has a lot to do with the fact that the migrant-outsider existence (or 'otherness') accentuates distinctive presence and practice—or 'lived faith.'"[59] Christian immigrants, in their capacity for adapting new and different ways of being church, expressing their faith, worshipping, praying, and passing on the faith across generations call us to "rediscover conceptions of the church as a pilgrim community."[60] Migrant Christians challenge long-established existing denominations into new ways of being church and also call these communities to resist the idolatry of the nation-state and to work toward building anti-racist communities.[61] And, although I cannot do justice to this topic in this chapter, many Christian migrants and their descendants in the United States stand alongside African Americans and other BIPOC communities as some of the most compelling challengers to white Christian nationalism.[62]

---

59 Jehu Hanciles, *Migration and the Making of Global Christianity*, 419.
60 Susanna Snyder, Joshua Ralston, and Agnes M. Brazal, eds., *Church in an Age of Global Migration: A Moving Body* (Hampshire, UK: Palgrave Macmillan, 2016), 7.
61 William T. Cavanaugh, *Migrations of the Holy: God, State, and the Political Meaning of the Church* (Grand Rapids, MI: William B. Eerdmans, 2011).
62 Andrew L. Whitehead and Samuel L. Perry, *Taking America Back for God: Christian Nationalism in the United States* (New York: Oxford University Press, 2020); PY Liu, "How White Christian Nationalism Contributes to the Marginalization of the Asian American Community" Americans United for Separation of Church and State,

Finally, churches demonstrate what Wesley Granberg-Michaelson has called the *"endlessly dynamic" nature of the Christian faith*:

> The astonishing ability of the Christian faith to embed its truth in the life of widely diverse and endlessly changing cultures is the key to its growth, durability, and vitality through time and across geographical space. Christianity rests on the conviction that God became flesh and blood in Jesus. This incarnational foundation projects Christianity into an ongoing pilgrimage, constantly asking how it finds expression and vital witness in the world's changing history and cultures.[63]

Christian migrants and their institutions call us to engage in the developing migratory context with depth and nuance, to center the perspectives and voices from within, and to better understand how to live out Christian witness and practice in this "age of migration."

BIBLIOGRAPHY

Adogame, Afe. "Transnational Migration and Pentecostalism in Europe." In *GloPent: Transnational Pentecostalism in Europe*. University of Birmingham, 2009.

———. *The African Christian Diaspora: New Currents and Emerging Trends in World Christianity*. London: Bloomsbury, 2013.

August 6, 2021; Janelle Wong, *Immigrants, Evangelicals, and Politics in an Era of Demographic Change* (New York: Russell Sage Foundation, 2018).

63 Wesley Granberg-Michaelson, *From Times Square to Timbuktu: The Post-Christian West Meets the Non-Western Church* (Grand Rapids, MI: William B. Eerdmans, 2013), 3.

Amelina, Anna. "Searching for an Appropriate Research Strategy on Transnational Migration: The Logic of Multi-Sited Research and the Advantage of the Cultural Interferences Approach." *Forum: Qualitative Social Research* 11, no. 1 (2010).

Ammerman, Nancy T. "America's Changing Religious and Cultural Landscape and Its Implications for Theological Education." In *Looking Forward with Hope: Reflections on the Present State and Future of Theological Education*, edited by Benjamin Valentin. Eugene, OR: Cascade Books, 2019.

Bauman, Zygmunt. "On Glocalization: Or Globalization for Some, Localization for Some Others." *Thesis Eleven* 54, no. 1 (1998): 37–49.

Biney, Moses O. *From Africa to America: Religion and Adaptation among Ghanaian Immigrants in New York*. New York: New York University Press, 2011.

Casanova, José. "Immigration and the New Religious Pluralism: A EU/US Comparison." *The New Religious Pluralism and Democracy* (April 21–22 2007).

Castles, Stephen. "Twenty-First-Century Migration as a Challenge to Sociology." *Journal of Ethnic and Migration Studies* 33, no. 3 (2007): 351–71.

———. "Understanding Global Migration: A Social Transformation Perspective." *Journal of Ethnic and Migration Studies* 36, no. 10 (2010): 1565–1586.

Cavanaugh, William T. *Migrations of the Holy: God, State, and the Political Meaning of the Church*. Grand Rapids, MI: William B. Eerdmans, 2011.

Choi, Hee An. "Challenges of Korean Immigrant Leadership in the Church." *International Journal of Practical Theology* 23, no. 2 (2019): 224–241.

Diamant, Jeff. *African Immigrants in U.S. More Religious Than Other Black Americans, and More Likely to Be Catholic*. Pew Research Center (2021). https://tinyurl.com/4ap9pds7.

Ebaugh, Helen Rose, and Janet Saltzman Chafetz, eds. *Religion across Borders: Transnational Immigrant Networks*. Walnut Creek, CA: AltaMira Press, 2002.

Esterline, Cecilia, and Jeanne Batlova. *Frequently Requested Statistics on Immigrants and Immigration in the United States*. Migration Policy Institute (2022). https://tinyurl.com/4tvuh9pu.

Faist, Thomas. *The Volume and Dynamics of International Migration and Transnational Social Spaces*. Oxford: Oxford University Press, 2000.

———. "Transnationalization in International Migration: Implications for the Study of Citizenship and Culture." *Ethnic and Racial Studies* 23 (2000): 189–222.

Foner, Nancy, and Richard D. Alba. "Immigrant Religion in the U.S. and Western Europe: Bridge or Barrier to Inclusion?" *International Migration Review* 42, no. 2 (2008): 360–392.

Fortuny-Loret de Mola, Patricia. "The Santa Cena of the Luz Del Mundo Church: A Case of Contemporary Transnationalism." In *Religion across Borders: Transnational Immigrant Networks*, edited by Janet Saltzman Chafetz and Helen Rose Ebaugh, 15–50. Walnut Creek, CA: AltaMira Press, 2002.

Garcia-Muñoz, Teresa, and Shoshana Neuman. "Bridges or Buffers? Motives Behind Immigrants' Religiosity." *IZA Journal of Migration* 2, no. 23 (2013): 1–23. https://doi.org/https://doi.org/10.1186/2193-9039-2-23.

Guest, Kenneth J. *God in Chinatown: Religion and Survival in New York's Evolving Immigrant Community*. New York: New York University Press, 2003.

Hanciles, Jehu. *Beyond Christendom: Globalization, African Migration, and the Transformation of the West*. Maryknoll, NY: Orbis Books, 2008.

———. *Migration and the Making of Global Christianity*. Grand Rapids, MI: William. B. Eerdmans, 2021.

Herberg, Will. *Protestant, Catholic, Jew: An Essay in American Religious Sociology*. Chicago: The University of Chicago Press, 1955.

Hervieu-Léger, Danièle. *Religion as a Chain of Memory*. New Brunswick, N.J.: Rutgers University Press, 2000.

Hirschman, Charles. "The Role of Religion in the Origins and Adaptations of Immigrant Groups in the United States." *International Migration Review* 38 (2004): 1206–1233.

Jeung, Russell, Carolyn Chen, and Jerry Z. Park. "Introduction: Religious, Racial, and Ethnic Identities of the New Second Generation." In *Sustaining Faith Traditions: Race, Ethnicity, and Religion among the Latino and Asian American Second Generation*, edited by Carolyn Chen and Russell Jeung. New York: New York University Press, 2012.

Kim, Kirsteen. "Mission's Changing Landscape: Global Flows and Christian Movements." *International Review of Mission* 100, no. 2 (2011): 244–267.

Kivisto, Peter. *Religion and Immigration: Migrant Faiths in North America and Western Europe.* Immigration & Society. Cambridge: Polity Press, 2014.

Kosmin, Barry A., and Ariela Keysar. *American Religious Identification Survey (Aris 2008) Summary Report.* Hartford, CT: Trinity College, 2009.

Krause, Kristine. "Spiritual Spaces in Post-Industrial Places: Transnational Churches in North East London." In *Transnational Ties: Cities, Migrations, and Identities*, edited by Michael Peter Smith and John Eade. Comparative Urban and Community Research. New Brunswick, NJ: Transaction Publishers, 2008.

Kwiyani, Harvey C. *Multicultural Kingdom: Ethnic Diversity, Mission and the Church.* London: SCM Press, 2020.

Levitt, Peggy. *The Transnational Villagers.* Berkeley: University of California Press, 2001.

———. "Praying across Borders: How Immigrants Are Changing the Religious Landscape." *MIGRACIÓN Y DESARROLLO* 8 (2007): 65–83.

———. "Crossing Boundaries of Religious Tradition." *Reflections* (Fall 2008). https://tinyurl.com/2ptphzd2

———. "Redefining the Boundaries of Belonging: The Transnationalization of Religious Life." In *Everyday Religion: Observing Modern Religious Lives*, edited by Nancy Tatom Ammerman. Oxford: Oxford University Press, 2007.

Levitt, Peggy, and B. Nadya Jaworsky. "Transnational Migration Studies: Past Developments and Future Trends." *Annual Review of Sociology* 33 (August 2007): 129–156.

Levitt, Peggy, and Nina Glick Schiller. "Conceptualizing Simultaneity: A Transnational Social Field Perspective on Society." *The International Migration Review* (2004).

Liu, PY, "How White Christian Nationalism Contributes to the Marginalization of the Asian American Community." *Americans United for Separation of Church and State*, August 6, 2021, https://tinyurl.com/3e7thxj7

Lugo, Luis. "A Land of Immigrants, a Shifting Religious Marketplace." *Reflections* (Fall 2008).

Min, Pyong Gap. *Transnational Culture Flow from Home: Korean Community in Greater New York.* New York: Rutgers University Press, 2022.

Nail, Thomas. *The Figure of the Migrant.* Stanford, CA: Stanford University Press, 2015.

Nanko-Fernández, Carmen M. "We Are Not Your Diversity, We Are the Church! Ecclesiological Reflections from the Marginalized Many." *Perspectivas: Hispanic Theological Initiative Occasional Paper Series,* no. 10 (2006).

Norton, Allison L. "Fanning the Pentecostal Fire: Faith Transmission and the Second Generation in African Immigrant Churches." In *African Pentecostal Missions Maturing: Essays in Honor of Apostle Opoku Onyinah,* edited by Elorm Donkor and Clifton Clarke. Eugene, OR: Wipf and Stock, 2018.

Reside, Graham. "The State of Contemporary Mainline Protestantism." In *The Future of Mainline Protestantism in America,* edited by James Hudnut-Beumler, Mark Silk, and Andrew Walsh. New York: Columbia University Press, 2019.

Saunders, Jennifer B., Elena Fiddian-Qasmiyeh, and Susanna Snyder. *Intersections of Religion and Migration: Issues at the Global Crossroads.* Religion and Global Migrations. New York: Palgrave Macmillan, 2016.

Sheringham, Olivia. *Transnational Religious Spaces: Faith and the Brazilian Migration Experience.* Migration, Diasporas and Citizenship. London: Palgrave Macmillan, 2013.

Silk, Mark, and Andrew H. Walsh. "Series Editors' Introduction: The Future of Religion in America." In *The Future of Evangelicalism in America,* edited by Candy Brown and Mark Silk. New York: Columbia University Press, 2016.

Snyder, Susanna, Joshua Ralston, and Agnes M. Brazal, eds. *Church in an Age of Global Migration: A Moving Body.* Hampshire, UK: Palgrave Macmillan, 2016.

Smith, Timothy L. "Religion and Ethnicity in America." *The American Historical Review* 83, no. 5 (1978): 1155–1185.

Twenty Years of Congregational Change: The 2020 Faith Communities Today Overview. Faith Communities Today. https://tinyurl.com/34vke3rz

Warner, R. Stephen, and Judith G. Wittner. *Gatherings in Diaspora: Religious Communities and the New Immigration.* Philadelphia, PA: Temple University Press, 1998.

Whitehead, Andrew L., and Samuel L. Perry. *Taking America Back for God: Christian Nationalism in the United States.* New York: Oxford University Press, 2020.

Williams, Raymond Brady. *Religions of Immigrants from India and Pakistan: New Threads in American Tapestry.* New York: Cambridge University Press, 1988.

Wimmer, Andreas, and Nina Glick Schiller. "Methodological Nationalism, the Social Sciences, and the Study of Migration: An Essay in Historical Epistemology." In *The Transnational Studies Reader: Intersections and Innovations,* edited by Sanjeev Khagram and Peggy Levitt. New York: Routledge, 2008.

Wong, Janelle. *Immigrants, Evangelicals, and Politics in an Era of Demographic Change.* New York: Russell Sage Foundation, 2018.

9

EXPLORING DIASPORA MISSION IN THE CONTEXT OF THE LATIN AMERICAN MISSION TO NORTH AMERICA WITH THE SECOND GENERATION

Alexia Salvatierra

INTRODUCTION

Christianity in North America is on the decline. The percentage of Americans identifying as Christian went down from 78.4 percent in 2007 to 70.6 percent in 2014, with only 60 percent of those aged eighteen to thirty reporting Christian faith.[1] However, the global picture is different. Christianity is holding its own at a little over one third of the world's population. In contrast to much of church history, the majority of Christians internationally are now either in or from the Global South and Global East. Declining faith in the United States is being revitalized and supported primarily by immigrant churches.

---

1 Pew Research Center, "America's Changing Religious Landscape," May 12, 2015, https://www.pewresearch.org/religion/2015/05/12/americas-changing-religious-landscape/

The majority of immigrant churches are characterized by a missionary faith. Immigrant churches are "bastions of fervent religiosity and 'communities of commitment', experiencing significant growth through innovative ministries."[2] They offer their core constituency a cultural home in their new land in which traditional values can be reinforced while economic opportunities and support are provided through social networks. The in-betweenness of Korean diaspora churches provides a variety of opportunities for mission.[3] These congregations are particularly successful in missionary outreach to immigrants. While 7.1 percent of the Asia Pacific region identifies as Christian, it is estimated that over 40 percent of US Asian adults identify as Christian.[4] Latin American diaspora churches play a similar role and display similar missional assets in Latinx immigrant communities in the United States.

Latin America is the home of a newly vital and growing Christian movement, even though Roman Catholicism in Latin America dates back to the conquest. While over 95 percent of the Latin American population report Christian faith, new non-Catholic Christian movements are growing rapidly—at three times the rate of Catholic churches.[5] In 1910, 1 percent of Christians in Latin America were not Catholic. In 2010, that number had grown

---

2 Jehu Hanciles, *Beyond Christendom: Globalization, African Migration, and the Transformation of the West* (Maryknoll, NY: Orbis Books, 2008), 283.
3 See Enoch Jinsik Kim, "Introduction," in this volume, XX.
4 Pew Research Center. "New Study Finds Asian Americans Contribute to Diversity of US Religious Landscape," July 19, 2012, https://www.pewresearch.org/religion/2012/07/19/new-study-finds-asian-americans-contribute-to-diversity-of-u-s-religious-landscape/
5 Philip Jenkins, *The Next Christendom: The Coming of Global Christianity* (Oxford: Oxford University Press, 2002).

to 20 percent and continues to accelerate.⁶ These new Christian movements in Latin America are sending informal missionaries to the United States in the form of immigrants. Almost half of the foreign-born population in the United States is Latinx.⁷ The fastest growing group in the evangelical church in the United States is Latinx. Many of these church members have come to the United States bringing a vibrant and contagious faith.

However, for both Korean and Latin American diaspora churches, the question for immigrant believers and for the fate of the churches in the United States is the extent to which immigrant faith is transmitted to the second and ensuing generations. In this paper, we will focus on this question through the lens of the Latinx church. We will also ask how this faith is most effectively transmitted. While our focus in the Latinx church and community, our findings and observations are potentially useful for the Korean church and community in the United States as well. Both church communities are struggling with their cultural and theological identities in the United States and seeking their new missional mandate.

THE IMPACT OF IMMIGRANT FAITH

Immigrant churches clearly make a difference in the faith and lives of immigrants. In addition to refuge and support, immigrant churches "provide a safe place from which to negotiate adaptation and incorporation into American society".⁸ As we examine the process of faith transmission to the second and ensuing

---

6 Todd M. Johnson and Kenneth R. Ross, eds., *Atlas of Global Christianity* (Edinburgh: Edinburgh University Press, 2009), 50–51.
7 "The Hispanic Population in the United States" US Census 2019.
8 Jehu Hanciles, *Beyond Christendom: Globalization, African Migration, and the Transformation of the West* (Maryknoll, NY: Orbis Books, 2008), 300.

generations, it is important to analyze the impact of immigrant churches on their surrounding communities. Post-immigration generations integrate increasingly into the broader society over time. A church that does not seek to impact the broader community is more likely to become irrelevant to those generations.

It is not a simple task for an immigrant congregation to impact its broader community. Beyond language barriers, the United States has a schizophrenic history with immigrants—welcoming and rejecting in waves, with a particular tendency to despise and exclude immigrants of color. When the United States is passing through an anti-immigrant phase, it is difficult for the contributions of immigrants to be recognized and received. However, the collective culture of immigrants from the Global South and Global East often results in an organic response to the needs of their neighbors. Interracial marriage, the location of immigrant churches in marginalized communities and the missionary spirit of immigrant churches further combine to encourage the development of outreach programs that witness to and serve their communities. Jehu Hanciles describes the broader outreach efforts of African immigrant churches as "witness as withness," accompanying their neighbors in their daily struggles.[9] In the Korean immigrant community, larger churches assist at-risk youth, domestic violence survivors, the homeless and children in need of educational scholarships.[10] Mexican immigrants have resisted the attempts to devalue them, partly by providing "culturally contextualized ministries and theologies that allowed

---

9   Hanciles, *Beyond Christendom*, 365.
10 Rebecca Y. Kim, "Making their Mark: Asian Americans and the California "Christian Landscape" in *Migration, Transnationalism and Faith in Missiological Perspective: Los Angeles as a Global Crossroads*, ed. Kirsteen Kim and Alexia Salvatierra (Lanham, MD: Lexington Books, 2022), 103.

for care for those on the racial and socioeconomic margins of U.S. Society".[11]

Immigrant faith also impacts broader church networks. The vitality of immigrant spirituality has led denominations to include ethnic music and fervent prayer practices in their worship services and at times, to partner with ethnic churches in global ministry programs.

IMMIGRANT CHURCH FAITH TRANSMISSION TO THE SECOND GENERATION

All churches must engage in the challenge of transmitting their faith to emerging generations, a particularly difficult task at this historic moment. However, immigrant churches have the added dynamics of intergenerational conflict and cultural tension. Yet, examples abound of second and third generation leaders in immigrant churches who are carrying the faith forward, adapting but not abandoning their Christianity. Hanciles identifies two aspects of the immigrant church with the power to attract and maintain the engagement of emerging generations. First, the ongoing discrimination experienced by immigrants, particular in communities of color, impacts younger generations as well and leads them to seek places where their culture is affirmed, and their identity appreciated. Second, immigrant churches in the age of the internet are increasingly transnational, which makes it possible for younger generations to actively encounter the faith of younger generations in their countries of origin. Parents are not stuck trying to communicate the faith that they received but are,

---

[11] Robert Chao Romero, "Mexican Americans and the Southern Errand" in Kim and Salvatierra, *Migration, Transnationalism and Faith*, 73.

rather, able to introduce younger generations to a vibrant faith being practiced currently.[12]

Second generation leaders are not simply receiving the faith; they are taking from the traditions of their elders and reshaping them for their current world. They are offering services in English and welcoming neighbors of all cultures, making spaces where they can feel comfortable. At the same time, they are carrying forward traditions of collective care, fervent prayer, vibrant music, and a global sensibility.[13] Second and third generations in the Korean church are creating a hybrid Christian expression with the potential to reach and serve other young people intersectionally.[14] Emerging Latinx generations are engaged in similar identity and missional formation.

THE SECOND GENERATION IN THE HISPANIC COMMUNITY

How do these dynamics play out in the Latinx community in particular? The decline of Christian faith in young people in the United States includes Latinx as well as other populations. However, the broad statistics do not reflect the nuanced differences that exist. In 2019, we completed a pilot study of Latinx millennial Christian leaders through the Centro Latino of Fuller Theological Seminary.[15] The bulk of the respondents shared a profound ambivalence about the faith of their parents and grandparents. While feeling alienated from certain aspects of church doctrine

---

12 Hanciles, *Beyond Christendom*, 301.
13 Kim, "Making their Mark," 105–106.
14 See Sebastian Kim, "Concluding Remarks," in this volume, XX
15 Alexia Salvatierra, Cynthia Erikkson, Marcos Canales, and Vanessa Martinez, "Latinx Millennials in the United States and Theological Education" (Pasadena CA: Centro Latino, Fuller Theological Seminary, 2019).

and practice, they generally held a deep respect for the ways in which their elders' faith had sustained them in the immigration process and in their struggles in their new country. They also felt connected to, and responsible for, their ethnic community. They did not want to walk away but rather struggled with how to find the right relationship with their communities of origin. Here are a few responses that describe the paradox well: On the one hand, "I am driven by beautiful stories of parents and grandparents"; "I respect the uninhibited faith of our elders, the power of prayer, the unshakeable faith that moves mountains"; and "My heart is for the Latino community." On the other hand, as one respondent said, "Latin American leaders in the church have come from Spanish speaking churches that resemble churches back home for our parents or churches that are stuck in two or three decades ago. And so, we are starting to reject conforming to that same mold"; or in the word of another, "I don't like the word relevant, but I think we'd really need to be aware of where we live, like our reality. And I think the church is so out of that. Out of touch. Yes. Literally."[16]

These young Latinx second-generation leaders shared painful stories about the ways in which their families' immigrant congregations did not fully welcome or trust them. Over 75 percent shared that they felt hurt in some way by the immigrant church. This was associated with fear and suspicion of millennials, lack of openness, legalism, judgment, shaming, black-and-white thinking, and attachment to tradition. As one young respondent said, "My mom was heard and free in the church—I never felt seen and heard." Even when there is some openness to their leadership, it is often experienced as incomplete. As another respondent shared: "They empower our calling but then they don't make a space for us to lead."[17]

---

16 Salvatierra, et al, "Latinx Millennials in the United States".
17 Salvatierra et al, "Latinx Millennials in the United States."

EFFECTIVE RESPONSES BY LATINX IMMIGRANT CHURCHES

Latinx immigrant churches respond to the challenge of the ambivalence of the younger second-generation in a variety of ways. Daniel Rodriguez's research focuses on best practices for Latinx immigrant churches engaging younger generations. His bottom-line conclusion is that the immigrant church must intend to incorporate and honor younger generations, recognizing that this necessitates changes in language and culture. As Juan Martinez states in *The Story of Latino Protestants,* young Latinx have polycentric identities[18] Immigrant churches that attract and keep younger generations view this complex identity as a missionary gift and not in itself a reason for suspicion of spiritual or theological heresy. Taking the language of younger generations seriously means offering services in English or bilingual services. Culture is a more complex issue.

As is true in the Korean context, the culture of the second generation is hybrid. Daniel Orlando Alvarez writes about hybridity as an interaction between two cultures which creates a third and new culture capable of acting as a bridge between the original cultures and opening up new space for the movement of the Holy Spirit. Juan Martinez describes the hybrid culture of young second-generation Latinx as having the following characteristics:[19]

- Influenced by the spiritual dynamism of the South (with a strong sense of the daily encounter with God) and with a clear desire to learn from Christian faith in the North, interacting with both and learning from both

---

18   Juan Francisco Martinez, *The Story of Latino Protestants* (Grand Rapids, MI: William B. Eerdmans, 2018). 321–322.
19   Martinez, *The Story of Latino Protestants,* 321–326.

- Transnational life experiences—creating a global consciousness

- Actively living out their identity as a bridge, relating well to people from different cultures, understanding themselves as part of an intersectional minority community

- Having a strong sense of an extended family network and responsibility toward their community while also cherishing the freedom of US-style individualism, allowing them to both individually progress and still bring their communities along with them

- Appreciating both formal and informal education

These young people are particularly equipped to minister to intermarried couples. Over 35 percent of US born Latinx are intermarried.[20] Their hybrid culture is also attractive to others of their generation beyond the Latinx community. The millennial generation is characterized by a hunger for authentic community, an appreciation for mystical experience, and global interconnectedness.

Both Rodriguez and Martinez note an additional characteristic of the second generation which is shared by their generation at large, a deep concern for and commitment to social justice. This is intensified for Latinx millennials by their direct and immediate experiences of unjust suffering, including poverty, discrimination, and a broken immigration system in the United States, as well as the legacy of colonialism in Latin American. A striking 100 percent of the young Latinx Christian leaders who participated in the Centro Latino study shared that their vocation included the

---

20 Pew Research Center, "Intermarriage in the U.S. 50 years after Loving vs. Virginia", May 18, 2017, https://www.pewresearch.org/social-trends/2017/05/18/1-trends-and-patterns-in-intermarriage/

desire to serve people in need or pain. Here are a few quotes from the study: "I want to be present in places of brokenness where God brings resurrection, grace, mercy." "I am out to embody justice, hospitality, love." "I have the DNA to minister with the oppressed." "I want to raise up leaders from the community who love the community." "I am called to create communities that are equitable with servant leaders."[21]

To incorporate the culture of second-generation Latinz, immigrant congregations need to let them lead, manifesting their own ideas in the programs that they design. Discipleship programs also must be designed to match their cultural orientation. In comparative case studies of Latinx immigrant churches that are successfully reaching and discipling the young second-generation, Rodriguez notes the following common characteristics:

- Identification by pastors of potential leaders who then receive ongoing whole life and whole family mentoring from the pastors
- Apprenticeship—accompanying the pastor(s) while they lead, leading under the pastors' supervision, taking on gradually increasing responsibility (culminating in planting a satellite church)
- Cell groups—small home Bible studies that encourage participants to apply the scriptures to their daily lives and develop deep relationships of mutual care and concern. These groups offer young Latinx a ground level opportunity to lead.
- Vibrant worship that includes leadership by young Latinx and a variety of music

---

21 Salvatierra et al, "Latinx Millennials in the United States."

- Regular training in consecrated teams which provide character development, spiritual formation, and ministry skills. In these teams, young leaders practice habits of fervent prayer, intentional relationship with the Holy Spirit, offering sincere personal testimony and developing of an "unswerving faith in the power of God to break the cycle of sin, suffering and death."[22]

- Active community ministries which impact the lives of neighbors, increase the well-being of the whole community and support a more equitable society

- Intensive long-term residential training programs for mission experience.

CASE STUDIES
La Iglesia de Restauracion, Los Angeles

Rene Molina, Jr. is a Latinx millennial who serves as a pastor in his father, Rene Molina's immigrant congregation, La Iglesia de Restauracion. Restauracion has approximately 2,500 members who worship in Spanish and a relatively new ministry led by Rene Jr. in English which includes several hundred millennial members. Rene Jr.'s discipleship program has the following components and characteristics:

- They follow the maxim: Jesus allowed his disciples to belong before they believed. They provide avenues where the second generation can identify their passion and contribute to the church's mission.

---

[22] Daniel Rodriguez, *A Future for the Latino Church: Models for Multilingual, Multigenerational Hispanic Congregations* (Donner's Grove, IL: Intervarsity, 2018), 135

- They integrate discipleship with evangelism. They state that they are the same and interconnected.

- They demonstrate to the second generation that God "has lots to do and say about social justice. We try to show that God is not only spiritual; he cares about every aspect of our lives."[23]

- They invest in their ministry with younger generations, ensuring that they have well-equipped and compensated staff serving them.

- They use available research data to ensure that their policies, processes, and structures are healthy for staff and participants.

- They collaborate with other training programs—e.g., Young Life, the LAPD—to provide skills training and character development.

- They intentionally use language that communicates well to younger generations (e.g., they do not call their program a discipleship program but rather a mentoring/support/leadership program.)

Rene Jr. summarizes his discipleship program for the second generation as "*mission integral* (holistic mission)." He says, "This is the secret sauce for the second generation."[24] Rene Jr. and Senior both affirm that the generations mutually need each other. Rene Jr. says that the first generation has fire and spiritual stability that the second generation absolutely needs. Rene Sr. says that the second generation has helped them to understand and connect

---

23   Rene Molina Sr. and Rene Molina Jr., Interview by Alexia Salvatierra, March 24, 2022. Fuller Theological Seminary.
24   Rene Molina Sr. and Rene Molina Jr., Interview by Alexia Salvatierra, March 24, 2022. Fuller Theological Seminary.

with the broader community, broadening and strengthening their overall ministry.

La Fuente Ministries

Marcos Canales's parents are also a ministry team from Peru. However, his church plant is independent from his parents' ministry. La Fuente Ministries is intentionally bilingual in all aspects of its life and ministry. While most members are Latinx millennials, they also provide a church home to multiple bicultural families. There are also a few key immigrant leaders from Marcos's parent generation who act as the informal godfathers and godmothers of the congregation. La Fuente Ministries has survived and thrived for eight years, including through the middle of the pandemic.

The bilingual character of La Fuente Ministries is a core pillar of its success, for reasons that go beyond simple accessibility. "In waiting for translation, the Spirit was re-forming our inclination toward dominance in 'moving things along' to reach a conclusion or decision. Even to this day, the value of waiting for one another in bilingual contexts has paved the way in our leadership processes, nurturing a sense of *familia* and attentiveness to Scripture and context."[25]

La Fuente Ministries has a strong commitment to honoring the gifts of the migrant generation while also moving into new territory to honor and support the faith of emerging generations. As their website reads, this ministry is willing to dwell and celebrate the intersection between the Latinx community and the Latinx church; between first generations and second generations; between the realities of race and culture; between

---

25   Alexia Salvatierra and Brandon Wrencher, *Buried Seeds: Learning from the Vibrant Resilience of Marginalized Christian Communities* (Baker Academic, 2022), 215.

Christian evangelism and God's justice; and between Spanish and English."[26] This complex welcome extends to the active utilization of the gifts of all. The leadership actively encourages the creativity of members who are supported in initiating projects like an outreach to day laborers in a local park or a support circle for a family seeking asylum. One of Marcos's favorite sayings is "Do less. Trust people more."[27]

The *mission integral* commitment that Rene Molina Jr. described as core to his ministry is also core to La Fuente. As one younger member said, "After the 2016 election, we were embarrassed to use the name Christian because of all the connotations that it carried in a polarized political reality. We said that there has to be a place where Jesus's politics, social justice and the church intersect. Once we experienced La Fuente's commitment to God's heart of justice for the immigrant, the orphan, and the widow, we found Jesus and we started to use the term Christian again."[28] This commitment is lived out l partnership with other churches, Christian ministry networks and organizational collaboration as well as in independent projects.

CONCLUSION

How are these observations and findings relevant for Korean churches? The well-being of immigrant churches is critical for the sustaining and growth of the Christian faith in the United States. In the face of the rapid decline of Christian faith and affiliation, the vitality of Christian movements in the Global South and

---

26 Zhenchao Qian, Daniel T. Lichter, and Dmitry Tumin, "Divergent Pathways to Assimilation? Local Marriage Markets and Intermarriage among US Hispanics," *Journal of Marriage and Family*, 80/1, 2018, 271–288.
27 Salvatierra and Wrencher, *Buried Seeds*, 209.
28 Salvatierra and Wrencher, *Buried Seeds*, 208.

Global East brought by migrants on their journeys are strengthening the mission of the church. These churches impact both the broader US church and missionary efforts in their local communities. The question that this chapter attempts to answer, in the particular context of the Latinx church in the United States, is whether that vital contribution can be transmitted and built upon by the second and ensuing generations.

The good news is that it is possible to transmit a vibrant and orthodox Christian faith from the immigrant church to the second generation. Perhaps even better news is that the second generation of both the Latinx and Korean immigrant church community can potentially carry out a powerful mission to a broader constituency of younger citizens of the United States. The challenging news is that the discipleship of the second generation requires an intentional commitment to change the habitual and traditional discipleship practices of the Latinx and Korean immigrant church to fully incorporate the language and hybrid culture of these generations, welcoming and utilizing their leadership. For both Korean and Latinx immigrant churches, reaching and incorporating younger generations will require a greater civic commitment toward a more just society. For many of these immigrant churches, the most difficult aspect of the shift will be the adoption of a more holistic and community-engaged ministry which includes active collaboration with organizations outside the church. Congregations that can make the shift, however, will find that the reward is more than they can imagine—not only for their own church life but for the gospel. We close with a scripture to remind us that this is neither a new challenge nor a new vision:

> David said to Saul, "Let no one lose heart on account of this Philistine; your servant will go and fight him." Saul replied, "You are not able to go out against this Philistine and fight him; you are only a young man, and he has

been a warrior from his youth." But David said to Saul, "Your servant has been keeping his father's sheep. When a lion or a bear came and carried off a sheep from the flock, I went after it, struck it and rescued the sheep from its mouth. When it turned on me, I seized it by its hair, struck it and killed it. Your servant has killed both the lion and the bear; this uncircumcised Philistine will be like one of them, because he has defied the armies of the living God. The Lord who rescued me from the paw of the lion and the paw of the bear will rescue me from the hand of this Philistine." Then Saul dressed David in his own tunic. He put a coat of armor on him and a bronze helmet on his head. David fastened on his sword over the tunic and tried walking around, because he was not used to them. "I cannot go in these," he said to Saul, "because I am not used to them." So he took them off. Then he took his staff in his hand, chose five smooth stones from the stream, put them in the pouch of his shepherd's bag and, with his sling in his hand, approached the Philistine. (1 Sam 17:32-40)

REFERENCES

"The Hispanic Population in the United States" US Census 2019.

Hanciles, Jehu. *Beyond Christendom: Globalization, African Migration, and the Transformation of the West* (Maryknoll, NY: Orbis Books, 2008).

Jenkins, Philip. *The Next Christendom: The Coming of Global Christianity* (Oxford: Oxford University Press, 2002).

Johnson, Todd M. and Kenneth R. Ross, eds. *Atlas of Global Christianity* (Edinburgh: Edinburgh University Press, 2009).

Kim, Rebecca Y. "Making their Mark: Asian Americans and the California Christian Landscape," in *Migration, Transnationalism and Faith in Missiological Perspective: Los Angeles as a Global Crossroads*, edited by Kirsteen Kim and Alexia Salvatierra, 93-112. Lanham, MD: Lexington Books, 2022.

Martinez, Juan Francisco. *The Story of Latino Protestants.* Grand Rapids, Ml: William B. Eerdmans, 2018.
Pew Research Center. "America's Changing Religious Landscape." May 12, 2015. https://www.pewresearch.org/religion/2015/05/12/americas-changing-religious-landscape/
Pew Research Center. "Intermarriage in the U.S. 50 years after Loving vs. Virginia." May 18, 2017. https://www.pewresearch.org/social-trends/2017/05/18/1-trends-and-patterns-in-intermarriage/
Pew Research Center. "New Study Finds Asian Americans Contribute to Diversity of US Religious Landscape." July 19, 2012. https://www.pewresearch.org/religion/2012/07/19/new-study-finds-asian-americans-contribute-to-diversity-of-u-s-religious-landscape/
Qian, Zhenchao, Daniel T. Lichter, and Dmitry Tumin, "Divergent Pathways to Assimilation? Local Marriage Markets and Intermarriage among US Hispanics", *Journal of Marriage and Family,* 80/1, 2018, 271–288.
Rodriguez, Daniel A. *A Future for the Latino Church: Models for Multilingual, Multigenerational Hispanic Congregations.* Donner's Grove, IL: Intervarsity, 2018.
Romero, Robert Chao. "Mexican Americans and the Southern Errand" in *Migration, Transnationalism and Faith in Missiological Perspective: Los Angeles as a Global Crossroads* edited by Kirsteen Kim and Alexia Salvatierra, 67–78. Lanham, MD: Lexington Books, 2022.
Salvatierra, Alexia and Brandon Wrencher, *Buried Seeds: Learning from the Vibrant Resilience of Marginalized Christian Communities* Baker Academic, 2022.
Salvatierra, Alexia, Cynthia Erikkson, Marcos Canales, and Vanessa Martinez, "Latinx Millennials in the United States and Theological Education." Pasadena CA: Centro Latino, Fuller Theological Seminary, 2019.

10

CONCLUDING REMARKS
The Identity and Mission of Korean American Churches

Sebastian Kim

The expansion of Christianity, according to conventional understanding of mission and church history, has been initiated and carried out with the enthusiasm and sacrificial works of missionaries, first in Europe and North American, and then in the rest of the world. In this understanding, local church history and their theologies are understood and interpreted in light of missionary or Western perspectives. The local churches are "expansions" of Western churches with certain aspects of cultural, socio-economic, and political variations. However, a recent study of world (or global) Christianity has demonstrated very different realities in local Christianity and has challenged conventional understandings of Christianity worldwide. While acknowledging the contributions of missionaries, Christianity is spread primarily by indigenous believers and developed by them in local ways. Christianity has always been geographically widespread and practiced locally in different communities across the world. Christianity is polycentric in every respect. In particular, it is an established fact by scholars that over the past century the growth of Southern Christianity has been remarkable and has created a "shift of the center of gravity" from Western regions to African, Asia, and Latin America.[1] And this shift is commonly acknowledged by recent scholarship on religions and sociology because the growth of Christian churches in the Southern hemisphere is set to continue, and this affects not only the demography within the Christian church but also the pattern of religious groupings and the characteristics of Christianity worldwide.[2]

Philip Jenkins, in his survey of the shift of the Christian presence to the South, convincingly argues that churches in the South have developed distinctive forms of Christianity that are shaping Christianity as a whole.[3] He identifies the distinctive characteristics of the Southern Christianity as traditional (not liberal) on social issues, conservative on beliefs and moral issues, and interested in supernatural and personal salvation rather than radical politics. Although in many ways she shares Jenkins's thesis, Grace Davie comes to a different conclusion and challenges the notion of Europe being a model for the rest of the world by arguing that the religious behaviour of Europeans is distinctive and peculiar to Europe. Therefore, the rise of Southern Christianity does not necessarily impact on Northern Christianity since both have developed distinctive characteristics of Christianity according to their own contexts.[4] I have argued elsewhere that the future shape of the church will not be a series of confrontational encounters or clashes of different forms of Christianity, as Jenkins suggests. Nor will it be the situation that the North and South will exhibit

---

1 Philip Jenkins, *The Next Christendom: The Coming of Global Christianity* (New York: Oxford University Press, 2002), 1–2.
2 See David Barrett, George Kurian, and Todd Johnson, *World Christian Encyclopaedia*, 2nd ed. (New York: Oxford University Press, 2001), 12–15.
3 Jenkins, *The Next Christendom*, 6–7, 214.
4 Grace Davie, *Europe—The Exceptional Case: Parameters of Faith in the Modern World* (London: Darton, Longman & Todd, 2002), 2–8.

such distinctive characteristics that there is little in common between the two as Davie argues. Rather, the different traditions and expressions of faiths will form a mosaic of Christianity as a whole, as each contributes their own distinctive color to the wider community.[5]

The microscope of the above discussion could be applied to the study of Korean and Korean American Christianity. In many ways, Korean American churches are the continuation of Korean churches in South Korea in terms of church organizations, leadership, worship patterns, theological orientations, views on socioeconomic and political issues, mission activities, and public engagements. On the other hand, Korean American churches exhibit their distinctiveness in all the areas due to their historical developments and issues they face in the American contexts. As "homeland politics" in ethnic communities in the United States, Korean American Christians are always aware of what is going on in the contemporary Korean peninsula and incorporate it into their life. They also try to digest and struggle to fine the meaning of being a diaspora community in an "exiled land" as the early Christian immigrant expressed.[6] Again, the perception of being diaspora differs significantly from the first generation and the second and third generations as the latter generations gain significant integration and confidence in the wider society. The issues of identity due to race and ethnic problems of American society are deeply challenging for Korean Americans, especially in recent troubles of racial tensions in the United States. As "shrimps among whales" in the East Asian geopolitical situation, Korean Americans yet again face the difficulties of asserting their identity.

---

5   Sebastian Kim, "The Future Shape of Christianity from an Asian Perspective," in *Global Christianity: Contested Claims*, eds. Frans Wijsen and Robert Schreiter (Amsterdam: Rodopi, 2007), 69–93.
6   See David Yoo, *Contentious Spirits: Religion in Korean American History, 1903–1945* (Stanford, CA: Stanford University Press, 2010).

Korean Americans over the years have gained a significant confidence and pride of successful *hallyu* (Korean wave), both coming from Korea and from the United States. But they also are struggling to come to the terms with the fragility of that pride when they encounter incidents like that of Itaewon in late 2022 when many young people were killed and the continued treat of nuclear warfare from the North Korea.

The Korean immigration to the United States was in the contexts of the introduction and growth of Protestant Christianity in Korea, which occurred during one of the most turbulent times in Korean modern history. Several major political crises happened during this period, including the Gapshin Coup (1884), the Sino-Japanese War (1894-1895), the Russo-Japanese War (1904-1905), the Japanese annexation of Korea (1910-1945), the Korean War (1950-1953), and the struggle for democracy of the 1970s and 1980s. Amid uncertainty and chaos, people desperately sought stability and security, and Christianity was accepted by many, not only for spiritual and religious reasons but also as a means of sociopolitical change.[7] After the two wars for the hegemony over the Korean peninsula, the influence of China and Russia were lessened and the power of Japan over the government of Korea and people increased. Life for ordinary people became harder because of banditry, cholera epidemics, famine (in 1900-1902), and Japanese migrants who were in a better position to take advantage of business opportunities. Many desperate Korean families, unable to make a living in Korea, moved abroad temporarily. Some trekked across the mountainous northern border to Manchuria and Siberia, where they braved extreme living conditions and Chinese warlords, and eventually transformed a

---

7   Sebastian Kim and Kirsteen Kim, *A History of Korean Christianity* (Cambridge: Cambridge University Press, 2015).

wilderness into productive farmland.⁸ Among them were Christians and, hearing their need, Canadian Presbyterian missionaries started work in North Gando in 1898. In 1903, with the diplomatic help of Horace Allen, one hundred and twenty Korean Methodists departed for Hawai'i where George Heber Jones had discovered through the global missionary network there was work on plantations. The new arrivals endured back-breaking work and basic conditions but by 1905, when further migration was forbidden, and with the help of two workers from their church in Korea, the Methodists had established a network of nine churches across the islands accompanied by schools.⁹

Since the initial migration to Hawai'i, then a territory of the United States, Koreans started to migrate to the mainland in California and other places. In the early twenty-first century, of the two-million-strong Korean community in the United States, 98 percent were migrants or descendants of migrants who arrived after 1968 when Korean emigration to the United States was regularized.¹⁰ It was estimated that more that 70 percent of Koreans were affiliated to Korean churches. Forty percent of these had gravitated toward the church and become Christians after arrival in the United States; four out of five attended the church more than once a week and they generously supported it.¹¹ Korean

---

8   James A. Foley, *Korea's Divided Families: Fifty Years of Separation* (London: Routledge, 2003), 6–10.
9   Yoo, *Contentious Spirits*, 8, 35-45; Dough K. Oh, "History of the Korean Diaspora Movement" in *Korean Diaspora and Christian Mission*, eds. S. Hun Kim and Wonsuk Ma (Oxford: Regnum Books, 2011), 181-196.
10   Wayne Patterson & Hyung-chan Kim, *Koreans in America*, 2nd ed. (Minneapolis: Lerner, 1991).
11   Steve Kang and Megan A. Hackman, "Toward a Broader Role in Mission: How Korean Americans' Struggle for Identity Can Lead to a Renewed Vision for Mission," *IBMR* (2012) 36/2, 72-76.

churches mushroomed from about forty Protestant congregations and one Catholic in 1972 to over four thousand and spread out from California across the nation. The largest churches—LA Youngnak Presbyterian Church and Sa-rang Community Church, both in Los Angeles, and New York Presbyterian Church—numbered several thousand members but most Korean Protestant churches were small—between twenty and fifty adults. Their pastors mostly described themselves as theologically conservative.[12] About 70 percent of congregation members said that they attend the church at least once and the reasons for coming to the church are: for worshiping God (85.9 percent); adapting to the American life (45.5percent); meeting other members (46.8 percent); good moral and ethical influence for children (40 percent); maintaining Korean language and culture (24.8 percent).[13] Forty percent of Protestant churches were Presbyterian and other significant denominational groups were Baptist, Methodist, Full Gospel, and Holiness. Other churches were independent or interdenominational.[14] Some churches existed as Korean congregations within US denominations—notably in the PCUSA, which recorded four hundred and thirty Korean-American churches with their own synodical structure in 2012, and in the Catholic Church where there were one hundred and thirty parishes with a specific ministry to Korean communities in 2010.[15]

---

12 Immigration Theology Institute 2011.
13 Je Hoon Lee, "The Status of Korean American Community's Religious Perspectives: Focus on Korean American National Survey 2008 University of Southern California School of Social Work" in *The Journal of Immigrant Theology*, Sang Chul Oh, ed. (Fullerton, CA: Institute of Korean American Immigration Theology, 2009), 147–59.
14 Kang & Hackman, "Toward a Broader Role in Mission," 72–76.
15 Mark Gray, Melissa Cidade, Mary Gautier, and Thomas Gaunt, *Cultural Diversity in the Catholic Church in the United States* (Washington, DC: Georgetown University, 2013), 22.

Although the second generation might drop out of the Korean-medium congregations of their parents, they might move to English-speaking congregations or, in the case of Protestants, Christian youth—or often church youth groups—set up new churches. Although second-generation Korean Americans had high rates of education, income, and mobility, they were still marginalized due to their race, so they were observed to develop a distinctive "hybrid" Christian expression of their own.[16] Second generation Korean Protestants were less conservative than the first generation and keen to become good citizens. They used the church as a platform for community development and outreach, including social service programs to non-Koreans.[17] Some of their churches were multiethnic congregations mainly made up of other Asians, in which Koreans played the leading role.[18] This might be partly a recognition by other Asians of the unique history of Korean Protestantism and it was probably also bolstered by the spread of Korean popular culture.[19] In this context Korean Americans developed a distinctive theology which was directed not at issues on the Korean peninsula but at the questions of identity and mission raised in the North American situation.[20] Korean Americans formed the largest non-white group in American Evangelical seminaries and some were in leadership roles of national

---

16   Sharon Kim, *A Faith of Our Own: Second-Generation Spirituality in Korean American Churches* (New Brunswick, NJ: Rutgers University Press, 2010), 160–165.
17   Elaine Howard Ecklund, *Korean American Evangelicals: New Models for Civic Life* (Oxford: Oxford University Press, 2006), 70, 117, 137.
18   Ecklund, *Korean American Evangelicals*, 39–44.
19   Sharon Kim, *A Faith of Our Own*, 161.
20   Paul S. Chung, Veli-Matti Kärkkäinen, and Kim Kyoung-Jae, eds., *Asian Contextual Theology for the Third Millennium: Theology of Minjung in Fourth-Eye Formation* (Cambridge: James Clarke & Co., 2007).

or international Evangelical organizations.[21] Min Kyung-seok discusses the challenges Korean American churches are facing such as: overcoming the suffering and humiliation of past and present experiences of poverty and discrimination; uncertainty of identity and the adjustment of cultural diversities and values; creating some common community in multicultural society; and maintaining dignity as a community.[22] However, while these challenges still prevalent in Korean American churches, the churches are already moving forward with vision and aspirations in their Christian lives by asserting their self-identity with confidence, working toward their missional and spiritual formations, and their intercultural engagements within the wider US society.

The aim of this book is to provide a forum for the scholars of Korean American church to address some of the key challenges and sociocultural and theological formations of identity as they continue to navigate their own place in society as immigrant churches and in relation to Korean churches in South Korea, mainline churches, and other ethnic and multiethnic churches in the United States. The discussions in this volume are arranged in three areas: identity formation; missional and spiritual formation; and inter-cultural formation. First, for identity formation, Choi Hee An argued for overcoming a Black-white binary in the discussion of race in the United States and anti-Asian violence, and the problem of setting up successful upper class Asians as a model minority. For this, she introduced the concept of "우리" (*woori*) as togetherness of the people with same side, collective assuring of individuals, and representation of the voices of powerless.

---

21 Sharon Kim, *A Faith of Our Own*, 5.
22 Anselm Kyongsuk Min, "Theological Reflections on Immigrant Life" in *The Journal of Immigrant Theology*, ed. Sang Chul Oh (Fullerton, CA: Institute of Korean American Immigration Theology, 2009), 46–70.

Furthermore, the idea of "깍두기" (*kaagdugi*) provides some alternative understanding of the identity of individual Christians, leadership, and the congregation. Examining the importance of food for Koreans, Nam Soon Song used "밥" (*bahb*) (cooked rice) as the bread of life and presented in as a fundamental element of Korean identity and argued that *bahb* represents the biblical and socio-cultural concepts of sharing, empathy, harmony, and vanity. In terms of the theological identity of Korean American churches, Helen Jin Kim examined the two protagonists of evangelical movements in the United States and in Korea and the way the two movements interacted with and influenced each other in the context of the Cold War strategy as well as for the task of world Christianity. As we have discussed earlier, the encounter of the churches in the North and the South has never been one-way traffic, it always resulted in shaping of the counterpart; they are interconnected and interdependent.

Regarding the spiritual formation of the Korean American churches, Euiwan Cho called for a post-pandemic ascetic spiritual formation. He identified that the problems the churches face during the pandemic tend to be self-pity, distraction, immediacy, and a palliative living. He calls for ascetic spirituality of inner withdrawal, stability, and radical honesty, which he argues some of the essential ascetic practice toward attentiveness toward God, self, and others in order to light "divine fire of prayer" in our daily lives and also the life of the congregation. For the missional formation of Korean American churches, Enoch Jinsik Kim pointed out immigration as God's missionary act, and as such, the initial formation of Korean churches in the United States plays an important role of forming "ethnic enclaves" for Korea immigrants by the sense of a welcoming community within an alien society. From a missiological perspective, however, he challenges the Korean churches to build bridges between ethnic groups and the wider society to make Korean American churches part of the dynamics of a global mosaic church and play its missional role to shape the mainstream churches and society, and furthermore to provide a positive influence on the churches in South Korea. Similarly, on the missional formation of Korean churches, Enoch Wan compared popular missiology and diaspora missiology and identified some of key stages of developing diaspora missiology among Korean diaspora churches, namely: mission to; through, by and beyond, and with the diaspora churches. He then emphasized the importance of mission through and beyond diaspora churches to reach out to the wider society and play the role of bridging the gospel for the *missio Dei*.

The third aspect of the current discussion is the intercultural formation of Korean Americans in the wider contexts of US society. For the issue of race, Daniel D. Lee sees race as a hermeneutical category rather than experience of discrimination or marginalization, and convincingly argued his case for race dynamics in the United States as critical for understanding not only US society but also the identity and ministry of Korean American churches. He examined the complexity of "ethnic nationalism," "model minority myth," and the idealized perception of the United States, and their interplay into the identity of Korean Americans and further suggested that for the understanding and overcoming of the Black/white binary paradigm, intergenerational gaps, and invisibility of Asian Americans, racial awareness is crucial for effective ministry within Korean American churches. Alison Norton, in her thorough examination of the relationship between immigration and congregational life, argued that immigrant churches, both Protestant and Catholic churches, play a vital role in revitalizing churches in the United States and create dynamic redrawing of the contours of American Christianity, in line with what Philip Jenkins argues as discussed in the early part of this chapter. Especially for the issues of transgenerational belonging, since immigrant churches experienced and demonstrated their resilience, adaptation, and change, these immigrant congregation have much to offer non-migrant faith communities regarding the process of intergenerational transmission. In the context of the United States, the growth of Latinx congregations, especially second generation and evangelical churches are significant in considering changing dynamics of immigrant churches. Alexia Salvatierra examined the importance of churches' response to the needs of the young Latinx second generation since they have distinctive identities, culture, and aspirations. She also identifies some of the key areas of the hybridity of these groups for effective ministry. This hybridity is shared by other immigrant congregations, such as the Korean American younger generation and these findings are important to intersectional, interethnic, and intercultural engagements in the United States.

In his book, *Contentious Spirits*, David Yoo argues that that the theme of "exile" is deeply rooted in the minds of the early Korean immigrant Christians to the United States as they identified themselves to the geopolitical fate of Israelites in the Hebrew Bible, and this provided the source of their hope and contention.[23] That said, though the early immigrants suffered and struggled in an alien land, as a minority that immigrated from a much troubled and divided nation, recent dramatic changes in the homeland, gained by democratization, economic developments, cultural dominance in the area of music, film, and drama, means present-day Korean American churches can exhibit much hope and confidence. More significantly, the Korean American young Christians are no longer bounded by the perceptions of their parents about the United States and Korea, but establish themselves as part and parcel of the mainstream society with certainty of the formation of identity, spiritual and missional, and intercultural dimensions. The recent developments of multicultural congregations led by Korean

---

23   Yoo, *Contentious Spirits*, 10–11.

American young leaders and missionary activities of local Korean American churches are some of the examples of these phenomenon. As the authors of this volume have indicated, the Korean American churches are in the cross road, on the one hand, dealing with racial tensions, ethnic discrimination, economic and political recognition in the wider society, and on the other hand, by identifying the distinctive characteristics of being a Korean heritage, working with the other ethnic groups, and to contribute to the wider society with their lessons of distinctive spiritualties and resilience. As the churches in Korea, in spite of their weaknesses and shortcomings, have demonstrated their sustaining faith commitments in the midst of suffering, persecutions, and hardship in Korean modern history, so the Korean American churches will set to fulfil the role of mission by affirming their identity in God who has been faithful to them in their struggles, visions, and commitments.

BIBLIOGRAPHY

Barrett, David, George Kurian, and Todd Johnson. *World Christian Encyclopaedia*, 2nd ed. (New York: Oxford University Press, 2001).

Chung, Paul S., Veli-Matti Kärkkäinen, and Kim Kyoung-Jae, eds., *Asian Contextual Theology for the Third Millennium: Theology of Minjung in Fourth-Eye Formation* (Cambridge: James Clarke, 2007).

Davie, Grace. *Europe—The Exceptional Case: Parameters of Faith in the Modern World* (London: Darton, Longman & Todd, 2002).

Ecklund, Elaine Howard. *Korean American Evangelicals: New Models for Civic Life* (Oxford: Oxford University Press, 2006).

Foley, James A. *Korea's Divided Families: Fifty Years of Separation* (London: Routledge, 2003).

Gray, Mark, Melissa Cidade, Mary Gautier, and Thomas Gaunt, *Cultural Diversity in the Catholic Church in the United States*. Washington, DC: Georgetown University, 2013.

Jenkins, Philip. *The Next Christendom: The Coming of Global Christianity*. New York: Oxford University Press, 2002.

Kang, Steve, and Megan A. Hackman. "Toward a Broader Role in Mission: How Korean Americans' Struggle for Identity Can Lead to a Renewed Vision for Mission," *IBMR* (2012) 36/2, 72–76.
Kim, Sebastian. "The Future Shape of Christianity from an Asian Perspective." In *Global Christianity: Contested Claims*, edited by Frans Wijsen and Robert Schreiter, 69–93. Amsterdam: Rodopi, 2007.
Kim, Sebastian, and Kirsteen Kim. *A History of Korean Christianity*. Cambridge: Cambridge University Press, 2015.
Kim, Sharon. *A Faith of Our Own: Second-Generation Spirituality in Korean American Churches*. New Brunswick, NJ: Rutgers University Press, 2010.
Lee, Je Hoon. "The Status of Korean American Community's Religious Perspectives: Focus on Korean American National Survey 2008 University of Southern California School of Social Work." In *The Journal of Immigrant Theology*, edited by Sang Chul Oh, 147–59. Fullerton, CA: Institute of Korean American Immigration Theology, 2009.
Min, Anselm Kyongsuk. "Theological Reflections on Immigrant Life." In *The Journal of Immigrant Theology*, edited by Sang Chul Oh, 46–70. Fullerton, CA: Institute of Korean American Immigration Theology, 2009.
Oh, Dough K. "History of the Korean Diaspora Movement." In *Korean Diaspora and Christian Mission*, edited by S. Hun Kim and Wonsuk Ma, 181–196. Oxford: Regnum Books, 2011.
Patterson, Wayne, and Hyung-chan Kim. *Koreans in America*, 2nd ed. Minneapolis: Lerner, 1991.
Yoo, David. *Contentious Spirits: Religion in Korean American History, 1903–1945*. Stanford, CA: Stanford University Press, 2010.

INDEX

AAPI hate, 14, 145, 162
accommodation, 102, 104
Achor, Shirley, 101
American Evangelical Empire, 45
American Forces Korean Network (AFKN), 143
American religious landscape, 171, 175, 177, 189
anti-Asian violence, 11, 151, 224
Antony, 78, 89
Apatheia, 82, 84, 90
asceticism 70, 77-81, 88
Asian American Advocacy Fund, 21
Asian immigrants, 6, 8-15, 101, 145, 176,
assimilation, 6, 101, 138, 145, 150, 156, 184,

bahb, 26-33
    bahb of life, 26-28, 37, 41
    cooking *bahb*, 36-41
    See also sharing *bahb*
belongingness, 4
Billy Graham Evangelistic Association, 46. *See also* Graham, Billy
binary, 9-14, 54, 63, 141, 147-8, 150-154, 224-226

Black Lives Matter, 14, 21, 145
Bright, Bill, 45

Campus Crusade for Christ, 45-47
Catholic Church, xiv, 174, 200, 222, 226
Chang Ahn, 46
Chinese Exclusion Act, 159
Choi, Susan, 46
Christian education, 26, 35-39
Christian mission, 72, 117, 123, 127, 131
Chung, Hye Kyung, 27
Cold War, 46-51, 62-63, 141, 225
Cold War Orientalism, 49-52
collaborative leadership, 18-21
Colorblind White Dominance, 147
Commission on World Mission and Evangelism, 35
communal, 2, 4-7, 15-16, 112, 156, 174, 181
congregations, 170-174, 178-184, 186-189, 222-223, 227
contextualization, 106, 121, 189
COVID-19, 11, 16, 19, 21, 40, 145, 162
cultural homogeneity of Korean society, 112

INDEX

Daoism, 146
Desert Fathers and Mothers, 77, 80, 82–90
diaspora churches, 200–201, 226
diaspora Korean culture, 111
diaspora missiology, 118–126
distraction, 2–3, 73, 75, 83
diversity, 143–144, 161, 163, 173–175

East-West Development Company, 96
ecclesiology, 94, 161, 170
embodied knowledge, 7
emerging generations, 203, 211
ethnicity
   ethnic identity, 8, 73, 105–143, 185
   ethno-racial pentagon, 141
ethnographic description, 111–112
exclusivism/exclusivity, 4, 15, 16, 22
Explo '72, 63, 64
Explo '74, 63, 64

faith transmission, 182, 184, 189, 201, 203
Fensham, Charles J., 34
first-generation Korean immigrants, 8, 14, 115
Foreign Student, The, 46
forgotten history, 46
Fuller Theological Seminary, 54, 55
future of Christianity, 171

globalization, 15, 106, 127, 172
glocal mission, 121, 126
God's mission, 30–35, 125, 225
Graham, Billy, 45, 61. *See also* Billy Graham Evangelistic Association

Great Commission, 48, 51, 54, 119, 121–128

hallyu, 220
hangukinron (한국인론), 114
harmony, 22, 32, 113, 114, 132
hermit kingdom, 33, 122, 125, 126
Holistic Christian missions, 131–132
honorary white, 145, 148–149, 163
Hull, John M., 35
hybridity, 119, 206

immediacy, 73, 75, 81, 87
immigrant church, 7, 14–20, 174, 188, 189, 191, 199–203, 205–206
immigrant congregation, 64, 205, 208
immigrant faith, 189, 201–203
in-betweenness, 105, 200
   double in-betweenness, 12
inclusivity, 14, 15–20
inhwa (인화), 113
intergeneration, 155
isolation, 14, 102–104

Japanese colonialism, 142, 146
Jenkins, Philip, 218, 226
jeong, 30–32, 112, 114

kibun (기분), 113
Kim, Joon Gon, 47–54, 54–64
kkagdugi (깍두기), 17–21
Korean American theology, 139
Korean diaspora congregation, 115
Korean Immigrant Christian Leadership, 16
Korean Immigrant Church, 16–22

INDEX

Korean Immigrant Identity
    Formation, 2-3, 7
Korean War, 46-49
Kyung-seok, Min, 224

Latin America, 200, 218
Latin American, 200-207
Latinx, 200-201, 204-209
Liberation Front, 138, 152
life-giving, 33-39
logismoi, 80, 82, 88
Los Angeles Riots of 1992, 158

mainline Protestant, 172, 174
marginality, 20-21, 139
marginalization, 14-16, 139, 156, 226
migrant church, 169, 182
migration, 96-99, 138-140, 170-172, 176, 190-192
Missio Dei, 34, 128-129, 131, 226
missiological implication, 127
missiological paradigm, 118, 130
missional Christian education, 39, 41
missional church, 33, 71
mobility, 73, 178, 190, 223
model minority myth, 11, 21, 145, 148, 149, 226

National Origins Act, 52
nationalism, 141-143, 146-147, 179, 191
neo-evangelical, 47, 61, 63
Newbigin, Lesslie, 34

Oahu, Hawai'i, ix
Orientalism, 49, 157
otherness, 7, 9, 10, 13-15, 17, 22

outsider, 149, 191

palliative life, 90
palliative living, 73, 75
palliative society, 75
panethnicity, 159
parochialism and racism, 112
patriarchal culture, 18
People v. Hall, 151
picture bride, 98
positionality, 8, 10
post-1965 immigration, 138, 156, 171-173, 177, 185-186
postcolonial identity, 14, 16
postcolonial self, xii, 3, 7, 14, 70-71, 76
post-Korean War immigration, 46
post-pandemic, x, 69-73, 225

racism, 9, 112, 139-140, 143, 146, 148-155, 158-162, 178
racial identity, 4, 15, 141, 149, 152, 154, 159, 164
racial justice, 9, 147, 151
racial segregation, 53
racial triangulation, 149
radical honesty, 70, 82, 87-90
red scare, 61, 147
religiosity, 175, 200
rule of reciprocity, 113
Russell, Letty M., 34, 36

Sargeant, Wendi, 33
Sayings of the Desert Fathers (Apophthegmata Patrum), 70, 81
second generation, 38, 47, 139, 154-157, 161, 185-188, 204-210, 213, 223, 227

self-pity, 73, 90, 225
Shamanism, 146
sharing bahb, 29–32, 34–35, 37
sociopolitical, 9, 10, 13, 15, 144, 220
spiritual formation, 70, 75, 77, 81, 86, 90, 209, 224–225

Takenaka, Masao, 27
third other, xi, 8, 13–14, 22
Third World Liberation Front, 138, 152
transnationalism, 178, 183
transnationalization, 180

Van Gelder, Craig, 34

WEC '80, 63, 64
white fundamentalism, xi, 49
white normativity, 140, 144, 145, 148, 158
withdrawal (anachoresis), 82
women's leadership, 16, 18–20
woori (우리), 3–7, 14, 175, 224
world Christianity, xiv, 67, 218, 225
World Council of churches, 35
World Vision, 45, 66

yellow peril, 149